What Leaders Ar... ...
HIGH PERF...

"Ted Engstrom is a man who liv... ... what he lives."

> Edward R. Dayton, Vice President-at-Large
> World Vision International

"*HIGH PERFORMANCE* will challenge and motivate you to demonstrate a life of excellence in your commitment to Christ, family, friends and colleagues. It teaches practical truth that will work in every facet of your life."

> Sylvia Nash
> Executive Director/Chief Executive Officer
> Christian Ministries Management Association

"Ted Engstrom is among the world's most respected authorities on personal leadership and successful living. For anyone who leads people in any capacity, and for all who desire to live a life of greater achievement and fulfillment, *HIGH PERFORMANCE* is a priceless treasury of ideas and resources to help you succeed."

> Steve Douglass
> Executive Vice President
> Campus Crusade for Christ International

"As one who has helped train thousands of Christians to be more effective leaders, I am confident that the principles of leadership and personal excellence found in this book will help any reader better achieve his or her God-given potential."

> Bruce Cook, President
> Rapha Southeast

"Enjoy *HIGH PERFORMANCE: The Best of Ted Engstrom*. THE BEST is wonderfully good."

> Anne Ortlund
> Author, Speaker

"Most of us read a book hoping to find a few nuggets — bring your wheelbarrow! This book is full of them. Ted Engstrom has crammed

30 years of lessons and insights into a unique combination of management insight and personal motivation."

Pat MacMillan, President
Team Resources, Inc.

"As a Christian leader, I am always striving for excellence and encourage others to do the same. Ted Engstrom offers many ideas to help you achieve excellence as a leader."

Florence Littauer, President
CLASS Speakers, Inc.
Founder, Christian Leaders and Speakers Seminars

"All who read this digest of Ted Engstrom's life values and apply it to their own lives will be more effective and more fulfilled. He has distilled the practical wisdom he has received from a lifetime of dependency on the Lord into a treasury of guiding principles that will enable many to serve, as Ted has, with personal joy and fruitfulness."

Howard Ball, President
Churches Alive International

"Ted Engstrom is a leader among leaders. This collection represents the best of this man's great heart and mind and is worthy material for those who are interested in becoming maximum Christians. I commend it to my brethren everywhere."

Adrian Rogers, Pastor
Bellevue Baptist Church
Memphis, Tennessee

"Ted has taught many of us the essentials and techniques of efficient management, but he is never too efficient to pray and weep with a brother. The best thing about this book is that you will get acquainted with a remarkable, gifted, godly, and—to thousands who know and appreciate him—a beloved man."

Robert A. Cook, President Emeritus
King's College

"Practical, pointed, and powerful in its reality. Ted is not a dreamer. He really tells us how to do things well in Christ's work, both personally and for the organizations we serve."

Stephen F. Holbrook, President
Princeton Management Associates

THE BEST OF

TED ENGSTROM

H·I·G·H
Performance

COMPILED BY ROBERT C. LARSON

Here's Life Publishers

Softcover edition, First printing, February 1992

Originally published in hardcover as *The Best of Ted Engstrom on Personal Excellence and Leadership.*

Published by
HERE'S LIFE PUBLISHERS, INC.
P. O. Box 1576
San Bernardino, CA 92402

Library of Congress Cataloging-in-Publication Data
Engstrom, Theodore Wilhelm, 1916-
    [Best of Ted Engstrom on personal excellence and leadership]
    High performance : 31 proven strategies for personal success /
compiled by Robert C. Larson.
        p.   cm.
    Originally published as: The best of Ted Engstrom on personal
excellence and leadership. 1988.
    Includes bibliographical references and index.
    ISBN 0-89840-350-2
    1. Christian leadership. 2. Motivation (Psychology). 3. Christian
life—1960- 4. Excellence—Religious aspects—Christianity. I. Larson,
Robert C. II. Title.
[BV652.1.E523   1992]   91-41860
158'.4—dc20   CIP

For More Information, Write:
L.I.F.E.—P.O. Box A399, Sydney South 2000, Australia
Campus Crusade for Christ of Canada—Box 300, Vancouver, B.C., V6C 2X3, Canada
Campus Crusade for Christ—Pearl Assurance House, 4 Temple Row, Birmingham, B2 5HG, England
Lay Institute for Evangelism—P.O. Box 8786, Auckland 3, New Zealand
Campus Crusade for Christ—P.O. Box 240, Colombo Court Post Office, Singapore 9117
Great Commission Movement of Nigeria—P.O. Box 500, Jos, Plateau State Nigeria, West Africa
Campus Crusade for Christ International—100 Sunport Lane, Orlando, FL 32809, U.S.A.

To my dear friend and colleague,
Ed Dayton,
who helped take so many chapters in this book
from idea to reality.

— Ted W. Engstrom

Special Thanks

This book would never have seen the light of day were it not for the generous permission granted by those companies that originally published the chapters of this volume. So a great debt of thanks goes to our good friends at Zondervan, Word, Regal, Thomas Nelson and Fleming H. Revell. These men and women have given their full cooperation to the reproduction of these materials in the spirit of Christian fellowship, and in a desire to see the message of these chapters reach an ever–expanding readership.

Section 1. Material in this section is taken from *Integrity* by Ted W. Engstrom with Robert C. Larson. Copyright © 1987 by Ted W. Engstrom and Robert C. Larson. Used by permission of Word Books.

Section 2. Taken from *The Pursuit of Excellence* by Ted W. Engstrom with Robert C. Larson. Copyright © 1982 by the Zondervan Corporation. Used by permission.

Section 3. Taken from *Motivation to Last a Lifetime* by Ted W. Engstrom with Robert C. Larson. Copyright © 1987 by Ted W. Engstrom. Used by permission of Zondervan Publishing House.

Section 4. Taken from *A Time for Commitment* by Ted W. Engstrom and Robert C. Larson. Copyright © 1987 by Ted W. Engstrom and Robert C. Larson. Used by permission of Zondervan Publishing House.

Section 5. Taken from *The Fine Art of Friendship* by Ted W. Engstrom with Robert C. Larson. Copyright © 1985 by Ted W. Engstrom and Robert C. Larson. Used by permission of Thomas Nelson Publishers.

Section 6. Taken from *For the Workaholic I Love* by Ted W. Engstrom and David J. Juroe. Copyright © 1979 by Ted W. Engstrom and David J. Juroe. Published by Fleming H. Revell Company. Used by permission. Also from *Strategy for Leadership* by Edward R. Dayton and Ted W. Engstrom. Copyright © 1979 by Edward R. Dayton and Ted W. Engstrom. Published by Fleming H. Revell Company. Used by permission.

Section 7. Taken from *Managing Your Time* by Ted W. Engstrom and R. Alec Mackenzie. Copyright © 1967 by Zondervan Publishing House. Used by permission.

Section 8. Taken from *The Making of a Christian Leader* by Ted W. Engstrom. Copyright © 1976 by the Zondervan Corporation. Used by permission. Also from *The Christian Leader's 60-Second Management Guide* by Ted W. Engstrom and Edward R. Dayton. Copyright © 1984 by Edward R. Dayton and Ted W. Engstrom. Used by permission of Word Books.

Section 9. Taken from *Your Gift of Administration* by Ted W. Engstrom. Copyright © 1983 by Ted W. Engstrom. Used by permission of Thomas Nelson Publishers.

Contents

SECTION 9: THE GIFT OF ADMINISTRATION

To the Reader

Whether you are a pastor, homemaker, student, craftsman, athletic professional, retired senior citizen, realtor or businessperson, this book is for you.

If you wonder how I dare invite such a wildly disparate, wide-ranging assortment of men and women into these pages it is because of this: Through years of management experience, Ted Engstrom has discovered that virtually every success-oriented man and woman—and certainly you who hold this book in your hands fit this category—wants to do two things. People such as you are willing to pay the high price to do all that is necessary to design a life, and not just make a living. You are also eager to further develop your interpersonal skills and expand your leadership potential to become a more effective, productive servant of God. These objectives are what this volume is all about.

If you are a pastor, you want to keep becoming the leader God wants you to be to your congregation, your community and your family. The pressures on your life are increasing. You are being requested to perform leadership tasks demanded of few other leaders. You're expected to "ring the bell" every Sunday morning with sermons clearly thought through and powerfully spoken—to say nothing of your being expected to be a professional counselor, apt administrator, one-person public relations firm—and a low handicap golfer if at all possible. If in the midst of your harried life you are in need of a boost—and perhaps even a challenge—this book can and will be your fresh source of personal development and management ideas.

If you are a mother, father or grandparent, your deepest desire is to present yourself as a model of God's love to your children and grandchildren. When the child-rearing gets tough—and communication *always* breaks down—you want to believe with all your heart the truth of the verse: "Train up a child in the way he should go, and when he is old he will not depart from it." If we've caught you as a parent at a tough time, cheer up.

Ted Engstrom will lift your spirits and give you hope.

If you're a businessperson, you've trained yourself to wade through the superfluous numbers so that your eyes fall repeatedly to the all-important "bottom line." Every day, profit and loss figures stare you in the face. Some weeks business is terrific. At other times you honestly wonder if it's worth getting out of bed in the morning. But you hang in there because you're not a quitter and you are determined to exercise your leadership and management skills. Right now, if you feel you could use some good, sound business counsel, that's in this book too. (In fact, you might even want to start your reading with Section 6: "Work, Goals and Problem Solving." I think these and other chapters will provide you with some key insights on how to stay on top in your business world.)

No matter who you are, no matter how young, how old, how experienced or inexperienced, the ideas in this book will help you gain a better understanding of yourself. You'll receive insights on how to motivate and work with others, and you'll learn how to further sharpen your leadership and administrative skills.

With the encouragement of many of his colleagues—and particularly the gentle nudging of good friends such as Dr. Bill Bright of Campus Crusade for Christ and Les Stobbe and Dan Benson of Here's Life Publishers, Ted Engstrom has consented to this gathering together of selected chapters from several of his previous books whose themes have been integrity, excellence, friendship, time management, goal-setting and administration. I believe you will find it invaluable to have this treasury of trustworthy advice at your side to inspire you, train you, and encourage you.

Throughout a lifetime of successful leadership, Ted remains a man of quiet strength and humility. In fact, it was only after a long period of persuasion on the part of Here's Life Publishers and myself that he agreed, reluctantly, to let us subtitle this book *The Best of Ted Engstrom.* After considerable reflection, he agreed to the republication of these chapters provided their reappearance be for one purpose only: *that the words of my mouth and the meditation of my heart be acceptable in Thy sight, O Lord, my Rock and my Redeemer.*

I urge you to read this book with that spirit in mind. When I asked Ted what his prayer is for this project, he suggested that I convey his thoughts directly to you, the reader:

"I pray your life may be filled with an integrity of conscience, word and deed that will cause those around you to beat a path to your door.

"I pray you will pursue an uncommon excellence in your dealings with your congregation, your community, your family, your students, your teachers and your friends.

"I pray if you should ever lose your motivation for service and decide to throw in the towel, that you will always give your challenge at least 'another five minutes,' believing that *it's always too soon to quit.*

"I pray you will always remember that true happiness comes only when your life remains dedicated to God and committed to serving others.

"I pray you will get a stronger, more resolute hand on managing your time, setting good, realizable goals and solving problems.

"And from the bottom of my heart, I pray you will keep exhibiting your leadership, management and administrative skills as your worthy service to a God who expects from you your very best."

I close with two of the most powerful words in the English language. *Thank you! Thank you* for taking the time to read this book. *Thank you* in advance for applying the principles in these chapters to your own life and ministry. *Thank you* for sharing its message with your friends. And *thank you* to a loving God for giving me the privilege of gathering together these life-changing thoughts in one volume.

ROBERT C. LARSON
Editor

The High Road to Integrity

Keeping promises. Telling the truth. Doing what's right at all costs. However you define the word "integrity," I think you'll agree it is a commodity in painfully short supply in our homes, businesses, politics and interpersonal relationships. Why is this so? What has happened to erode our commitment to truth? What can we do about it?

In these chapters from *Integrity,* we will look at some of the fundamental reasons why our IQ (integrity quotient) is at an all-time low. We'll also suggest some practical ways to help you pursue the high road of integrity in every area of your life.

*How the integrity crisis is
hitting ever closer to home.*

1

One Nation Under Greed?

W̲e Americans pledge allegiance to "one nation under God" and then often conduct our lives as if we believe in "one nation under Greed." The currency in our pockets says, "In God We Trust," but which god? New cars, vacation homes, investments, prestige and notoriety all develop heartbeats of their own, and rise up to demand our worship.

How did our nation get this way? And what can we do to affect a change?

OPENING THE FLOODGATE

It seems ironic that as I write this chapter we are observing the anniversary of a watershed event in American ethics. It was early Saturday morning on 17 June 1972. A guard named Frank Wills noticed the catch on a door leading from his building into its garage had been taped so it would not lock. Thinking someone in the building had put it there, he tore off the tape. On his next rounds, Wills found the catch had been retaped. This time he called the police. The officers went to the eighth floor and started down. On the sixth floor, they surprised five men rifling files. Although they were dressed in suits and ties, they wore surgical gloves and carried walkie-talkies.

The newspapers didn't make much of the incident. It just didn't have the feel of a front-page news story. At least not yet.

The following Monday, President Nixon's press secretary Ronald Ziegler called it "a third–rate burglary," but with that small start began the biggest political scandal in American history.

In the ensuing years, the fallout from the Watergate incident would cause the first resignation of a president, the coincidental first resignation of a vice president, and the trials and jailing of many top administration officials including the attorney general, the White House chief of staff, the head of the president's domestic counsel and his White House lawyer.

The White House attempted to hide its role in the affair and payoffs were made to the burglars.

In a conversation with his chief of staff, H.R. Haldeman, six days after the burglary, President Nixon agreed to a plan whereby the CIA, on a pretext that its operations might be compromised, would tell the FBI not to investigate Watergate further.

John Dean, the White House counsel who was involved in the planning of the political espionage effort, tried to tell Nixon how deeply mired the White House had become. When it became apparent prosecutors were closing in, Dean told them the whole story.

The House Judiciary Committee held hearings to decide whether to recommend that Nixon be impeached, and voted yes on three of five charges. Then came the final blow: Among the tape recordings Nixon had to release was the Haldeman conversation of 23 June 1972, dubbed the "smoking gun."

Two years later, on 8 August 1974, Nixon told the nation he had lost his political base. He resigned as of noon the next day.

Many observers feel this event served as a critical turning point in America's moral conscience. Soon after the fall of Nixon a groundswell of sentiment spawned new interest in campaign reform and political honesty.

But how long did it last?

A recent poll by *U.S. News and World Report* and Cable News Network showed that more than half of the 1,006 adults surveyed think people are less honest today than they were ten years ago. Seven out of ten say they are dissatisfied with current standards of honesty—the largest proportion since 1973, at the height of the Watergate scandal.[1]

And those polled seem to be particularly suspicious of public figures. Three out of four say they rarely or never lie to family members, and substantial majorities of married respondents think their spouses are almost always honest with them. But only 30 percent feel that congressional leaders always or almost always tell the truth; only 38 percent believe the President "tells it like it is."

This reminds me of the old backwoods story. Seems a farmer needed an extra hand for a moment. "Will you hold my horse?" he said to a well-dressed stranger.

"Sir," said the stranger, "I'll have you know that I'm a member of the U.S. Congress."

"Oh, that's all right," said the farmer. "I'll trust you anyway."

Despite their dim view of what's going on in the outside world, those surveyed in this same poll indicated they personally still highly prized integrity. Overwhelmingly, they ranked it as the most important characteristic in a friend—well ahead of intelligence or even common interests. Those same respondents were firm in their convictions that others, up to and including public officials, should be held to high standards of honesty and integrity. Seven out of ten said the President of the United States should *never* lie to the American public.

Yet as I wrote this chapter the news was filled with new revelations of President Reagan's alleged mishandling of the Iran-Contra arms and hostage affair. Senior staff members, cabinet members, military leaders, secretaries, and numerous others paraded before the congressional committee on television interpreting and inventing the truth. Many sought to uncover yet another "smoking gun" in the hand of the President.

LEADERS TURNED LOSERS

Americans have been given ample cause for alarm. In a recent cover story on "Ethics," *Time* magazine ran the following revelation: "More than 100 members of the [then-present] Administration have had ethical or legal charges leveled against them. That number is without precedent."[2]

Not counting those embroiled in the "Iran-amuk" crisis, the infamous included: a Chief of the FAA who resigned when grand juries probed his earlier business dealings; a Food and Drug Administration commissioner who resigned while under investigation for overlapping reimbursements for travel; a National Security Adviser who resigned amid controversy over a $1,000 "honorarium," and an EPA assistant administrator who was convicted of perjury concerning preferential treatment for a former employer, to cite but a few.

Our Congress may be loud and boisterous when it comes to investigating the integrity of the President's men, but it doesn't always make the same noise about its own internal investigations. In the more secluded recesses of the Capitol, the House Committee on Standards of Official Conduct and the Senate Select Committee on Ethics are investigating allegations of misconduct by its own. At the time of this writing at least five members have been accused of ethical and legal transgressions that make them potential targets for committee investigation. Allegations range from bribery, payroll and campaign-fund infractions to the possible leaking of classified information to foreign sources.

Despite the 1978 Ethics in Government Act, critics think Congress is too slow to respond, or that they shroud their deliberations in silence.

"The problem is, it's very hard for peers to judge peers," says Fred Wertheimer, president of Common Cause. "The system ends up shielding the member; it becomes his protector."

What seems right to the White House is often wrong to

Congress. And what seems right to Congress is often wrong to the public. Leaders in power are no different from the rest of us. No matter how much we try to hide our actions, our integrity (or lack of it) always shows through.

PERSONAL REFLECTION

The natural reaction is to look at these transgressors, hike up our skirts and turn smugly away in righteous indignation. But before you and I assume the role of prosecutor, judge and executioner, let's take a look at ourselves.

I'll start with me. One short incident will serve to remind me of my need to examine my own motives and actions.

It was back in 1944 while I was serving both in the U.S. Army and as editor of *Christian Digest* magazine for Pat and Bernie Zondervan. We were on a troop train. Before my conversion I had enjoyed an occasional poker game, but for reasons of conscience had given it up soon afterward. However, this trip was long and the train was slow, so when a couple of the fellows invited me to join them for a few hands, I hesitated only a moment before saying, "Deal me in."

I knew I shouldn't be playing. My conscience was smarting the whole time. But then nobody was going to recognize me so why not keep playing? During the game, I noticed a young man who stood to watch me play for a while, then moved on. After the game was over, this same young soldier approached again.

"Are you Ted Engstrom?" he asked.

"Yes," I replied.

"Are you the Ted Engstrom who writes that column in the *Christian Digest?*"

"Yes, I am. Why? Have we met?"

"No, we haven't met, but I read that column all the time."

About now I could feel the flush of embarrassment and consternation rising with more intensity than the thrill of four

21

aces.

"Well, I want you to know that I've lost all respect for you." Then he turned and walked away from me (and perhaps the Lord). I never saw that soldier again.

No big deal? Hardly. It started as an innocent little game to kill time, but I soon discovered the stakes were much higher. Now it was no game and the issue had grown as large as my entire ministry and a brother's spiritual well-being. I've never forgotten the pain and sadness of that moment.

It's sobering to think how quickly the smallest personal decision can escalate into a large group concern. I'm sure the people whose pictures appeared in that *Time* article could all tell similar stories about the innocent beginnings of their ordeals.

It's obvious the Watergate debacle didn't bring lasting reform to the secular world, so it should come as little surprise that previous problems in the pulpit didn't prevent our current religious difficulties.

SEDUCTION AND ADULTERY

One of the first celebrity preacher scandals involved sex and a clergyman who—like today's group of miscreants—also enjoyed "the good life." Before and after the Civil War, the Rev. Henry Ward Beecher was the most famous preacher in the land. His oratory drew crowds of thousands to his church in Brooklyn each week. Some called him "the greatest preacher since Saint Paul." He reportedly earned the princely (and unheard of) sum of $40,000 per year. Delighting in his treasures, Beecher enjoyed carrying with him uncut gems and openly endorsed commercial products ranging from soap to watches. Then in 1874 Beecher's friend and protégé, Theodore Tilton, accused the beloved preacher of seducing his wife. The trial was such an attraction that admission tickets were sold to the public. And the outcome? The jury failed to reach a verdict and Beecher's influence and popularity continued undiminished for another thirteen years until his death.

FALLEN "QUEEN OF HEAVEN"

The next notorious case of an imperfect pastor in America occurred some fifty years later. She was flamboyant and attractive—a seemingly necessary mix for the flapper age of the Roaring Twenties. Aimee Semple McPherson wore flowing white gowns as she held court in her $1.5 million church in Los Angeles where she was surrounded by choirs, bell-ringers and an eighty-piece xylophone band. One afternoon in May of 1926, at the peak of her career, McPherson went for a swim in the Pacific and disappeared.

Thirty-six days later she emerged in a Mexican border town, claiming to have wandered through the desert after escaping from kidnappers. Police, noting that the ordeal had left her shoes unscuffed, turned up evidence that the preacher had in fact spent most of the time in a Carmel, California cottage with a former employee, himself married. McPherson was charged with "conspiracy to commit acts injurious to public morals."

Though the case was eventually dropped and the "Queen of Heaven's Flock" remained loyal, McPherson died at the age of fifty-three of an "accidental overdose" of barbiturates.

You and I would like to think experiences such as this teach us something. I'm sure they do. But not always as much as we would like.

At the same time that revelations of alleged government misdeeds were hitting our headlines, the Christian world was both shocked and embarrassed when the head of a popular Christian TV ministry resigned in disgrace after acknowledging sexual misconduct. Subsequent investigation revealed an addiction to opulence that misappropriated millions of dollars in donations and put the ministry in jeopardy of bankruptcy and legal action.

Less than a year later, yet another TV evangelist was caught visiting a motel with a prostitute. Acquaintances admitted he had struggled with a history of sexual misconduct, and in a tearful confession to his home church he confessed his wrongdoing and begged forgiveness. Yet only three months later,

23

he was back in the pulpit.

DONOR DOLLARS

In the late 1970s I had the privilege and pain of reviewing our country's charitable giving practices. This experience led to the formation of a national council. The country had undergone a prominent scandal some years earlier involving the Pallottine Fathers. In 1975, two reporters for the *Baltimore Sun* discovered that the Pallottine order, mailing as many as a hundred million letters a year in charity appeals, was funneling large sums into a variety of other operations — monetary and political. They collected millions of dollars that donors thought were going to the poor. This deception — along with several other public disclosures — spurred many religious organizations into a closer examination of their financial dealings.

More than 150,000 inquiries a year poured into the Better Business Bureau concerning the "honesty" of charitable organizations.

In December 1977, representatives of thirty-two evangelical Christian groups met in Chicago to decide on their response to mounting pressure for reform. Over the next few months, a steering committee developed standards which would be applicable to evangelical groups and sought to communicate with others who were not at the original sessions. In March 1979, the Evangelical Council for Financial Accountability (ECFA) was formed, representing more than 1,100 evangelical organizations with a total 1975 income of $1 billion from 25 to 30 million donors. It was my privilege to serve as chairman of the board of the ECFA for its first three years.

Today, this organization accounts for approximately $1.5 billion in donations. Unfortunately the American Association of Fund-Raising Council estimates that religious causes collect around $37 billion. Who oversees the remaining $35.5 billion?[3]

America's experience with greed and integrity breakdown is by no means the first. The events which led to the collapse of the Roman Empire are startlingly similar to the events occurring in our nation today.

The following seven-step sequence was recently distributed as a warning to America by the Arthur S. DeMoss Foundation. I find its conclusions revealing and sobering.

Historical Sequence

1. *Strong Families*: Rome was founded on high moral standards. Each father was respected as the head of the family. In the early republic, the father had legal authority to discipline rebellious members of his family.

2. *Home Education*: The education of the children was the responsibility of the parents. This further strengthened the children's honor and respect for their parents and also deepened the communication and understanding between parents and children.

3. *Prosperity*: Strong Roman families produced a strong nation. The Roman armies were victorious in war. The wealth of conquered nations increased Roman prosperity and prestige.

4. *National Achievements*: Great building programs began in Rome. A vast network of roads united the empire. Magnificent palaces, public buildings, and coliseums were constructed.

5. *Infiltration of "The Lie"*: "The Lie" was first given to Eve in the garden of Eden: "ye shall be as gods, knowing—and deciding for yourselves—good and evil" (Genesis 3:5). As families prospered, it became fashionable to hire educated Greeks to care for the children. Greek philosophy, with its humanistic and godless base, was soon passed on to the Roman families. Women demanded more rights and, in order to accommodate them, new marriage contracts were designed, including "open marriages."

6. *Big Government*: By the first century A.D. the father had lost his legal authority. It was delegated to the village, then to the city, then to the state, and finally to the empire. In Rome, citizens complained about housing shortages, soaring rents, congested traffic, polluted air, crime in the streets, and the high cost of living. Unemployment was a perennial problem. To solve it, the government created a multitude of civil service jobs, includ-

ing building inspectors, health inspectors, and tax collectors.

7. *Decline and Persecution*: The problems of big government only multiplied. Meanwhile, a flourishing New Testament church was established in the Roman Empire through the preaching of the apostle Paul and others. The final act of the Roman Empire was to bring great persecution to these Christians.[4]

Our moral decline hasn't reached these proportions yet by any means. But I think it's important to know where the barbs and hooks of integrity breakdown can lead.

IT'S ONLY NATURAL

Earlier I posed the question, "How did we get this way?" How did we move so much closer to becoming "one nation under Greed"? Quite simply. We came by it naturally. "The *natural man* does not receive the things of the Spirit of God," Paul tells us in 1 Corinthians 2:14. "For they are foolishness to him; nor can he know them, because they are spiritually discerned."

Admittedly, it's far easier to hustle the "quick buck" rather than the "slow cents." And conditions will remain this way until we apply the instruction that Paul adds in the next verse. "But he who is spiritual judges all things" (1 Corinthians 2:15). It is said that about 200 years ago, the tomb of the great conqueror Charlemagne was opened. The sight the workmen saw was startling. There was his body in a sitting position, clothed in the most elaborate of kingly garments, with a scepter in his bony hand. On his knee lay a New Testament, with a cold, lifeless finger pointing to Mark 8:36: "For what shall it profit a man, if he shall gain the whole world, and lose his own soul?"[5]

I also asked at the beginning of this chapter, "What can you and I do to *change* our own methods and motives? How can we earn a lasting profit and judge with the spiritual judgment that promotes integrity?"

That question is too profound to answer with a single chapter. More of the answers unfold as we spread out this map of truth in the pages that follow.

Where can we turn for accurate direction
in the moral choices we face?

2

When "Wrong" Becomes Right

Why does it seem that one person's delight is another's disgust? How much easier it would be to lead a life of integrity if we could all agree on the definition of "acceptable behavior."

We Christians have a concise package of Ten Commandments. But we also have many times that number of denominations to interpret them for us. So it's little wonder that wherever we look, the windows of truth become layered with semantic and theological fog.

This is an age of mind–numbing paradox. Our country began "with a firm reliance on the protection of Divine Providence." But today it's against the law for children to pray in public school. What seemed right for the preservation of the nation to one generation is now illegal to another.

Recently the state of California paroled a prisoner who was convicted of raping a fifteen–year–old–girl and chopping her arms off below the elbow. Though his victim is now condemned to a lifetime without her hands, Lawrence Singleton served less than ten years in prison. The law released him. Officials have not been able to find a community that wants the man within their city limits. What seems right to the authorities appears wrong to the public.

Here lies the core of integrity. How do we know what's right?

Even the little matters confound us in their own subtle ways. Parents spend two years teaching children how to stand up and speak for themselves. Then they spend another eighteen years teaching them to sit down and be quiet.

"Mind your own business! But remember you are your brother's keeper."

"The early bird gets the worm. But haste makes waste."

"To err is human. But one mistake and you're through."

Life is filled with contradictions. And we don't always resolve them as well as we might.

"FACTS ARE ENEMIES OF THE TRUTH"

Don Quixote makes a humorous remark in the play, "The Man from La Mancha." He used it to hide from the fact that his beloved "Dolcinea" was actually a common barmaid and the dreaded dragon was nothing more than a windmill. When confronted with such "facts," Don Quixote responded, "Facts? Facts are enemies of the truth."

I've heard it said, "You can prove anything from the Bible." True, there are those who would use the facts of Scripture to support their own ideas. Satan himself tried this ploy against Jesus. "If you are the Son of God, throw Yourself down (from the pinnacle of the temple where they were standing). For it is written: 'He shall give His angels charge concerning you,' and 'in their hands they shall bear you up, lest you dash your foot against a stone.' " Satan was indeed quoting "the facts of Scripture"—Psalm 91—but he was using it as an enemy of the truth. Jesus retorted with another overriding passage, "It is written again, 'You shall not tempt the Lord your God' " (Matthew 4:5–7).

If facts can be enemies of the truth, then it should come as no surprise to you and me that good intentions can be enemies of integrity.

STATISTICALLY MISSPEAKING

Statistics are often used as enemies of the truth. They say statistics never lie. But you find a lot of liars quoting statistics! It's all too easy to leave out data or compare apples with oranges. And once an erroneous statistic is spread around it becomes like toothpaste—virtually impossible to put back into the tube.

Recently I discovered I had fallen victim to a statistical cliché—one that is easy to remember, popular, and wrong. Let me use this occasion to correct a misconception and illustrate once again how "facts" can actually become enemies of the truth.

It's been widely quoted that about one out of two American marriages will end in divorce. This idea is "one of the most specious pieces of statistical nonsense ever perpetrated in modern times," says pollster Louis Harris. Government figures and a recent poll by the Louis Harris Company show that only one in eight will end in divorce. And in any single year, only about 2 percent of existing marriages will break up.[1]

Yes, Census Bureau figures do show about 1.2 million divorces for 2.5 million marriages during an average year. But "one critical element is left out of the equation," observes Mr. Harris. "A much, much bigger 52 million other marriages just keep flowing along like Old Man River."

This whole episode reminds me of the old adage from H.L. Mencken. "There is always an easy solution to every human problem—neat, plausible, and wrong."

EYEWITNESS MYOPIA

Since we have to be cautious about statistics for direction, what can we rely upon to keep us wholehearted, sound and unimpaired in character? Surely, seeing is believing?

Maybe.

Elizabeth Loftus is an expert witness who has testified in hundreds of cases where eyewitness testimony is crucial. But her experience as a professor of psychology and adjunct professor of law at the University of Washington in Seattle lends little support to the assumption that "seeing is believing."

"As a psychologist who specializes in memory, I know that the human mind is subject to distortion," she writes in an article for *Newsweek* magazine. Loftus informs us, "People often remember things differently from the way they really were. And contrary to the popular belief that traumatic events tend to create an indelible 'fixation' in the mind, such traumas are often associated with memory problems. There is, in fact, a body of research challenging the value of eyewitness memory."[2]

Professor Loftus then summarizes the story of three innocent citizens who served time in prison because of erroneous eyewitness testimony. One account involves a Roman Catholic priest who was falsely identified by seven witnesses in a series of holdups in Delaware and Pennsylvania. They swore to tell the whole truth and found it impossible.

So how reliable is the human mind for control and direction of its own life? How reliable is an umbrella in a hurricane? Scripture leaves little doubt. "There is a way which *seems right* to a man. But its end is the way of *death*" (Proverbs 14:12). To reiterate the point, this warning is repeated verbatim by the same inspired author two chapters later in Proverbs 16:25.

"But surely," some may argue, "if I wander around long enough looking for the right answers I'll stumble onto the truth." Unfortunately one of the major prophets takes major exception to that delusion. "O Lord, I know the way of man is not in himself; it is not in man who walks to direct his own steps" (Jeremiah 10:23).

The book of Judges recounts the happenings in Israel when "everyone did what was right in his own eyes" (Judges 21:25). It was one of the bloodiest eras in their history.

HUMANISM – SPIRIT ANSWERS FROM THE WRONG REALM

To further trouble the waters and muddy the distinction between wrong and right, we find ourselves surrounded by the intellectual waves of secular humanism. Here is a philosophy that worships the use of human intellect by rejecting God and canonizing reason as "supreme." Though less obvious than ancient "gods" of wood and stone, such idolatry is equally destructive to integrity.

Secular humanism has its roots in the eighteenth century "Enlightenment" which taught that man is the master of personal fate and captain of his soul. We see this heresy taking root in the educational system from preschool to postgraduate institutions. But we often overlook its sinister shadow in other circles.

Here are some of the humanistic issues that impair our ability to distinguish right from wrong. These are paraphrased from an article by Donald Bloesch which appeared in *Eternity* magazine.[3]

WELFARE LIBERALISM

The ideology of welfare liberalism, which seeks to solve human problems through social engineering, is one manifestation of secular humanism. But the ideology of free enterprise capitalism (classical liberalism), which believes the free market contains all the solutions, is definitely another. Messianic socialism, with its dialectical materialism, is one of the more poisonous fruits of secular humanism.

The Moral Majority, other fundamentalists, and evangelical groups concentrate unduly on the left–wing expressions of these issues. But secular humanism isn't the only pseudo–religious reflection we see in the contorted glass of human reason. Other distortions obscure the path to integrity.

NATIONALISM

Easy to overlook is the threat of nationalism. This sentiment enthrones the values and traditions of the nation or *Volk* (people). It elevates the national or racial heritage over the autonomous individual (as in classical liberalism) or the political party (as in communism). While secular humanism subverts the family by endorsing sexual freedom, "nationalism" (though

31

posing as the family's defender) subordinates it to the interests of the wider community, the nation–state, which is adorned with a kind of mystical aura.

American fundamentalism has been unable to perceive or appreciate this threat from the political right. This may account for fundamentalism's lack of credibility when it addresses issues that should command the attention of all people of moral sensitivity, (including pornography, "value–free" sex education, and abortion).

TECHNOLOGICAL MATERIALISM

We should also consider the threat to our value system imposed by technological materialism. Jacques Ellul has called this the dominant ideology in the modern industrialized nations. According to this world—and life—view, the prime virtues are utility, efficiency, and productivity. People who make no visible contribution to the betterment of society, such as the aged, the retarded, and the severely handicapped, are pushed to one side or even regarded as expendable.

Whereas a great many secular humanists are inner-directed and stress personal integrity, technological materialists are other–directed, emphasizing loyalty to the organization, whether it be the state, corporation, or union. While a significant number of secular humanists prize individuality and freedom, technological materialists encourage the dependence of humanity on technology.

MYSTICISM

A more subtle challenge to integrity is mysticism—that perennial temptation to turn away from the pursuit of pleasure and power in search of union with the Eternal. The penetration of Eastern religions into the industrial West has presented a new alternative for tens of thousands of people. Mysticism is usually a world–denying type of philosophy, but some neo–mystics stress immersion in the world, finding God in the depths of human existence. Whereas secular humanism celebrates the fulfillment of the self, mysticism emphasizes the loss of the self in the collective unconscious, the cosmic process, or the undifferentiated unity.

Mysticism is especially prevalent among those in our churches and theological schools who are intent on recovering spirituality. It is also found among radical feminists, particularly those who are trying to reinstate the nature religion of witchcraft.

NIHILISM

Perhaps most sinister of all is the mounting peril of nihilism—the denial of all norms and values. Nihilism is particularly fostered by the technological mentality, which elevates efficiency over ideology and religion. Technocrats try to give technology a rational direction, but the temptation is almost irresistible to sacrifice ends for means. Moreover, a technology without aim or purpose, a soul-less science, is more destructive than constructive.

Indeed, the social agenda of nihilism is generally the overthrow of all existing social institutions and all norms. Nihilism ushers in the new barbarians, who are intent on destroying rather than creating, but they destroy in vain hope that something new and durable will result. The dramatic rise in international terrorism is a manifestation of the unleashing of the spirit of nihilism.

Nihilists, like mystics and occultists, are generally irrationalists, even as secular humanists and technological materialists are supreme rationalists. If the modern age is correctly characterized by what Francis Schaeffer calls "the flight from reason," it seems that nihilism, fascism, and nationalism may be greater threats than secular humanism to behavior and integrity. (End of paraphrase.)

WHERE DO WE TURN?

Since we cannot automatically trust every "ism" and spirit; since we must beware of our own steps and our own mind to determine what is right and what is wrong; since we cannot trust eyewitness testimony and statistics; since we cannot rely upon conventional wisdom of the world around us, where *can* we turn for accurate direction in life? How can anyone be expected to lead a life of integrity if everyone uses different rules? Personally I count it a miracle that modern society can hold together at all with strains such as these tearing at the fabric of its value system.

What this means to you and me in our search for integrity is that we must "prove all things" and "try the spirits" as admonished by the apostle Paul.

For times such as these, let me suggest three rules to live by that can help us be men and women of integrity.

RULE #1: GIVE OF YOUR BEST IN THE WORST OF TIMES

In times such as these, our best defense is friends who keep us honest. One of my close friends, Russ Reid, and I were having lunch the other day. Russ is a long–time business associate, one whom I encouraged during the birth of his advertising agency. In the years since, he has helped us significantly at World Vision.

As we talked, the subject quickly turned to integrity. After all, I was writing a book on the subject and needed as much input from my friends as I could get. Russ reminded me that within the broad category of integrity, the "sub–category" of *accountability* was perhaps the greatest prize of all. He reflected that when Christian leaders, pastors, educators, homemakers, and others hold their power loosely and listen to the counsel of others, they become more open and accountable. However, when they become tight–fisted with their thinking, and when they choose to "go it alone" the results are usually devastating. We need each other. There simply must be others with whom we consciously share our most intimate thoughts.

Russ's words set the tone for our lunch as we opened up to each other even more—taking the risk of choosing to be vulnerable. We talked about the need for accountability with our families, friends, and fellow workers. We further agreed that accountability starts with *yours truly* — with an honest appraisal of who we are, of what makes us tick. This includes a long, hard look at our own ideals and motives. The process must begin with a "self-inspection" tour. After all, if you and I are not honest with ourselves, how will we ever be authentic to others? However, when you and I give an accurate account of what we think and what we do, then those around us can come to rely on us with confidence.

Another colleague and close friend, Dr. James Dobson, founder of Focus on the Family, stresses the importance of getting together to review plans and review actions. "Men need to ask themselves, 'How can I be a better husband, father, and worker?' Women need to sit down and discuss how they can help each other meet the needs of family and friends."[4]

We need help from each other. About the only thing we can do well by ourselves is fail.

The need for such accountability through our friendships is even greater for those in leadership positions.

Bill Hybels, pastor of the Willow Creek Community Church in South Barrington, Illinois, says, "I walk with a group of three brothers. I share much of my personal life and they are free to correct me. In fact, they delight in correcting me. This keeps me accountable."[5]

The 2/4/6 Club

Many years ago I heard another friend of mine, Pastor Ray Stedman, talk about a special group of men he had gathered to meet with him on a weekly basis. These men were not all members of his congregation, but were close friends who held each other accountable in their spiritual walk. He said his experience with that small group was one of the most meaningful in his life.

After thinking about it, and realizing the need for such accountability in my own life, I talked to my pastor about it. Dr Ray Ortland was interested. He expressed similar deep needs and feelings, so we met a couple of times to discuss the concept.

Then we invited several men to meet with us. Some of the original group dropped out, but ultimately there were six of us who met together periodically for more than ten years in a local restaurant. We called it the 2/4/6 Club, indicating that there were six of us, who met on the second and fourth Friday mornings of each month for breakfast. We met at 7 A.M. for approximately an hour and a half.

It was not a prayer group—although we did pray together. It was not a Bible study group—although we did spend time in the Word. It was a time of meeting and growing together, appreciating each other and sharing our individual spiritual pilgrimages. There was no appointed leader and no agenda. We met to share experiences, to laugh and to weep. We rejoiced in our successes. We also shared and were open about our failures.

Those meetings have literally changed my life.

ECFA—The Other Half of Stewardship

This need for accountability goes beyond our friends and personal lives.

I had the privilege, along with George Wilson of the Billy Graham Association, of co-founding the Evangelical Council for Financial Accountability in 1979 to protect donors from unscrupulous practices. "Part of the problem is that we've only been taught half of stewardship," said Arthur Borden, present president of the ECFA. "We've been taught how to give but not where to give, or what to expect from the organization we're supporting."[6]

Before being accepted into the Evangelical Council for Financial Accountability, potential members must show they meet several tough criteria.

How badly are these integrity "rules" needed today? A recent telephone poll conducted by Media General–Associated Press of 1,348 adult Americans revealed the following: Slightly more than half—53 percent—said they didn't believe money collected by television evangelists generally went to good causes. *Only 27 percent* believed the money was used for good purposes.[7]

Tough standards are desperately needed today. For more information about the reputable organizations that have joined the ECFA, I encourage you to write for a complete listing of all 400 (plus) members. The address for the Evangelical Council for Financial Accountability is P.O. Box 17511, Washington, D.C. 20041.

And the Inside, Too

Giving of our best in the worst of times means being wholehearted from the inside out.

Cliff Jones tells an amusing story about a close friend in Boston: "This man is intellectual, capable, and before he retired, he was the head of a prominent company. Some years ago, he was bothered by a toothache. This puzzled him because he had always brushed his teeth regularly. Upon visiting his dentist he was genuinely surprised to learn that people are supposed to brush on the inside as well as the outside of their teeth. He had been religiously cleaning only the front!"[8]

A bit hard to believe, but true. It illustrates our proclivity to clean the visible exterior and to assume the inside, which we cannot see, will somehow take care of itself. Christ encountered this same phenomenon with the Pharisees. They wanted to clean the outside of the platter and leave the inside full of vile and disgusting motives (Matthew 23:25).

We can overcome this attitude as long as we remain aware and vigilant.

RULE #2: LOOK UP TO THOSE BENEATH YOU

One of the major undercurrents eroding integrity is pride. It's "common thinking" to look down on those beneath us. Yet the wisdom of both man and God is filled with admonitions about esteeming others better than self. But how can we do this if we feel we really *are* better than another? Such is the case with parent over child, veteran over newcomer, boss over employee. How does a "superior" person build integrity by making others feel elevated?

David Ogilvy, founder of the advertising giant, Ogilvy and

Mather, reinforced the importance of this principle among his executives by sending a Russian doll to each person newly appointed to head an office in the Ogilvy Mather chain.

The doll contains five progressively smaller dolls. The message inside the smallest one reads: "If each of us hires people who are smaller than we are, we shall become a company of dwarfs. But if each of us hires people who are bigger than we are, Ogilvy and Mather will become a company of giants."[9]

One way to look up to those beneath you is by giving them room to grow into giants.

One of the giants of the business world is IBM. Did it become this way by looking down on the little guy? I found an enlightening interview with a legend at IBM, F.G. (Buck) Rodgers, former vice–president of marketing, and company dynamo for thirty–five years. His observations and philosophies are worth putting into practice.[10]

> Question: The IBM philosophy of business has become almost legendary. What makes it so special?
> Rodgers: It is based on three beliefs: first, respect for the individual; second, to give the best service of any company in the world; and third, to expect excellence from what people do. This was the idea of Tom Watson, Sr. when he started the business back in 1914.
> Question: What is the core of your belief system, if you had to sum it up in one basic principle?
> Rodgers: The thing I stress all the time is that you have to do a thousand things 1 percent better, not just one thing 1,000 percent better. It's doing the little things well, returning phone calls, saying "thank you" to people. It sounds like a simplistic cliché, but that is the reason one organization or one person is successful and another is not. The secret is that everybody knows what they ought to be doing, but the ones who practice daily excellence are the real difference makers.[11]

Much of that excellence stems from placing the needs of the customer (beneath you) *above* your own. In fact, earlier in this interview Buck Rodgers explained that a "company's organization structure should be inverted, with the customer at the top and sales reps and management underneath." Rodgers' commitment to the customer even went so far as to give priority to appointments with customers when they conflicted with meetings in the IBM executive suite.[12]

Five Rules for Dealing With Others

A research organization polled 500 executives, asking them what traits they thought were most important in dealing with others. From the information received, five basic "rules" were formulated. I like them because each one helps enlarge the other person. They are:

1. Always give your people the credit that is rightfully theirs. To do otherwise is both morally and ethically dishonest.

2. Be courteous. Have genuine consideration for other people's feelings, wishes, and situations.

3. Never tamper with the truth. Never *rationalize*. What you might *like* to believe is not necessarily the truth.

4. Be concise in your writing and talking, especially when giving instructions to others.

5. Be generous. Remember that it is the productivity of *others* that makes possible your executive position.[13]

People have greater motivation to understand and apply these principles in business—where the dollars count. But these concepts are equally important among family and friends. Families such as yours and mine are in dire need of help from above. It could easily start with big sister, Mom, or Dad. (That's you and me.) Looking up to those beneath you is one of the stepping stones of integrity.

RULE #3: STAND UP FOR YOUR CONVICTIONS

Those beneath us are but part of our world. Another strata exists over our heads. These include parents, older brothers and sisters, the boss (or bosses), police, city hall, the IRS, your pastor, to name but a few. And sometimes it feels as if all of these are looking over our shoulders and breathing down our necks at once.

When I say "stand up" to these superiors, I'm not talking about insubordination, hostility, or rebellion. I'm talking about esteem and conviction.

Some people may look down on you because they have personal problems dealing with their own authority. Others may look down on you because they care about you and want to help you become larger than they are (like the Russian doll). In either case, our reaction must be the same. We should stand up for what we believe. That way if we're right we'll gain ground. If we're wrong, we'll find out sooner than if we had made no stand at all.

This story by Nido Qubein illustrates my point.

An Eastern bishop was accustomed to paying an annual visit to a small religious college. On one such visit, the bishop engaged in an after–dinner conversation with the college president. The religious leader offered the opinion that the millennium could not be long in coming since everything about nature had been discovered, and all possible inventions had been made. The college president disagreed, stating that he felt the next fifty years would bring amazing discoveries and inventions. In his opinion, human beings would be flying through the skies like the birds within a relatively short time.

"Nonsense!" shouted the bishop, "Flight is reserved for the angels!"

The bishop's name was Wright. He had two sons—Orville and Wilbur.[14]

Fortunately for American aviation, the bishop's two sons were willing to join the college president in "standing up" for their beliefs and convictions.

As important as holding ground when you're right is the willingness to give ground when you're wrong. The challenge we all face is knowing which attitude is appropriate.

Fortunately, we're not left to our own guesswork. In matters of conviction and integrity, we have ample direction—as this remark from Abraham Lincoln demonstrates: "All the good from the Savior of the world is communicated through this Book; but for the Book we could not know right from wrong. All the things desirable to man are contained in it."

I've wrestled often with questions of integrity. Here are some passages from "the Book" that helped me keep my eye on the north star of conscience:

> By pride comes only contention, but with the well–advised is wisdom (Proverbs 13:10).
> The law of the wise is a fountain of life, to turn away from the snares of death (Proverbs 13:14).
> Poverty and shame will come to him who disdains correction, but he who regards reproof will be honored (Proverbs 13:18).
> He who walks with wise men will be wise, but the companion of fools will be destroyed (Proverbs 13:20).
> Faithful are the wounds of a friend, but the kisses of an enemy are deceitful (Proverbs 27:6).

There are dozens of other passages that will help you decide when to dig in your heels or when to hang up your boots. In fact, I agree with President Lincoln in recommending that you read the entire Book. But these passages have been useful to me in sorting out these matters of integrity. I'm confident they can benefit you as well.

Dr. E.M. Griffin gave an interesting comment when addressing a writer's conference at Wheaton College several years ago. It purportedly came from Ted Kennedy's speech writer:

"Those are my views. If you don't like them, let me know and I'll change them."

That's the exact antithesis of everything I want to convey in this chapter. It tells you what will *not* work as a new rule for the new millennium ahead. But let's take a brief look once again at what *will work* for you and for me:

1. Give of your best in the worst of times.

2. Look up to those beneath you.

3. Stand up for your convictions.

The Pursuit of Excellence

When you buy a new car you want to know the workmanship was done by competent, highly trained men and women who were committed to excellence in their work. When you attend a sporting event, you expect to see top athletes perform as if excellence flowed in their veins. When you hear a lecture, read a book, listen to a business proposal or observe actors on stage, you look forward to every facet of the presentation being carried with unabashed excellence. You want the performers to stretch you to your creative limits . . . to take you as far as you are able to go.

It's the same with trees! If someone were to ask you, "How tall will a tree grow?" your answer would have to be, "As tall as it can." After all, trees just don't grow half–way. And neither must you. Starting today, you, too, can *grow all the way* as you make a commitment to live a life of quality and excellence that will take you to your own outer limits of personal development—the kind of growth that will free you up to become an even greater servant to others.

In these chapters from *The Pursuit of Excellence* you will read stories that will challenge you to go even beyond those limits of excellence. You will be encouraged to give up your small ambitions and *go for it* as never before. In so doing you're bound to make some mistakes. But you will also learn that *what does not kill you makes you stronger.*

Enough said. Welcome to the exciting world of the pursuit of excellence.

*It takes action to achieve excellence—
there are no shortcuts to quality.*

3

Give Up Your Small Ambitions

An American Indian tells about a brave who found an eagle's egg and put it into the nest of a prairie chicken. The eaglet hatched with the brood of chicks and grew up with them.

All his life, the changeling eagle, thinking he was a prairie chicken, did what the prairie chickens did. He scratched in the dirt for seeds and insects to eat. He clucked and cackled. And he flew in a brief thrashing of wings and flurry of feathers no more than a few feet off the ground. After all, that's how prairie chickens were supposed to fly.

Years passed. And the changeling eagle grew very old. One day, he saw a magnificent bird far above him in the cloudless sky. Hanging with graceful majesty on the powerful wind currents, it soared with scarcely a beat of its strong golden wings.

"What a beautiful bird!" said the changeling eagle to his neighbor. "What is it?"

"That's an eagle—the chief of the birds," the neighbor clucked. "But don't give it a second thought. You could never be like him."

So the changeling eagle never gave it another thought.

And it died thinking it was a prairie chicken.[1]

What a tragedy. Built to soar into the heavens, but conditioned to stay earthbound, that eagle pecked at stray seeds and chased insects. Though designed to be among the most awesome of all fowl, he instead believed his neighbor's counsel: "Hey, you're only a prairie chicken. . . Come on, let's go find us some insects."

ACCEPTING THE STATUS QUO

Right now, you may find yourself in a situation much like that changeling eagle. You know you are designed to perform tasks far greater than you've performed to date. You know you have the ability to move well beyond your present self–imposed limitations. But for some reason, you do not choose the path of excellence.

You say, "After all, it's so much easier to scavenge for insects than to soar among the heavens. It's so much easier to accept the status quo than to venture out." Of course it is. It's also easier to enjoy long, nonproductive lunches and attend seminar after seminar on "how to do it" than to sit down and get the job done.

But that which is easy and nondemanding is seldom truly fulfilling. And it is 180 degrees away from the path toward personal excellence.

As we work out a strategy for pursuing excellence in these chapters, I think you'll realize that today is the today to start giving up your small ambitions. Right now, you can begin living your life with a vigor, enthusiasm, and intensity you never before imagined. Starting today, you can begin to draw from your own deep inner resources and cut a swath through mediocrity that will give your life a whole new significance. The results of your efforts may so surprise you that you'll wonder why you waited so long. You'll also find that your mind, stretched to a new idea or new action, will never retreat to its original dimension.

But a word of caution: Every truly worthwhile achievement of excellence has a price tag. The question you must answer for yourself is, How much am I willing to pay in hard work, patience, sacrifice, and endurance to be a person of excellence? Your answer is important, because the cost is great. But if you are willing to be the person you were meant to be, I think you will discover that *for you* the sky is the limit, because each one of us is called by God to become personally involved in an act of creation. Excellence is not restricted to sex, age, race, or occupation. This means a life of excellence is for *you*.

You may be a pastor, a student in seminary, a carpenter, an executive, a teacher. You may be a mother who every day tries to relate to two- and three-year-olds. You may be a parent of teenagers (a special prayer is said here for you). You may be young, or you may be in retirement. Whoever you are, today *is* the first day of the rest of your life—a day of new resolve and new beginnings. What will you make of these precious hours? Are you going to live the half life of a prairie chicken, scratching for seeds and insects? Or will you choose to soar, to build a personal reputation for excellence . . . to live your life as God intended, knowing that He loves you dearly and that He wants the very best for your life? I hope you'll accept the challenge to make this day a truly new day.

THE HIGHEST AND THE BEST

J.B. Phillips paraphrases Philippians 1:10 as follows: "I want you to be able always to recognize the highest and the best, and to live sincere and blameless lives until the day of Christ." In the New International Version the apostle's prayer is that we "be able to discern what is best."

The highest and the best—this should be the goal of every man and woman of God.

Be the best person you know how to be, in your personal life and on the job.

If you're not stretching yourself and your talents, ask yourself why not. And then do something about it.

Give up your small ambitions. Believe a big God: Remember that "God is greater"!

Get angry with your own mediocrity, and then do something constructive to get yourself out of the same old rut.

Don't wait for the seventh wave of success to carry you on to the comfort of the shore. That's the thinking of the irresponsible and the lazy. With God as your strength, take responsibility for your own actions and begin living life with a fresh point of view.

An exciting life of excellence awaits you — and it can begin today.

The admonition of the apostle Paul in Colossians 3:17 is to the point: "And whatever you do, in word or deed, do everything in the name of the Lord Jesus, giving thanks to God the Father through him." No greater standard for excellence can be found anywhere!

Again the apostle says in Philippians 4:8 (NIV): "If anything is excellent . . . think about such things."

But among many Christians, there are some serious tensions in the pursuit — or nonpursuit — of excellence. There are conflicts over what is highest and best. Some people feel the church should be a nickel–and–dime operation. Others choose to mortgage their grandchildren's future on the building of lavish cathedrals. Often, there's a curious mix.

I once visited a beautiful chapel on a new church college campus. In contrast to three obviously expensive chandeliers was a hand–drawn Sunday school attendance chart taped on the foyer wall. Twenty–five hundred dollars for chandeliers, but the best they could do to communicate what was happening to *people* was a crude graph.

WE ARE CALLED TO EXCELLENCE

A few years ago, we at World Vision were strongly criticized for purchasing first–quality plumbing for a new building (a long–term investment that has paid good dividends). But at the time, to some, it seemed "too good." There's also been occasional criticism for our having carpeting in many of our offices, instead of linoleum. "It looks too posh," one said. "It doesn't look Christian," said another. (I've never quite figured out what a Christian carpet might look like!) Someone else offered, "It won't be a good witness. It looks too nice."

Well, I couldn't disagree more. Somewhere in my files I have the actual yearly cost breakdown of how much World Vision has saved in linoleum wax alone. But that carpet also reduces noise and distraction, and thus helps our staff get the work done in considerably less time. As far as the Christian witness is concerned, we believe that appearance *is* important. We make no apologies for first–class appearance, because we as Christ's people are called to excellence. Further, we believe we are to *set the standards* of excellence for ourselves and others.

But "clothes don't necessarily make the person," and there is always the issue of confusing shadow with substance. Carpet on the floor will not hide shoddy work at the desk. That is why the quality of excellence must pervade our entire lives. It's so much more than just appearance. Scripture reminds us, "Let all things be done decently and in order."

In his book *Making It Happen,* Charles Paul Conn writes:

> Whatever it is
> However impossible it seems
> Whatever the obstacle that lies between you and it
> If it is noble
> If it is consistent with God's kingdom, you must
> Hunger after it and stretch yourself to reach it.

Have you ever watched a dramatic movie about mountain climbing, where the camera follows the climbers close up as they inch their way into the heavens, grasping and reaching for every little crevice of rock which in turn gives them a new footing to move up still a few more inches? And haven't you felt, *Wow. I could never do that. You've got to be born a mountain goat to make that kind of a climb.* But some of you *have* tried it, haven't you? And you've actually lived to discuss the experience. Sure, it was tough, exhausting, and frightening. But you did it. You moved beyond yourself. You gave up the comfort of the common plateau and headed toward greater heights. And you made it!

But mountains aren't the only challenges. What about your everyday life? How exciting are your sixteen waking hours each day? Are you constantly challenging yourself, straining your muscles? Or are you settling for less than the best?

If so, is it because you feel uneasy with the idea of having the best, being the best, or doing something that is truly outstanding? Do you find it easier to handle "excellence" if you can shift the responsibility for it onto someone else—or *onto the Lord*: "The Lord has really blessed his ministry," or, "The Lord really gave her great gifts"? Do you even feel somehow less spiritual if there is direct praise for a job done with *excellence*?

"To God be the glory" is more than the poetry of a song. It's the truth. God is the source of all our strength and to Him all glory and honor is due. But God has always chosen to use people like you and me. Frail? Yes. Prone to mistakes? Of course. Perfect? Never. But with all the things we can list that are wrong with us, there is still one overriding cry from the heavens: "I love you, and you are my children." When it comes to people, God never has made junk. And besides that, as Ethel Waters used to say, "He's never been guilty of sponsoring a flop."

EXCELLENCE: OUR DUTY, OUR WITNESS

Striving for excellence in our work, whatever it is, is not only our Christian duty, but a basic form of Christian witness. And our nonverbal communication speaks so loudly that people often cannot hear a single word we say.

Dr. David McClellan, professor of psychology at Harvard, says: "Most people in this world can be divided into two broad groups. There is that *minority* which is challenged by opportunity and is willing to work hard to achieve something, and the *majority*, which really does not care all that much."

Which camp are you in? Are you willing to work at being good at something? Really good? Are you willing to spend your life building a reputation? Or will you settle for the life of a prairie chicken and never even come close to fulfilling your potential?

Dr. Melvin Lorentzen reminds us that "We must stress excellence over against mediocrity done in the name of Christ. We must determine to put our best into the arts, so that when we sing a hymn about Jesus and His love, when we erect a building for the worship of God, when we stage a play about the soul's pilgrimage, we will not repel people but attract them to God."

Perhaps part of our problem is just some defective theology. Many of us have difficulty living with the biblical truth that a sovereign God is doing it all—and the parallel truth that man has not only been given complete responsibility *for* his actions but is commanded to *take action*! This is part of the tension between theology and living, a tension that will never be—nor should it be—resolved. The following story may illustrate what I mean.

A pastor once made an investment in a large piece of ranch real estate which he hoped to enjoy during his years of retirement. While he was still an active pastor, he would take one day off each week to go out to his land and work. But what a job! What he had bought, he soon realized, was several acres of weeds, gopher holes, and rundown buildings. It was anything but attractive, but the pastor knew it had potential and he stuck with it.

Every week he'd go to his ranch, crank up his small tractor, and plow through the weeds with a vengeance. Then he'd spend time doing repairs on the buildings. He'd mix cement, cut lumber, replace broken windows, and work on the plumbing. It was hard work, but after several months the place began to take shape. And every time the pastor put his hand to some task, he would swell with pride. He knew his labor was finally paying off.

When the project was completed, the pastor received a neighborly visit from a farmer who lived a few miles down the road. Farmer Brown took a long look at the preacher and cast a longer eye over the revitalized property. Then he nodded his approval and said, "Well, preacher, it looks like you and God really did some work here."

The pastor, wiping the sweat from his face, answered, "It's interesting you should say that, Mr. Brown. But I've got to tell you—you should have seen this place when God had it all to Himself!"

EXCELLENCE TAKES DISCIPLINE

It takes action to achieve excellence—deliberate, careful, relentless action. There are no shortcuts to quality.

In his fine book, *Excellence*, John Gardner says: "Some people have greatness thrust upon them. Very few have excellence thrust upon them . . . They achieve it. They do not achieve it unwittingly by 'doing what comes naturally' and they don't stumble into it in the course of amusing themselves. All excellence involves discipline and tenacity of purpose."

Simple? No. Costly? Yes. Worth it? You bet.

*Here's how you can turn failures
into successes.*

4

"Mistakes" Are Important

One of the greatest obstacles we face in attempting to reach our potential is the fear of making a mistake—the very human fear of failure. And yet *excellence* is built on failure, usually one failure after another.

The genius inventor Thomas Edison was one day faced by two dejected assistants, who told him, "We've just completed our seven hundredth experiment and we still don't have an answer. We have failed."

"No, my friends," said Edison, "you haven't failed. It's just that we know more about this subject than anyone else alive. And we're closer to finding the answer, because now we know seven hundred things not to do." Edison went on to tell his colleagues, "Don't call it a mistake. Call it an education."

What a marvelous perspective. I don't know how many additional tries it took before Edison achieved success, but we all know that eventually he and his colleagues *did* see the light. Literally.

Whether you are an inventor, a housewife, a student, a pastor, or a business executive, you must adopt the same principle that guided Edison in his laboratory work: Learn from your mistakes and keep going. In fact, don't call them mistakes at all; call them *education*.

I cringe when I recall some of the horrendous mistakes I have made during my lifetime. I have made gross errors in judgment and have been insensitive toward people I really loved. I have unintentionally bruised colleagues and employees. But I've tried to evaluate those mistakes down through the years so that I could learn from them. I hope I have.

I am not alone, however. I am in the company of millions. Because who among us has gone through a single day without committing some error, some mistake?

EVERYONE MAKES MISTAKES

I'd like you to consider doing this little exercise. Take a few minutes today or tomorrow to carefully observe yourself and people around you. For the sake of this exercise, watch them carefully and see if they make any mistakes. Here's what you may find:

The cashier at the supermarket rings up the wrong amount for your head of lettuce and has to correct the error on the tape.

The mechanic forgets to tighten that last nut on your car and you leave the repair shop with an annoying rattle in your car.

Your small daughter is learning how to walk and makes mistake after mistake as she forever tumbles to the carpet.

Your spouse is harsh with you over breakfast and in the evening tells you that he/she couldn't wait to put things right.

You inadvertently run a red light and immediately start praying that the police are patrolling in another part of town.

Mistakes. Errors in judgment. Some simple, some critical. As we look around us, we notice that no one is immune. And yet when we look at ourselves, we tend to be mercilessly critical. We speak of ourselves as failures, instead of as having failed in that one task. We're like the proverbial cat who, having sat on one hot stove, swore never to sit on any stove again.

Someone has quipped, "If Thomas Edison had given up that easily, you and I would be watching television in the dark." But he didn't give up, not even after seven hundred "learning experiences." All great discoveries have come about through trial and error. So will yours—whether it's a cure for cancer, a new technique for communicating with teenagers, or a better mousetrap.

I've always been encouraged by the words of Charles Kettering: "You will never stub your toe standing still. The faster you go, the more chance there is of stubbing your toe, but the more chance you have of getting somewhere." And, like the turtle, you really will go nowhere at all unless you stick your neck out. So it's back to our basic decision to *act*. To do *something*. I've heard psychologists say that action—any kind of action—is also a tremendous cure for depression, even if it's no more than a walk around the block.

Today is a good day to start believing that you don't need to live a life of quiet desperation, fearful of any new challenge. Starting today, you can begin to enjoy using and developing your gifts. For a start, you may want to risk something small—like a toe rather than a neck.

For example, if you've always wanted to write, then write something: a short article, a poem, an account of your vacation. Write it as if it were going to be published; then submit it somewhere. If you're a photographer, gather your best pictures together and submit them as entries in a contest. If you think you're a fair tennis player or golfer, enter some tournaments and see how you do. You may not win the top prize, but think how much you'll learn and experience just by trying.

Or perhaps you've always felt weak in math, or foreign language, or bookkeeping. Enroll today in a basic, nonthreatening course at a local college or a community night school program. The fact that you may have received a poor grade in the subject at 16 has little bearing on how you'll handle the subject matter at age 25, 30, 50, or 65.

Have you wanted to learn to play the piano? You can! Line up an instructor, set up a schedule for lessons, and set aside forty–five minutes a day for practice. In a year you'll be amazed at how well you will do.

Gourmet cooking appeals to you? Get some new recipe books; experiment with one meal each week. So what if the soufflé is scorched the first time? The second one will be better. Before you know it, your culinary delights will be lauded and in demand—at least by your family.

LEARN FROM FAILURE

Franklin D. Roosevelt once said, "It is common sense to take a method and try it. If it fails, admit it frankly. But above all, *try something.*" It's the only way you'll ever begin to realize your God–given potential. And it can be the glorious beginning in your pursuit of a life of excellence.

Don't be afraid of failure. It's by failure that we learn and profit. Ted Williams, one of the greatest baseball batters of all time, failed six times out of ten in his best year when he batted .400! Learn from your failures and mistakes, and move on.

Let me give you two personal examples of how I failed miserably, but how, through sticking with it, I made something good of those mistakes.

One Sunday morning, many years ago, I was scheduled to preach in a sizable Indiana church. It was Mother's Day, although I had paid scant attention to that. Upon arriving at the church, the pastor reminded me that it was Mother's Day and said that he hoped I would address the congregation with this particular day in mind. Most unwisely, I agreed that I would. While the congregation sang the hymns, while the choir sang the anthem, and while the ushers received the offering, I prepared a new sermon using the acrostic M–O–T–H–E–R. Rarely has a poorer sermon been preached! I blush to this day as I recall that Sunday morning. But I learned! I learned always to seek the mind of the Lord in preparing a message and, having done this, stick with it.

On another occasion, I was scheduled to address a large youth rally in Portland, Oregon. I arrived at the meeting utterly fatigued, after traveling and speaking for a number of days. I suffered from a severe cold and a splitting headache. Within minutes after beginning to speak, my voice faltered. I began to sound like a croaking frog and finally had no voice at all. I had to sit down in utter defeat, the address barely begun! What did I learn? Get some rest before a message; always have a lozenge available; and make certain that a glass of water is near the pulpit! Thank goodness that experience has not been repeated.

Don't simply commence to get ready to begin to live. Start now. Today. Don't prepare indefinitely to take that course, or teach that Bible class, or ask for that promotion. Do it now. If you're scared to death, admit it. You'll find that the admission alone will quiet your heart and unwrinkle your brow.

Paul Tournier, the well-known Swiss psychiatrist, has said, "God's plan is fulfilled not just through the obedience of inspired men, but also through their errors, yes, their sins."

The Bible is replete with examples of how God turned people's failures—and forgiven sins—into great triumphs. That's His business.

DAVID'S FAILURE → TRIUMPH

Look, for example, at King David. David failed to discipline his sons, and as a result a whole chain of sorry events occurred. David failed to discipline Amnon after his immoral relationship with his sister, Tamar. This led David's other son, Absalom, to avenge his sister by killing Amnon. Finally, the entire kingdom was totally disrupted when Absalom led a rebellion against his father.

Great warrior that he was, perhaps David lacked what many today are calling "tough love." He had an obvious strong emotional attachment to his children, as when he wept for Absalom after he was killed leading a rebellion, but somehow he could not bring himself to discipline his children as was needed.

We also recognize that David failed to control his physical

57

passions. When David added to his sin with Bathsheba the sin of murder of her husband Uriah, a faithful warrior in his army, he demonstrated a basic character flaw in not being willing to own up to sinful behavior soon enough to avoid adding another sinful act as a coverup.

Yet, despite his great failures, David stands as one of the truly great men of God and of all time. He was a man after God's own heart in his devotion to Him and in his eagerness to honor Him and seek His glory. He did not shake his fist at God after a failure but repented and earnestly prayed that God's spirit would never be taken from him.

SARAH'S FAILURE → TRIUMPH

Now look at Sarah. In her day, being childless in marriage was often construed as being a failure. A wife's purpose and role were very closely related to rearing children and maintaining the family name and heritage. Sarah had to bear this sense of failure until she was ninety years old. An example of how deeply affected and hurt she was by this sense of failure can be seen in her harsh treatment of Hagar when she was able to bear the child Ishmael. Hagar fled to the wilderness in her despair at Sarah's treatment of her.

At the age of ninety, Sarah was undoubtedly a frustrated, disappointed, and bitter woman. It is understandable how she could laugh, though she denied it, when she overheard God telling her husband, Abraham, that she would bear a child. Yet Sarah is listed in the "Hall of Fame of Faith" in Hebrews 11. Her faith grew, and she drew strength from her deep faith in God. The apostle Peter uses her as a key example in his teaching of how wives are to relate to their husbands in honor and obedience (1 Peter 3:6).

SAMSON'S FAILURE → TRIUMPH

Samson is another example; his failures are most evident in his relationships with women. Against the advice of his parents, he chose to marry a woman who evidently did not worship the Lord. This led to much bloodshed between his people and the Philistines and eventually to the death of his wife and her father.

Samson later entered into an immoral relationship with a harlot in the city of Gaza, and the people of that city sought to take his life. And, of course, what follows is the familiar story of the Philistines persuading the beautiful Delilah to entice Samson into telling her where he received his great and unusual strength. He made a game out of the whole situation, leading her along into many false assumptions about the source of his strength. But, finally, persistent Delilah persuaded him to tell her the truth. This led to Samson's capture and imprisonment and eventually to the gouging out of his eyes. Yet, Samson was used greatly by the Lord in helping to rescue Israel from the tyranny of the Philistines. And despite his failures, he was God's man, presiding over and judging the nation of Israel for twenty years.

PETER'S FAILURE → TRIUMPH

Turning to the New Testament, we find the apostle Peter, who drew stern rebukes and was told of the shameful denial that he would make of his Lord. At one point, when Jesus was talking about the death that He would die, He perceived that the very thoughts of Satan were coming out of Peter's mouth. And, of course, the three denials of Peter in the course of one evening, disowning any allegiance or association with Jesus, are familiar to all.

Though he was irresistibly attracted to being with Jesus, for he knew that He held the very words of life, Peter could not readily accept the ways of Jesus. Even after Jesus had ascended to heaven, Peter had great difficulty in accepting many of the things he had been taught by Jesus. The apostle Paul found it necessary to rebuke Peter and tell him face to face that he was showing prejudice and false standards in dealing with Jews and Gentiles. Yet, who could deny the greatness of Peter, the man who gave pivotal leadership to the early Christian church and was at the forefront of the earliest recorded people movements to Christ. His two New Testament epistles, which relate to bearing up under suffering, have provided great comfort and endurance for Christians throughout the centuries. His loyalty and devotion to Jesus Christ in his latter years have been an inspiration to all believers for two millennia.

JONAH'S FAILURE → TRIUMPH

And finally, there is Jonah. The reluctance of Jonah to do what God had asked him to do stands out as a glaring example of great stubbornness and rebellion, and perhaps fear. His was no passive resistance, but rather an active effort to get as far away from the place and purpose of God as possible. He was told to go to the great city of Nineveh and proclaim God's great displeasure with the wicked and godless ways of the people there. When Jonah finally got turned around, in a most unusual manner, and did what he was told to do, he displayed a selfish anger with God and the people of Nineveh. Rather than rejoicing that they had repented and were responding favorably to God, he displayed a great deal of contempt and selfish anger toward both God and the Ninevites. Then Jonah went outside the city gates, and in his despair—and perhaps exhaustion—asked that his life might be taken.

Still, Jonah remains one of the great examples of a man delivered and used by God, almost in spite of himself. It is recorded that a whole city of people, favorably affected by Jonah's preaching, turned away from their sins. And Jonah's prayer for deliverance, one of the great prayers of the Bible, was even quoted by the Lord Jesus Christ in His earthly ministry.

TURNING FAILURES INTO TRIUMPHS

God does not expect perfection; He expects obedience. And through obedience He can turn failures into triumphs.

Each of these Bible characters was unique. So are you. Develop your own style. No one has had the life experiences you have had; no one has the contributions to make that *you* can make. So it's not a question of being better than someone else.

60

Excellence demands that you be better than yourself.

Some people are outgoing, while others are introspective. Some are thinkers rather than doers. Some are leaders; some are followers. Some are ahead of their times; many are behind. Some are musical geniuses; most are not. Some are great preachers; many are not. But whatever category you are in, right now you can make that single, deliberate move toward a life of excellence.

We are all aware of true and challenging illustrations of hosts of people who have triumphantly overcome seemingly impossible handicaps and disabilities. Let me illustrate with just two familiar and moving examples. The first is my friend Joni Eareckson.

At the age of eighteen, Joni became paralyzed from the neck down after a diving accident in shallow water at Chesapeake Bay. She had total quadriplegia, the result of a diagonal fracture between the fourth and fifth cervical levels.

Joni survived the critical first few weeks but soon came to the point of total despair and frequently wanted to commit suicide. Her reasons were understandable. Her appearance was grotesque—at least to her. Her weight had dropped from 125 to 80 pounds, her skin was jaundiced, her head had to be shaved to help hold her in a brace, and her teeth had become black from medication. Added to that was her sense of extreme limitations and her fear of the future. However, she let Christ turn that tragedy into triumph, those limitations into unlimited opportunities, and her fear into fortitude.

She has since done some utterly remarkable things. For example, she learned to draw and paint by holding a pen or brush in her teeth, and her work is truly remarkable. She refused to remain cloistered, and began accepting numerous speaking engagements, including appearances on television programs such as the "Today" show. As a result she has spoken to tens of thousands of people, telling her story and encouraging them to find the hope and purpose which a life in Jesus Christ makes possible. And she has developed a ministry called Joni and Friends, which seeks to encourage others who are handicapped and to increase the understanding of those not handicapped.

The second person I want to remind you of is Helen Keller. At the age of nineteen months, because of illness, Helen became totally blind and deaf and speechless. Needless to say, it would have seemed that she had no future.

But Helen was a highly spirited girl and was tremendously encouraged by the loving care of her mother. When Helen was seven, the "beloved teacher," as Helen called her, came into her life. Anne Mansfield Sullivan was greatly responsible for unleashing in Helen Keller the great desire to express herself.

Through Anne's help, Helen went on to graduate cum laude from Radcliffe College. Helen had been determined to attend college years earlier, and it was due to her own insistence that she was finally enrolled. Devoting her life to helping others deprived of sight and sound, she traveled all over the world on their behalf, giving lectures. She wrote several articles and books including an autobiography. Her contribution inspired Mark Twain to observe that the two most interesting characters of the nineteenth century were Napoleon and Helen Keller.

IT'S UP TO YOU

What about you? Whether *your* handicap is physical or emotional, today can be the day you begin to chip away at that granite mountain of self–defeat. You can read books about how to do it. You can attend seminars on assertiveness training. You can discuss your plans for change with your friends and pray about it until the cows come home. But ultimately it's up to you to take action.

And to take action that is productive you must know who you are . . . and what you are. It is my hope that today you will recognize that God made you in a special way for His special purpose. He wants you to be all He meant you to be. And He wants you to perform with class.

It was said of Jesus, "Behold, He does all things well." A Jesus of mediocrity, a Jesus of the average, is not the Jesus of the Bible. And if we want a model of one who took risks and lived a life of excellence, we can find none better than the life of our Lord.

He confronted the religious leaders of His day, mincing no words. (Very risky.)

He claimed to be the Son of God. (This ultimately cost Him His life.)

He took a whole series of shopworn religious legal statements and suggested that they could best be summed up as: Love your God, and love your neighbor as yourself. (Tampering with sacred tradition.)

He spent huge amounts of time with so–called second–class citizens: tax collectors, prostitutes, lepers, disabled, Samaritans. (Misguided indeed.)

He was furious when His Father's house was turned into a noisy marketplace. (Tampering with temple economics.)

He had the audacity to reach out and heal the sick on the Sabbath. (Couldn't He lay off for just one day?)

He encouraged the little children to come to His side so He could tell them He loved them, too. (Judea was hardly a child–centered society.)

And during His last days on earth, He chose to love those who persecuted Him, mocked Him, and exposed Him to every human indignity imaginable.

During the latter part of His earthly ministry Jesus also said that His followers—you and I—would do greater things than He had done. Have you ever wondered if He really meant that? If He did, then we need His discipline and His courage. We need His anger at injustice and His untiring concern for those who suffer. We need His capacity for taking risks. And we need to know more of His great love.

SECTION

3

Motivation To Last a Lifetime

What do you think of when you hear the word "motivation?" Does your mind conjure up an image of the "carrot and the stick?" Do you think of *money* as the primary force for motivating people? Or do you fall into the camp that believes sincere *verbal appreciation* is one of life's greatest motivators—just telling people what a good job they've done? There are perhaps as many ways to motivate people as there are people. And that's what makes our challenge so challenging.

However, much of what motivates us to action is little more than *herd mentality*. It's on the bestseller list, so we read it. It's on the cover of our favorite magazine, so we wear it. It's featured in a gardening magazine, so we grow it. A superstar touts it on television, so we buy it, or rent it, or eat it, or fly in it.

But the real motivation you and I need to pursue is the kind that keeps us going for a lifetime. And that's what these chapters taken from *Motivation to Last a Lifetime* are all about.

*Fourteen proven ways to start the energy
and ingenuity flowing.*

5

How to Get and Stay Motivated

D r. Victor E. Frankl, survivor of three grim years at Auschwitz and other Nazi prisons, has recorded his observations on life in Hitler's camps:

> We who lived in concentration camps can remember the men who walked through the huts comforting others, giving away their last piece of bread. They may have been few in number, but they offer sufficient proof that everything can be taken from a man but one thing; the last of the human freedoms—to choose one's attitude in any given set of circumstances, to choose one's own way.
>
> And there are always choices to make. Every day, every hour, offered the opportunity to make a decision, a decision which determined whether you would or would not submit to those powers which threatened to rob you of your very self, your inner freedom; which determined whether or not you would become the plaything of circumstance, renouncing freedom and dignity to become molded into the form of the typical inmate.
>
> . . . Even though conditions such as lack of sleep, insufficient food and various mental stresses may suggest that the inmates were bound to react in certain ways, in the final analysis it becomes clear that the sort of person the prisoner

became was the result of an inner decision, and not the result of camp influences alone. Fundamentally, therefore, any man can, even under such circumstances, decide what shall become of him—mentally and spiritually.[1]

Some of you who hold this book in your hands know firsthand the suffering of those concentration camps. Most of us escaped the terror of that blight on human history. But whether we've been forced to endure the horror and indescribable pain of personal torture or not, all of us can grapple with Dr. Frankl's statement that fundamentally, under life's most trying pressures, it is the obligation of every man and woman to decide what to do with his or her life—mentally and physically. No exceptions. Period! Such a decision then gives way to what life is really all about—discovery.

What a tremendous, invigorating word—*Discovery!* More colorful than "find" or "locate" or "come up with." The word "discovery" has intrigue. Mystery. It implies that something valuable—even precious—is temporarily hidden from normal view, just waiting for us to dig until we find it.

This book can help you start to make the kinds of personal discoveries that will affect how you live the rest of your life. You may be a high school, college, or seminary student, a realtor, clergyman, housewife, computer expert, electrician, executive—it doesn't really matter. Because what is written in these pages is meant for you.

Consider this. If you were to participate in an archeological expedition, you would need certain essentials, including the strong mental desire to *believe* something is there to discover, and the assurance that the treasure, no matter how hidden, will yield to your desire to bring it to the surface.

Then you would need specific tools—made just for digging in the way *you* choose to dig. Without the right tools you may not make any discovery at all.

The task of digging would have to take absolute priority over every other activity in your life. You cannot scrape a few inches of dirt for five minutes a day and expect to make much of a discovery. You might uncover a few commonplace arrowheads—but you would, in all probability, *miss the gold*. And every day, good, sincere, well–meaning people everywhere are missing the gold.

Our search in these pages is not for gold or oil or ancient Spanish pieces–of–eight, although what we find could well be worth a hundred—even a thousand—times more than such wealth. Rather, we are about to discover ways to determine—and put into action—what can motivate us to become the very best God intends us to be. And when we make that important discovery, only the sky above will be our limit.

GETTING–AND STAYING–MOTIVATED

Let us initially talk about self–motivation, and let me suggest fourteen ways to begin the process.

1. *Determine values.* Motivation is always closely related to our own value systems, desires, needs, and ambitions. So we ask ourselves: What do I value most? What consumes my time? What are my deepest needs? How am I doing in fulfilling them?

We've read stories of men and women who have left high–level, lucrative, executive positions to run grocery stores or fishing tackle shops in the mountains. Whether it was a mid–life crisis or just a determination to get out of the rat race, their decisions to make a change started with the questions: What do I value most? How can I go about getting that for me?

2. *Realize motivation is continuous.* We are always motivated in some direction—good or bad—to do something. So right now, as we begin, let's ask ourselves: What is my direction? Where am I heading? If money or location or health or anything else were not obstacles, what would I do with my life—beginning today?

Another way to ask ourselves that question might be: What would I like to have written on my tombstone? Since that would be my final statement, it obviously would be an important one concerning the direction I had wanted my life to take.

3. *Seek wisdom.* We must recognize and understand that

divine wisdom is the only thing that has true value. In James 1:5, the apostle James admonishes us: "If any of you lacks wisdom, he should ask God, who gives generously to all without finding fault, and it will be given him." Wise counsel indeed! Read the words of Solomon the Wise. God enabled him to share practical wisdom with each of us — even these millennia after God revealed His wisdom to His servant Solomon.

4. *Be realistic about limitations.* We must be sure to set goals within our reach. Attempting the impossible will destroy our motivation overnight. Rome wasn't built in a day. Neither is a career . . . nor a life that's worth living.

Yes, we must stretch ourselves, but we must also ask, Is this goal I'm contemplating in sync with who I am? Will I be compatible in this new environment? Does my intuition tell me I may be overextending myself and my abilities in this?

We are neither Superman nor Wonderwoman. And if we feel we must do everything, sooner or later we will make the startling discovery that we are doing absolutely nothing of lasting value.

5. *Be willing to take some risks.* We cannot be afraid to try new ideas and new methods and we need to challenge with a vengeance such killer phrases as, "You're on the wrong track"; "The boss ought to get a chuckle out of *that* idea"; "Hey, I can tell you, the twelfth floor isn't going to like it"; "Someday there may be a need for this"; and the biggest putdown of all, "What are you, some kind of nut?"

Don't forget! All the new ways of doing things have not yet been discovered. So take some risks, find a better way. Maybe you will invent a new mousetrap in the process!

6. *Make lists.* If each of us had to make a decision today that would change the direction of our lives, what would it be? Would we start our own business? Take an overseas assignment? Work in a halfway house for kids in trouble? Would we finally sit down and write that novel? Start a course in accounting at night school? Take flying lessons? Start big. Think blue sky. No limits.

Make a list of your grandest dreams and then put it

aside—but don't forget it. Make another list with the heading "Things I can start doing today." Be specific, clear, and realistic. A good and effective, easily described plan (written so both you and others can understand it) is highly motivational.

7. *Pray.* We must lay our plans before the Lord. Years ago I took Psalm 32:8 as my life verse. "I will instruct thee and teach thee in the way that thou shalt go; I will guide thee with mine eye" (KJV). The knowledge that God does instruct, teach, and lead His children step by step and day by day is a constant encouragement to me. He is far more interested in us, our plans, our future, and our well-being than we are ourselves, and we must pray about what we think God has for us in this process. He is as much concerned about the minutia in our planning as He is about the final results. More is accomplished by prayer than by anything else this world knows. Prayer must be an integral part of our desire for redemptive motivation in our life.

Who can explain prayer? We have direct access to the Maker of the universe. We can call on Him, counsel with Him. God, in His Word, continually invites us into His presence. "Call on me . . . " We have an advocate with the Father, even Jesus Christ the righteous one. God's way of working always is in answer to believing prayer!

8. *Divide the project into manageable parts.* After we've given thought and prayer to our direction, we must ask ourselves: How can I break this up into manageable pieces so I can handle it effectively? Remaining consistently self-motivated throughout life comes from rewarding ourselves with successes every day. But if we overload our circuits, our system will begin to close down—physically and emotionally. When that happens we will frustrate ourselves into a corresponding loss of productivity. So initially, we must take only bite-size chunks and not try to finish a six-month project in six weeks. Being realistic with ourselves about our abilities will pay off in the long run.

9. *Take action.* Procrastination is the death blow to self-motivation. "I'll do it later . . . after I get organized" is the language of the unsuccessful and the frustrated. Successful, highly motivated men and women don't put it off. They know

their lives are no more than the accumulation of precious seconds, minutes, and days—golden moments never to be recaptured.

Just three words, *Do it now*, can propel us on to achievements we never thought possible. *Do it now!* is a worthy motto for all of life. Start prospecting a new client, *now*. Love your spouse, *now*. Today unused is lost forever, and tomorrow may never come.

10. *Consider the negative consequences of inaction*. After establishing practical goals and objectives for our lives, we need to remind ourselves of the horrors of letting ourselves down—financial loss, depression, loss of momentum in business, deteriorating health, taking our frustrations out on loved ones.

When we choose to *do it now*, we cut through our work like a machete going through high brush. When we choose not to act, our inaction takes on a life of its own and inflicts its punishment on us.

11. *Take advantage of energy peaks*. All of us need to learn to schedule our most important tasks during those times when our body and mind are functioning at top level. Some of us are morning persons, others don't get going until midnight. Some need naps, others don't. Only you know when you work at your best and highest level.

It may be helpful to make an "energy chart" for the month. At the end of each day, make a note of those periods of time when you did your most productive work. Was it after a nap? After lunch? After a stimulating conversation with an associate or with one of your children?

This regular, personal survey of our top moments will help give us the insights to keep us self-motivated for a lifetime.

12. *Trust in a big God*. God is without limits. Nothing is impossible with Him. He is the author of true creativity. All creation is His, including every idea our minds can conceive. He keenly desires to give us the ability to make the right choices in our lives.

13. *Become accountable*. Find some other person—or a

small group of people—whom you trust and who trust you. There is a great deal of pleasure in being held accountable, yet many of us fear this exposure. It is good to share our victories with others. But at the same time, most of us know that the joy of anticipated success can turn to ashes in the day of failure. Yet, success is only possible if the potential for failure exists.

There are three kinds of accountability. The first is determined by the society into which we are born. To be a part of our society, we must accept the accountability society places on us. We are, of course, expected to do certain things correctly and according to schedule. Taxes will come due every April. Stoplights will turn red. The consequences of ignoring these occurrences are powerful incentives for us to perform well. Accountability is assumed. It is a given, not an option.

We accept the second kind of accountability when we join an organization, whether it is part of our vocation or something like our local church. When we accept a job, we automatically accept responsibility to our superiors, peers, and subordinates. We may play different roles at different times, one time as leader, another time as follower, but accountability is always part of the job. Too often in our service we forget that.

The third kind of accountability is that which we voluntarily make to others. In many ways it is the most effective. We all seem to perform better against the goals we set for ourselves. This kind of accountability can operate in a number of ways. At the organizational level, it works for the superior who not only invites his subordinates to share in setting their own goals but who invites his subordinates to hold *him* accountable for *his* goals.

At the one–to–one, person–to–person level, we should seek to be accountable to someone for as many areas of our life as possible and to permit others to ask us to hold them accountable. I have a friend who often asks the simple question, "What can I pray about for you this week?" I soon learned that he intended to accept responsibility not only to pray about that need, but later to ask, "How did it go?" I quickly learned not to be too glib with my prayer requests!

73

14. *Be optimistic.* Success is won by people who know it can be done. One of the greatest salesmen of all time, W. Clement Stone, has said repeatedly, "What the mind can conceive and believe in, the mind can achieve." And Stone is right!

Do we believe it? Do we dare believe it? If we do, it will change our lives. We will be able to aim higher and reach further than we ever thought possible, because the motivated optimist, under the Holy's Spirit's guidance, is getting things done when others are still wondering if they *can* be done.

Optimists are self–motivated by inspiring themselves to action. They believe in who they are and in what they are doing. They make mistakes and learn from them. They achieve success but don't take for granted that success will come again. They set long–range objectives, but they also encourage themselves with daily personal rewards.

Optimists know that with God's help they can be the people they were created to be. We can be open, free, caring, spontaneous—with the daily awareness that successful living is, with God's help, an endless journey in self–discovery and personal fulfillment.

*Nine guidelines for a lifetime of
personal fulfillment.*

6

Finding the Right Motives to Keep You Going

Several years ago *Newsweek* ran an immensely valuable two–page piece entitled "Advice to a (Bored) Young Man" in its "Responsibility Series." Despite its title, its counsel is to us all— man or woman, young or old.

Died, age 20; buried, age 60. The sad epitaph of too many Americans. Mummification sets in on too many young men at an age when they should be ripping the world wide open. For example: Many people reading this page are doing so with the aid of bifocals. Inventor? *B. Franklin*, age 79.

The presses that printed this page were powered by electricity. One of the first harnessers? *B. Franklin*, age 40.

Some are reading this on the campus of one of the Ivy League universities. Founder? *B. Franklin*, age 45.

Others, in a library. Who founded the first library in America? *B. Franklin*, age 25.

Some got their copy through the U.S. Mail. Its father? *B. Franklin*, age 31.

Now, think fire. Who started the first fire department, invented the lightning rod, designed a heating stove still in use today? *B. Franklin*, ages 31, 43, 36.

75

Wit, Conversationalist, Economist, Philosopher, Diplomat, Printer, Publisher, Linguist (spoke and wrote five languages). Advocate of paratroopers (from balloons) a century before the airplane was invented. All this until age 84.

And he had exactly two years of formal schooling. It's a good bet that you already have more sheer knowledge than Franklin ever had when he was your age.

Perhaps you think there's no use trying to think of anything new, that everything's been done. Wrong. The simple, agrarian America of Franklin's day didn't begin to need the answers we need today. Go do something about it.[1]

Newsweek then suggested that the reader tear out the page and "read it on *your* 84th birthday. Ask yourself what took over in your life; indolence or ingenuity?"

I'm not suggesting you tear out this page, but we all need to keep it handy. There's no reason, however, to wait until our eighty-fourth birthdays. How about looking at it every birthday—or every month—or every week for the rest of our lives!

Benjamin Franklin found motives to keep him going for a lifetime of service to his country and to his fellow-man. And with each success his motivation became even stronger.

JUST AS MUCH OPPORTUNITY

Are you saying, "Come on, now, you can't expect me to be a Benjamin Franklin." Or are you thinking, "Now there was a great man. And I have just as much opportunity to make my life count as he did." I hope it's the latter. Because, for one thing, it's true.

We do have as much opportunity. And those diamonds still can be found in our own backyard. We just need to know where to dig.

So we need to ask ourselves: What are my motives? What makes me want to dig and discover and explore and learn? What are my objectives, my goals? What contributions am I making—or do I plan to make—to my family, my society, myself?

We will never know the thrill of a life well lived until we engage ourselves in the lifelong pursuit of motives that keep us going.

If Thoreau was right in saying "all men lead lives of quiet desperation," and if that is the story of our lives, then we may as well take early orders for our epitaphs, which might read:

> Here lies John . . . here lies Mary
> From very young to very old
> They always did what they were told.

In all their years of living on this earth they never chose to learn how to live. Instead of soaring to the heavens, pressing, pushing, extending themselves just a little further, they chose to stay earthbound.

All of us knew athletes in high school or college who had tremendous natural ability—who could have been true "stars" in their sports—but who just didn't have the drive or urge or willingness to push themselves, and thus remained "second–stringers." We also know of people with truly brilliant minds who could be successful scientists or researchers or leaders in one of many disciplines, but who simply won't pay the price for such readily achievable success. Tragic!

GUIDELINES FOR PERSONAL FULFILLMENT

Let's look at some guidelines that are essential for a lifetime of personal fulfillment.

1. *Keep your reservoirs full.* We must store up compassion, encouragement, forgiveness, and hope so we will have enough to give to others when they need it.

What an example Mother Teresa in Calcutta is for each of us. Born of poor Albanian parents in Yugoslavia, she determined early in life to give herself completely to God in order to minister to "the poorest of the poor" in the wretched slums of that Indian city. And for decades she has unreservedly shared of herself so that thousands rise up and call her blessed. A Nobel Prize winner, she remains the simple, modest peasant woman, who, through her deep and unswerving devotion and commitment, has been motivated to this exemplary service for our Lord Jesus Christ.

Mother Teresa said that each of us has a mission to fulfill, a mission of love, but that it must begin in our homes . . . in the place where we are, with the people with whom we are the closest, and then spread out. What wise advice this is indeed.

2. *Work on your character.* Many men and women are so concerned with their reputations that they give little or no thought to the development of their most important possession: their character. Do we know who we really are? Are we well-defined persons? Have we established standards for our lives on which we simply refuse to compromise? (Remember, reputation only functions under favorable circumstances; character functions under unfavorable circumstances.)

If answering such questions is difficult, try this exercise. Pretend you are a reporter on special assignment to do a cover story on you. That's right, you.

For a full working day, you the reporter will cover you the person. What will you discover as you follow yourself to the office, the gym, the kitchen, the television set? Report accurately all you see.

Although much of what you observe may make you want to put your pencil and pad down, you are required to complete the assignment.

Observe yourself in the supermarket lane marked "10 items only" when the person in front of you has eleven items (you know because you counted them).

At the office, report on how you treat your employees, how you talk on the telephone, how "sincerely" you sign your letters, and how your pulse rate rises when the IRS says you are being audited.

Would you be willing to make your story a cover story? What kind of man or woman emerges? Do you like what apparently motivates you?

In my forty-year ministry, I have traveled annually to

every nook and cranny and corner of the world, and I have met "unsung" heroes whose exemplary character, dedication, and determination to be at their best for God (even though seemingly no one would be aware of it) have challenged me time without number. But God sees and knows. And in eternity that's what will really matter!

3. *Seek good health.* Maybe it's time you reactivated that membership in your local Y, or started playing tennis or golf again. How long has it been since you've had a physical? Do you like the profile you see in the mirror each morning? Or ought you to lose a few pounds?

Here on earth, your body is a most prized possession. If it is not functioning properly, it's going to be difficult to be motivated about anything.

We know our bodies inevitably become what our minds harbor. In fact, the correlation between the "state of the mind" and "physical condition of the body" is so strong it's now estimated that 70 percent of all Americans go to doctors for treatment when they have nothing physically wrong.

Reports indicate that 52 percent of American men and women are seeing psychologists or psychiatrists or are going to great expense at a vast assortment of mental health clinics— when it's essentially their thinking that's all wrong.

Spiritual balance is often neglected as a factor that affects our emotional life and brings about stability. Recognize how vital it is to spend time with God, in His Word, and in fellowship with fellow believers. We dare not stand alone. God has committed Himself to us. Draw daily upon His reserves.

4. *Be enthusiastic about life.* "But I can't get worked up about things; it's just not my nature," some say. "I work hard all day, like to come home and watch a little TV, and then go to bed. It's just not like me to get all excited about anything."

Well, we had all better find *something* to excite us—and we'd better find it fast. At least we can be grateful we got up this morning. Lots of people didn't! When we breathed on the bathroom mirror today, it fogged up. That's terrific. That's something to get worked up about.

But we can't stop there. Now that we've confirmed we are alive, we must do something with this wonderful day, these precious minutes. We must find something to live for—perhaps even something to die for. It will change our lives.

5. *Be a person of faith.* Do we have the kind of faith that can move mountains? Perhaps they won't be the Sierras or the Himalayas. But what about the mountains of pain, worry, fear, and hopelessness all around us?

William Carey, often called the father of modern missions, was such a person of faith. Carey left his cobbler's bench in Britain almost two centuries ago to serve as a pioneer missionary in India. He knew no one there; he had no idea what he would face; he had no knowledge of the languages. When he died, after more than forty years of ministry in India, he had translated the Bible into three major Indian languages, had founded what has become the largest newspaper in India, had established the strong and effective Baptist Church Union in India, had done more than any seminary in India, and had done more than any individual to bring the message of the gospel of Christ to that sub–continent. He was one simple cobbler who took God at His word, and his obedience immeasurably affected an entire subcontinent.

6. *Be a friend.* We all know barbers and beauticians are often the best "poor person's psychologist." They listen while they cut and comb. Over the years they often become real friends with their clients.

We can be the same kind of person to our friends by helping them focus on what is bothering them. We can help put their problem in perspective, perhaps even suggest another way of looking at the disturbing issue. But we must take time to listen and make ourselves available. All the empathy, all the skill in the world are of no value if the person who needs our ear cannot get it. Times to listen can obviously be scheduled, but most of the important times come quite unexpectedly. Accept them when they come—and learn from listening.

80

Many people are still reluctant to seek counseling, and this is where we can help. We can listen with sympathetic gestures and mannerisms. By listening and caring we may help a friend overcome many unsettling fears. Have you noticed that those who often motivate us to action are usually those closest to us—our friends? And similarly, as we build friendships, we become "enablers" in the arena of motivation as we encourage our friends to participate in profitable and redemptive activities.

For serious problems, professional help is obviously necessary. But we don't need a wall filled with diplomas to be the best friend a person ever had.

7. *Learn to be calm under pressure.* A liberal endowment of patience is essential when pressures mount, as they inevitably will. The impatient person will become weakened and defective. "Be strong—and of a good courage" is God's word to Joshua—and to us.

The story is told of a young boy who wanted desperately to become a singer, but his teacher gave him no hope, telling him, "Son, you sound like the wind in the shutters!" but the boy's mother believed in her son—so much so that she sent him to another teacher. To pay the cost of her son's lessons she often went without shoes—sometimes even without food. The boy was Enrico Caruso. He became the greatest tenor of his time—because his mother loved him, had faith in him, and exercised patience.

8. *Be curious about life.* Develop an exploratory mind. Read. Ask questions. Listen. The exploring mind and heart adds spice to life. Those who turn over stones find the serendipities that make life fascinating. Let your curiosity "get the better of you" sometimes. It becomes the salt and pepper of life. Curiosity may have killed the cat, but it also enhances our lives.

9. *Invest in yourself.* This is the only way we will be able to invest in others. Each of us is that important. There are no unimportant people in God's economy. Somewhere along the line a strange idea has developed that in order to be humble we also have to be mediocre. Where we get such an idea is a mystery. It

certainly does not come from Scripture. Over and over again God selected ordinary people and made them extraordinary. Whether it was Moses of the Old Testament, with his heritage and palace training, or Paul in the New Testament, with his knowledge and organizational ability, God made them the best. And He will do the same for us. Know that this is so and accept the very best that God has for you. You are important!

The list could go on. But this is a start in the right direction in establishing goals and motives to last a lifetime. Much of what we've said thus far refers to self-growth—keeping our *own* reservoir full. But the highest motives of all are those that cause us to reach out to others.

Still, the best-laid plans—the strongest, most God-honoring desires—do go astray. That's when it's time to ask the next question: What do I do when I've lost my motivation?

*Seven steps to rekindling the spark
in your life.*

7

What to Do When You've Lost Your Motivation

The sales manager of the Fido Dog Food Company grasped the podium firmly as he prepared to speak to his salespeople at their weekly motivational meeting. In voice loud and clear, he shouted, "Ladies and gentlemen of Fido Dog Food Company, who's got the best packaging in the country?"

As expected, everyone cheered, "We do!"

The sales manager continued, "Who's got the best, most dynamic, most aggressive sales force?"

"We do!" came the enthusiastic reply.

Finally the boss asked, "Then why is it we're number seventeen out of a total of eighteen dog food companies in this country?"

Silence. People cleared their throats, searched for windows to look out of, played with their pencils.

Finally, a squeaky voice at the back of the room broke the silence with the memorable words, "Sir, it's because dogs don't like us!"

And not only do dogs shift with the times, change their desires, get burned out or turned off; it happens to us all.

Once we knew where we were going. We pursued our goals with a vengeance. Now we're not so sure. Self–doubts have eroded our confidence. We've begun to slip and we really don't know why. Once satisfied, enthusiastic, and highly motivated, we're now depressed, ill–at–ease, and plagued with the vague sense of having "missed the boat."

TO PUT THINGS RIGHT . . .

What action can we take to put things right? Let's look at some possibilities:

1. *Read inspirational books; listen to motivational cassettes.* These will help inspire us to action. No matter how bright, gifted, or intelligent we are, we can always use the insights of someone else. If we observe any person who has achieved success, we discover a person who has *worked at staying motivated*. Motivation is not automatic.

If we lose our drive and feel we are all washed up, with no more worlds to conquer, perhaps we've just lost our perspective. Because there still are worlds to conquer — hundreds of them — and there's one just waiting for each of us to discover.

We may have to take a thousand steps before we find it; but unless we take those thousand steps, we may never find that world waiting for us. So let's get a map and start moving. It's no sin to spend *some* time down in the dumps, but there is nothing saintly about *staying* there.

The Bible continually illustrates for us those men of faith who, at some point, seem to have lost their motivation. Look at Jonah on his way to Nineveh. Or Moses during his "backside of the desert" experience. Or Peter as he denied his Lord. These men were about to give up, but as God moved upon them they became, once again, highly motivated. It can be so with us during our inevitable low periods. Our God is our Motivator!

2. *Recognize that you are always in the process of change.* A Greek philosopher said, "It is not possible to step twice into the same river." The water moves downstream, never to return. The man or woman brings new experiences to every new situa-

tion. Things may look the same, but they never are.

We may think we are working in the same office we worked in five years ago, but we're not. We may think we have the same boss, but we don't. Everything is in flux, and whether we realize it or not, this constant change has its effect on us all.

Those who think we are not living through times of traumatic change should spend an evening reading *Future Shock* or *The Third Wave* by Alvin Toffler or *New Rules* by Daniel Yankelovich.

Management expert Peter Drucker writes compellingly of these changes in what he calls our "Turbulent Times." Seminars on how to cope with change are promoted at every turn. Change, obviously, is threatening but inevitable. A highly motivated person understands this and continually adjusts to it.

The literature that describes our rapidly changing present and inevitable future continues to pound away at one thought—things will never be the way they once were, no matter how much we may long for the "good old days."

Perhaps our sense of "lost motivation" is no more than a resistance to the changes that come into our lives uninvited. Of the total number of Americans out of work, 50 percent of them will not find the jobs they are seeking, for those jobs will never again exist. Retraining, for them, is essential for economic survival.

That may be where *you* are. The old shoe no longer fits. The new wine splits the cask that held the old wine without spilling a drop. We all change—and will continue to change. We may not welcome it, like it, or even enjoy it. But we must accept it! If not, we're destined to live out our frustrations like good old Charlie Brown, who complained, "How can I do new math with an old math brain?" It doesn't take much reflection to know the answer: Learn new math!

3. *Don't try too hard.* Even though change is a necessary and inevitable part of life, we often try to cope with it in the wrong way. For instance, some of us may try too hard to become a success, becoming, instead, burned out. A pastor tries to infuse

85

life into a struggling, non–responsive congregation. A mother with the words "Super Mom" on her license plate frame works hard to do everything—cook, bake, clean, be chauffeur for soccer and Little League and, on top of all that, tries to be the perfect wife. Pastor, wife, student, secretary—it doesn't matter—we may simply be trying too hard.

If you feel you are, the "slight edge" principle may help.

If you are an executive, work for a 12-percent increase in your company's production by raising it one percent each month. A 12-percent increase may be frightening, even intimidating. But one percent a month is manageable—and possible.

Spend just fifteen minutes a day on a subject that will enhance your present position. Become an expert. Read every book on the subject you can lay your hands on. Spend time in the stacks at the library. Quietly become the most well–informed person in your field. You can do it—and it will only take fifteen minutes a day. But you must do it every day. It's a sure way to recapture a motivation to serve you for a lifetime.

Spend an equal time in the Scriptures each day. Ask God to give you the insight, energy, compassion, and wisdom you need. Check frequently the wisdom of Solomon in Proverbs; identify with the sweet singer of Israel, David, in the Psalms. It's still true: "Seek and you will find; knock and the door will be opened to you" (Matthew 7:7). Maybe it's time for you to start believing what you say you believe.

In his book *The Range of Human Capacities*, well–known psychologist Dr. David Wechsler says, "The differences that separate the masses of mankind from one another—with respect to any one or all of their capabilities—are small. As compared with other ratios or orders of differences met in nature, they are pitifully insignificant."[1]

Wechsler's message is clear. The successful person is usually only a little bit better than the one who fails. Why? Because he or she has chosen to take the "slight edge." Small differences—big results. This is one of the best antidotes we know for frustration and lack of motivation.

4. *Don't wish for life to get easier; pray to become stronger.* Isaiah 40:31 should be a daily reminder of what happens when we go to the source of all true strength: "But they that wait upon the Lord shall renew their strength; they shall mount up with wings as eagles; they shall run, and not be weary; and they shall walk, and not faint" (KJV).

That is the secret of living. But to the believer it shouldn't be a secret at all. It's the heart of the Christian faith. A return to *real living*. No longer do we need to prop ourselves up with things we *hope* will carry us through. No. Pray for God's strength, and then believe it will come to you. We've gone through thousands of years of history since Isaiah made his declaration, but it remains as fresh as today's headlines: My strength comes from the Lord who made heaven and earth.

He also made you. And He made you to succeed. Judged by the world's standards, not every incident of life can be termed a success, of course. But God's will for us is, as we daily walk with Him, that we will have success as He marks it—in the satisfaction of knowing that we are "the apple of His eye."

5. *Take a vacation.* Football coach Vince Lombardi once said, "Fatigue makes cowards of us all." That's true, isn't it? How many times have you just been too tired to plug ahead? Too wiped out to continue even another five minutes?

Perhaps you need to spend a few days walking a quiet beach, exploring the beauty of God's handiwork. Grab a handful of sand through your fingers. Remember God already has those grains counted. Then reflect a bit more. That same God knows and loves *you!*

Or head off for the mountains, the wilderness. Enjoy the beauty of silence. Let the Father speak to you in the stillness—away from the telephones, copy machines, telexes, soccer games, or preparations for the morning sermon. Carve out a few extra hours for a good book or for some special—and extra—time with the Lord.

Don't wait until next year to take such a vacation. Do it now, even if it is for only a few hours, days, or a weekend at a time. It will do more good than worry, aspirin, or black coffee.

6. *Re–evaluate goals.* Write down who you were ten years ago, five years ago, last year at this time. How have you changed? Are you reading the same kinds of books? Do you have new friends? Do you still want the same things, value the same relationships?

You may discover you have changed more than you thought possible.

It is terribly important that we continually review our goals, our objectives, because they, as well as we, do indeed change. Dr. Ari Kiev, clinical professor of psychiatry at Cornell University, in his fine little book *Strategy for Daily Living*, says:

> The establishment of a goal is the key to successful living. In my practice as a psychiatrist, I have found that helping people to develop personal goals has proved to be the most effective way to help them cope with problems. Observing the lives of people who have mastered adversity, I have noted that they have established goals and sought with all their efforts to achieve them. From the moment they decided to concentrate all their energies on a specific objective, they began to summit the most difficult odds.

7. *Practice, practice, practice.* Fritz Kreisler, the famed concert violinist, maintained a rigorous, no–nonsense, eight–hour–daily practice schedule throughout his long, outstanding musical career. Often he would be asked why he needed to carry on such vigorous practice sessions. After all, wasn't he the best — without peer?

Kreisler had but one reply to such a question: "If I neglect to practice for a month, my audience knows the difference. If I neglect it for a week, my wife knows the difference. If I neglect practice for a day, Fritz Kreisler knows the difference."

When we think we've made it, we probably haven't. For often, when we've been blessed with even moderate success, we're tempted to lay down the tools that brought us to where we are. Tools such as perseverance, humility, caring for others, the ability to listen and empathize—and just plain hard work.

Paul Meyer, an authority on self–improvement through personal motivation, gives five danger signals that indicate our motivation is not what it once was.

Doubt—questioning our ability to do the job. Self–confidence is lost; worry and confusion take over.

Procrastination—putting off important decisions; hesitating to take considered risks; hoping the problem will take care of itself.

Devotion to false symbols—surrendering to egotism and status seeking; coveting the title of the job instead of concentrating on better ways and new ideas for actually doing the job; desiring to be a "well–thought–of " person instead of a thinking one.

Complacency—surrendering to the inner urge most everyone has to "take it easy"; being satisfied with "good enough" instead of "good," and with "good" instead of "excellent."

Loss of purpose—failing to make mental provision or concrete plans for going anywhere else; reaching the first goal becomes the end of the career instead of another beginning.[2]

If you are saying, "You're talking about me," please read on, because simply recognizing the problem is a problem half solved. And those who are willing to take some risks, are willing to start believing in themselves once again, will soon discover that life really does begin when they finally commit to get moving.

A Time for Commitment

You and I were designed for commitment, and we will never find true fulfillment in our lives until we give ourselves completely to a cause greater than ourselves. But before this can happen, it's critical that we come to grips with our own value. Further, we must see ourselves as we *can* be, and then take the risk of doing all we can to become all we *will* be.

In 1858, a small, frail lad was born to a rich family in New York. Along with feeble eyesight, he suffered from asthma so bad that he sometimes couldn't blow out the bedside candle. Nevertheless, he became one of the most powerful men on earth.

You'll read about this amazing man — and many others who seemingly did the impossible — in this section taken from *A Time for Commitment*. So if you are ready to take your commitments seriously, read these chapters that will challenge you to quit shuffling about in the shallows, and to wade the deep, uncharted waters that cry out for your unswerving commitment.

What are you committed to? Is there anything that means everything to you?

8

Designed for Commitment

While cleaning out her husband's belongings, a widow discovered dozens of keys she couldn't identify. Were they relics from worthless projects long forgotten? Or were they claims to important treasure? How would she ever find out? After exhausting all suggestions, the best she could do was admonish readers of a national newspaper column to take better care of important keys—disposing of worthless ones and marking those of value.

Ironically, our job in this search for the hidden key to personal fulfillment is much the same. Perhaps the key we seek is right there in plain sight. Or perhaps it's become obscured in the midst of all the other "important" things in life. But when you find and use that key called *commitment*, you'll open doors of opportunity you never thought possible.

What is commitment? Who needs it? And why?

You may have heard the story of the chicken and the pig. The two were walking side by side along a country road when they noticed an announcement tacked on the bulletin board of a little country church. The sign read: *Ham and Eggs Breakfast this Sunday at 7:30 A.M. All are invited.*

The pig turned to the chicken and said, "Will you look at that! For you, that's no more than a day's work. But for me, it's total commitment."

I can understand the pig's position. Commitment *is* costly, demanding careful focus and discretion. We can't be committed to just anything. Yet recently, we've had a heavy dose of books that focused on how to "Look out for #1" and "How to be your own best friend." But there seems to be an imbalance between those books and the ones that talk about the excitement of being committed to a cause, an idea, or a person. As we continue, we'll see how beneficial, even necessary, it is to improve ourselves to prepare for the greater challenges beyond.

ONE MAN'S COMMITMENT

Within ten miles of our World Vision headquarters in Monrovia, California, stands a living tribute to one man's personal commitment to a greater challenge—the Jackie Robinson Center in Pasadena.

In 1945, the time was long overdue for including Blacks in major league baseball. But the pioneer had to be a rare combination of talent and tact—someone with the athletic ability to speak for itself and the will power to stand back and let it do so.

"It won't be easy," said Branch Rickey of the Brooklyn Dodgers. "You'll be heckled from the bench. They'll call you every name in the book. The pitchers will throw at your head. They'll make it plain they don't like you, and they'll try to make it so tough that you'll give it all up and quit." Then he added sternly, "But you won't fight back, either. You'll have to take everything they dish out and never strike back. Do you have the guts to take it?"[1]

Jackie Robinson had the "guts." He courageously endured a storm of abuse for the chance to unlock a new door of opportunity for his race. Venting his hostility through spectacular swings and incredible catches, he became the 1947 National League Rookie of the Year and the 1949 Most Valuable Player, entering baseball's Hall of Fame with a lifetime batting average of .311.[2]

In 1974, the city of Pasadena erected the Jackie Robinson Center in his old neighborhood. Here the first Black in major league baseball continues to provide opportunities for young players even now, more than a decade after his death. All because of commitment.

THE NEED FOR COMMITMENT

Promise, submit, permit, mission, remit are cousins to the word "commit." "Send" or "let go" in Latin is *mitto* and *missus*. Combined with *co*, ("together"), commit means "to send together." The prefix and root do not work alone; neither do you.

Without the committed care of our parents, we would have quickly perished as newborns. But consider the infant's potential. Although as infants we were unable to feed ourselves, we are designed to produce food for others; although unable to stand, designed to run; although unable to lift a doll, designed to raise a family. We all grow into a potential that was at first incomprehensible to us.

For many people, placing the needs of someone else ahead of their own is as foreign an idea as chewing a carrot is to a toothless tot. Yet just as new teeth push through the gums, the need for commitment and personal fulfillment often drives people to bite off more than they can chew.

In 1858, a small, frail lad was born to a rich family in New York. Along with feeble eyesight, he suffered from asthma so bad that he sometimes couldn't blow out the bedside candle; nevertheless, he became one of the most powerful men on earth.

At eleven or twelve years old, Theodore Roosevelt's father told him that building a good mind alone would not ensure success but that he must build himself a powerful new body to match it. Theodore spent thousands of hours chinning himself, lifting weights, and rattling a punching bag. It's little wonder he rose like a rocket in the world of politics: Elected to the New York Legislature at twenty–three; candidate for mayor at twenty–eight; U.S. Civil Service Commissioner under two presidents; president of the police commission of New York; national hero as leader of the Rough Riders in the Spanish–American War at forty; then, in just three busy years, governor of New York, vice–president, and president. In 1905 Teddy Roosevelt received the Nobel Peace Prize for his efforts in helping to end the Russo–Japanese War. At five feet nine inches, Roosevelt was a small man, made large through commitment.[3]

Achievement like his may seem beyond our commitment quotient; however, let's not be deceived by what we are. Instead, be challenged by what we are designed to become.

In the early fifteenth century, Spain realized it could never compete as a world power with all of its internal rivalries and foreign influences. Spanish leaders designed a commitment that would solidify their country. Two of the most influential and antagonistic families, the Aragones and the Castiles, agreed to end decades of hostility through a planned marriage. In 1479, King Ferdinand II of Aragon and Isabella of Castile united the nation as king and queen. Due to this commitment, the exploits of Christopher Columbus were possible. Later, monarchs from this "designed commitment" elevated Spain to an apex of power as the richest and most powerful nation in Europe.[4] As is often the case with human designs and politics, this commitment was not without its subterfuge and strife. But it still illustrates the power behind the reality: Individuals, as well as nations, are designed for commitment.

Other figures of history have met even greater designs. These heroes were committed before birth and by name. God said, "Let us make Adam in our image after our likeness" (Genesis 1:26, KJV). The Hebrew word for "man" in this passage is the name/description *adam* (red mud). Isaac was designed to inherit the promises of God (commitments) even though his mother–to–be had long since passed the age of childbearing. Cyrus of Persia was called by name almost one hundred years before he was sent to fulfill God's comments for Babylon (Isaiah 45:1). John the Baptist received his commission before he was conceived (Luke 1:13). And Christ was "foreordained before the foundation of the world" to become our Savior (1 Peter 1:20,

KJV).

WHAT ARE YOU COMMITTED TO?

But what about us today? We live in a time when commitment is not the most popular word in our national vocabulary. The divorce rate continues to climb, while marshals lock up delinquent fathers for nonpayment of support. Personal debt is at an all-time high, while the rate of bank failures is the worst since the Great Depression. We are truly the in-and-out society, where a fad is in one minute and out the next. We even throw things away because it's cheaper than fixing them. Somehow, we feel a commitment to anything will, by definition, be uncomfortable, even painful—too much of a demand on our time, money, or energies.

What are you committed to? Is there *anything* that means *everything* to you? What are you living for? You may respond, "Well, I don't have much time to think about commitment. You see, I've got to get up early every morning, eat breakfast, go to work, come home at six o'clock, have a bite to eat, watch a little TV, go to bed, and that's about it." Or you may say, "There just aren't enough hours in the day for all I want to do. There are friends to see, exciting work to do, games to play, sunsets to watch, children to enjoy, and a big world to understand." Which category do you fit into? Are you somewhere in between?

Even though we are not created just to get by in life, we often give that appearance. Built with the potential for unlimited movement and growth, we seem determined to settle for much less. To seek personal fulfillment and growth, the first clue we discover is one that's obvious to others and obscure to us— YOU. Although perhaps not apparent from your perspective, from the way you look now, or from what you've done before, YOU are part of an unbroken chain of continuous commitments. Designed for commitment, you are the key to the personal fulfillment of yourself and those around you. Anything short of that will diminish the sacrifice and commitment scores of people have already invested in your ability to serve.

97

This key can open the gate to vast new fields of achievement for you. Those who understand the meaning of the game, who have tasted the thrill of victory, who have made the greatest gain now stand ready to help you do the same.

How perseverance will help you overcome almost any obstacle.

9

No Pain, No Gain

Of all the storytellers in America, I'm still convinced that my friend of many years, Art Linkletter, remains one of the best. Here are two true stories Art told recently that underscore the value of commitment.

The first one is about an unattractive, scrawny boy from California. As Art tells it, "He was a sickly ninety–seven–pound high school boy in San Francisco, so discouraged by his size and continuous bad health that he seldom went out. And no wonder—girls considered him a mess. He wore thick glasses, arch supports, a shoulder brace. Finally he quit high school in complete, total despair about his prospects for a future.

"Then one day, while wandering around in his neighborhood, he attended a health lecture by the late Paul Bragg. The boy was inspired, impressed by the message of hope, and decided he could make some changes in his life.

"So he became a believer in determination. He put himself through a rigorous change in lifestyle and diet. He stopped eating junk food, ate nutritious meals, began two hours of daily exercise to strengthen his body. He re–entered high school with his newly found confidence.

"Yes, Jack LaLanne was on the road to a brilliant and lucrative career in health programs. He has won many international athletic awards and is even known as Mr. Exercise the world over."[1]

Quite a success story! How did Jack LaLanne do it? He quit feeling sorry for himself, believed that he had the potential for something better, then he acted. That was the key: *He had the courage to act.*

Essentially the same thing happened to another young person in Cedar Rapids, Iowa. Art tells the story of Wendy Stoker, a nineteen–year–old freshman at the University of Florida.

"Last year she placed third, just 2 1/2 points from first, in the Iowa girls' state diving championships. She'd worked two hours a day for four years to get there.

"Now at the University of Florida, she's working twice as hard and has earned the number–two position on the varsity diving team, and she's aiming for the national finals. Wendy is carrying a full academic load, finds time for bowling and is an accomplished water–skier.

"But perhaps the most remarkable thing about Wendy Stoker is her typing. She bangs out forty–five words a minute on her typewriter—*with her toes.*

"Oh, did I fail to mention? Wendy was born without arms."[2]

Her gain, too, is the product of commitment.

I mention these stories for two reasons: First, stories of courage, discipline, and commitment are good reminders that we are never stuck in our own situations, regardless of what they may be. Under the guidance of God's Holy Spirit, what we can conceive and believe, we can achieve. We have choices—the greatest of which is the choice of attitude. Jack LaLanne *chose* to do something about his unimpressive, ninety–seven–pound–weakling body. Wendy Stoker *chose* to commit herself to a goal as though she had no disability at all.

Secondly, these stories encourage us to look beyond our own perceived disabilities to the full potential that pulsates within us—that driving force that waits to express itself to the fullest. But the idea of full potential is little more than a hollow phrase until we fill it with gain.

GRABBING FATE BY THE SHOULDERS

How painful would it be to fall off Mount Everest? That's how Lee Iacocca described his "gut–wrenching" shove from the "grand–hotel suite" office as president of Ford Motor Company to a scruffy transition desk in a company warehouse. He had every reason to give up. He was fifty–four years old, financially secure enough for retirement, and unemployed for the first time in his thirty–two–year career with a single company. Filled with anger, resentment, and humiliation, Iacocca faced a decision.

"There are times in everyone's life when something constructive is born out of adversity. There are times when things seem so bad that you've got to grab your fate by the shoulders and shake it. I was full of anger and I had a simple choice: I could turn that anger against myself, with disastrous results. Or I could take some of that energy and try to do something productive."[3]

Lido Iacocca, the son of an Italian immigrant, then went on to rescue one of America's major auto makers from bankruptcy, pay back an unprecedented federal loan guarantee for one billion dollars seven years early, and rescue 600,000 jobs.

Have you ever grabbed your fate by the shoulders? Shaken it? If not, you can be sure that fate will seize you and shake you.

Look at these statements about some super–achievers. "He possesses minimal football knowledge. Lacks motivation," a so–called expert once said of Vince Lombardi. "Can't act! Slightly bald! Can dance a little!" read Fred Astaire's first screen test in 1933. Referring to Albert Einstein, someone quipped, "He doesn't wear socks and forgets to cut his hair. Could be mentally retarded." What shield protected them from fate's seizures?

Commitment.

THE KEY TO VITALITY

I'm convinced that unswerving commitment to a person, a cause, or an idea is the single quality that gives life its vitality. Think how Thomas Edison felt when he dreamed of a lamp that could burn invisible energy. He could have quit, and no one would have blamed him. After all, he had more than ten thousand failures in that one project alone. Chances are you and I haven't had that many failures during all our lifetimes combined.

The Wright brothers wanted to do more than repair bikes in their Dayton, Ohio, bicycle shop, so they dreamed of a machine that could ride the sky. Some laughed at them; otherwise said it was not God's will for men to fly. But Orville and Wilbur determined to follow their dream. On December 17, 1903, near Kitty Hawk, North Carolina, history was made as the first power–driven airplane roared into the sky.

Daniel Webster could not make a speech until after years of disciplined effort but became one of America's great orators. George Washington lost more battles than he won but triumphed in the end. Winners never quit, and quitters never win. A cliché, but still true. If you don't believe it, consider these examples:

- John Bunyan wrote *Pilgrim's Progress* while languishing in the Bedford Prison in England, locked up for his vocal views on religion.
- Helen Keller was stricken deaf, blind, and dumb soon after birth. Did she quit? Hardly. Her name already stands alongside those of the most respected people in history. She knew what courage and discipline were all about. We call it commitment.
- Charles Dickens began his illustrious career with the unimpressive job of pasting labels on blacking pots. The tragedy of his first love shot through to the depths of his soul, touching off a genius of creativity that made him one of the greatest authors of all

time.

- Robert Burns was an illiterate country boy; O. Henry, a criminal and an outcast; Beethoven, deaf; Milton, blind. But once they mastered their own weaknesses and committed themselves to service, they strengthened the soul of all humanity.

Are you prepared to master your own weakness? The three greatest words in the English language for fulfillment are DO IT NOW. Work on your commitments prayerfully. Don't wait. DO IT NOW.

GAIN WORTH THE PAIN

Here's a short list of valuable objectives. How many of these are worth as much to you as the ability to type was to Wendy Stoker, the girl without arms?

- having a healthier, happier marriage
- being more open and understanding with your children
- creating more family times together
- losing weight and getting back into condition
- traveling throughout the United States
- becoming more active in your local church or community organizations
- volunteering to help the needy in your community
- attending adult education classes at the local college
- learning to play a new sport
- becoming a foster grandparent to orphaned children or to youngsters who have no grandparents

I'm sure you've already thought of other categories. Perhaps now would be a good time to lay this book aside for a few minutes to expand that list. Let your thoughts run free. Make your list of potential commitments as long as possible. Then, take some time to write your objectives in order of their priority. You'll be amazed how much this will reveal about your interests, your desires, and your opportunities.

Then, act.

Ultimately, we become the people we choose to be. Although we live together, each of us grows alone. What are we willing to exact from ourselves? It's been said that we're all self-made individuals; however, *only the successful will admit it!*

What's the opposite of no pain . . . no gain? Can we slump back into complacency, assuming we won't get hurt if we don't strive for gain? Unfortunately, no gain . . . *more* pain is true as well. Consider this warning from an unknown poet:

> I bargained with Life for a penny,
> And Life would pay no more,
> However I begged at evening,
> When I counted my scanty store.
>
> For Life is a just employer,
> He gives you what you ask,
> But once you have set the wages,
> Why, you must bear the task.
>
> I worked for a menial's hire,
> Only to learn, dismayed,
> That any wage I had asked of Life,
> Life would have willingly paid.

Are you wasting your life on mere pennies? To what gain are you committing your pain? Hopefully, to something great and wonderful—something larger than yourself. Are you prepared to commit the courage and discipline necessary to make your dreams come true? I hope so. If you're not, you're missing the greatest thrill of all.

Too difficult? Too many obstacles? Too much hard work? We've never hinted that a life of commitment would be easy. But it will be rewarding. Jesus Christ—the One who endured the pain of death to gain your life and mine, the One who looks us straight in the eye and sees beyond our infirmities to the ultimate potential—He is still able to tell us, "All things are possible to those who believe."

Do you believe? If you do, it's going to change your life.

*The positive results of committing to God
and His Plans.*

10

Surprised
by Joy

If I'd known I was going to live this long, I woulda taken better care of myself." I smile every time I think of those profound words spoken by entertainer Jimmy Durante. "If I'd only known . . . " I suppose we all feel that way at one time or another. How often do we say, "If only someone would have told me . . . if I'd just had that insight?" If, if, if . . .

Let's suppose for a moment this is your last day on earth. You have been asked to reflect long and hard on your life, your job, your interests, your relationship to your friends, to your family, to God, and to your church; and then to talk about your life's priorities. What would you say? Would you paraphrase Durante's words by lamenting, "If I'd known I was going to live this long, I would have been more serious about my commitments"? Or would you be able to close your eyes for the last time, feeling content, ready to say good–bye?

I've heard it said that you're not really ready for life until you know what you want to say when you're dead, that is, on your tombstone. That's an interesting idea to pursue for a moment. You fill in the blanks. "Here lies _____, known for his/her commitments to _____."

If this is truly what you are committed to, how are you

doing? How did you do yesterday? What has been your progress today? A friend of mine has a little slogan on her desk that asks, "Is what you are about to do bringing you closer to your goal?" I ask you the same question about your commitments.

Earlier, we talked about the pain and discipline needed for a productive commitment. We noted how people like Helen Keller, Thomas Edison, John Bunyan, the Wright Brothers, and others struggled through what seemed like insurmountable odds in pursuit of their commitment and ultimate success. In this chapter, we'll look at some of the payoffs that come our way when we burn the destructive fortresses of hesitation, half-baked enthusiasm and lethargy, and instead build bridges of decision, excitement, perseverance, and single-minded commitment.

I'm afraid too many see commitment as drudgery — something that will cramp their style and keep them from having a good time. Many people want the results of commitment; however, most are unwilling to pay the price. Like a man from Texas once remarked, "Preacher, you've done quit the preaching and gone to meddlin'."

TOO YOUNG? TOO OLD?

Why are we so eager to improve our circumstances, but so reluctant to improve our lives? Some say, "I'm too young to get all worked up and committed to anything!" Still others say, "I'm over the hill . . . time is no longer on my side." Benjamin Franklin didn't seem to have that problem. He was eighty-one years old when he helped create the Constitution of the United States; at sixteen, a newspaper columnist. The great Mozart was seven years old when he published his first composition. George Bernard Shaw was a crusty ninety-four when one of his plays had its first performance. William Pitt was in his mid-twenties when he became prime minister of Great Britain; Golda Meir, seventy-one when she was elected prime minister of Israel. No one is too old or too young to make a significant contribution. Age has absolutely no bearing on ability. You and I can choose to live a life of commitment at any time with an attitude that says *I*

106

can and I will. There are simply no more excuses. Period! Look at this profound message.

> If you think you are beaten, you are.
> If you think you dare not, you don't.
> If you like to win, but you think you can't,
> It is almost certain you won't.
>
> If you think you'll lose, you're lost.
> For out of the world we find,
> Success begins with a person's will—
> It's all in the state of mind.
>
> If you think you're outclassed, you are.
> You've got to think high to rise,
> You've got to be sure of yourself before
> You can ever win a prize.
>
> Life's battles don't always go
> To the stronger woman or man,
> But sooner or later the one who wins
> Is the one WHO THINKS "I CAN!"

Dorothy McKinney was content to remain a practical nurse at Miami's Jackson Memorial Hospital. But after seven years on the job, her co-workers recognized something better. They encouraged Dorothy to enter training and become a registered nurse. "I was just doing a job, but others saw potential," she says. "My cocky attitudes changed toward being able to help somebody." With that encouragement, Dorothy was surprised to become supervisor of the orthopedics and neurology sections, to receive the 1983 Outstanding Nurse Award, and to be interviewed for a national magazine.[1]

The greatest literary artist in American history and one of our foremost novelists, Nathaniel Hawthorne, not only owed his success to the daily inspiration of his wife, but also to his only opportunity to compose first his mind, then his masterpiece. If it had not been for Sophia, perhaps we would not remember Nathaniel. After he lost his job in the customhouse, he went home a broken-hearted man to tell his wife that he was a failure. To his amazement, she beamed with joy and said, "Now you can write your book!" When he bitterly responded,

"Yes, and what shall we live on while I am writing it?" the astounding woman opened a drawer and took out a mysterious hoard of cash. "Where on earth did you get that?" he gasped. "I have always known that you were a man of genius. I knew that some day you would write an immortal masterpiece. So every week, out of the money you have given me for housekeeping, I have saved something; there is enough to last us one whole year." Thoroughly surprised, Hawthorne sat down and wrote one of the finest literary pieces in the Western Hemisphere—*The Scarlet Letter.*[2]

Once you have rightly directed your attitude, the possibilities are endless for living out the joy that soars on a life of commitment.

RESULTS YOU CAN SEE

The first, and perhaps most obvious, result of our commitment to a loving God is *personal growth.* It's been said that God's reward for a job well done is to give us a bigger job to do. Similarly, commitment, even at its struggling, most fledgling level, contributes to personal growth and enhances our capacity to grow even more.

Internal peace that results from decision is another by-product of commitment. Be hot or cold, not in-between because there is no peace in indecision. Someone once said, "On the beach of hesitation bleach the bones of countless millions who sat down to wait and waiting, died." Ever wonder why the big fish vomited Jonah? The disobedient preacher was *lukewarm*! Commitment and lukewarmness fly in the face of each other; commitment and a deep sense of internal peace go hand in hand.

When you commit yourself to God and to His plans, there is yet a third result. *Your life takes on purpose.* You discover a reason for living. Suddenly, you are more than flesh and bone. You are a person of destiny and purpose, echoing these words of the poet Goethe, "Knowing is not enough; we must apply. Willing is not enough; we must do." Then, you begin to do it with an enthusiasm and desire you never had before. Why? Because you are living your God-ordained design for commitment. You are making commitment work for you.

The pleasure you gain from action is intimately tied to your level of service to others. I like what my friend Charles "Tremendous" Jones says: "Work as hard as you can, get as much as you can, give as much as you can." That's happiness. That's fulfillment.

Often, people say, "I'm unhappy," as if happiness were somehow supposed to be the ultimate purpose of life. I've found just the opposite. Usually I'm happiest when I'm not even thinking about being happy. Happiness and joy are always by–products of my commitment to a task, a person, or an idea, often in the midst of intense struggle — even pain. But without question, my greatest happiness comes in service to others and in my commitment to projects, people, and plans bigger than myself.

SPIRIT JOY

For the follower of Jesus Christ, there is no end to the service we can provide to those around us. It makes no difference how old we are, where we live, or the state of our physical health. *There are simply no excuses for not living a life of commitment to what is worthy, honest and just.* But it's not something we dare do with our own strength alone. Secular humanism continues to be the underlying philosophy of the world today; nevertheless, this system cannot endure. We need a divine Savior every day. Once our commitment to Jesus Christ is secure, then and only then are we ready to receive the greatest joys imaginable. It's as true today as it was for the people who needed that loving touch from the Man of Galilee more than two thousand years ago.

"These things have I spoken to you, that my joy might remain in you, and that your joy might be full" (John 15:11, KJV). The joy that He experienced in serving the world of His day is waiting for us today.

The Fine Art of Friendship

If you want to be that "one–in–a–million friend" to someone, these chapters from *The Fine Art of Friendship* may be what you are looking for. These pages will encourage you to have a greater appreciation of the value of being a good listener, of sharing common interests, of being generous with encouragement and praise and, perhaps most important, emphasizing the positive qualities in those whom you would have as friends.

In a day when there is a growing imbalance toward "looking out for Number One," it is our hope that the stories, insights and practical examples in these chapters will help you refocus on what has seemingly become a lost art—*the art of being a friend.*

"Give every man thine ear, but few thy voice."
— William Shakespeare

11

Learn To Listen!

If we don't invest the time, effort, sweat and tears to develop close relationships, we could well miss out on life's greatest blessings. I know, because it almost happened to me right in my own living room.

It was a cold, rainy night. My son Gordon, now thirty-eight years old but then twenty–one, finally came home around 1 A.M. after a long evening of smoking marijuana with his friends. I was livid, embarrassed, distraught, and afraid. How could this young man whom we loved so much do this to his mother and me? It wasn't fair; it wasn't right. It was happening to other parents, but who would have ever thought it would have reared its ugly head in the Engstrom family?

We couldn't understand why. But this particular evening I held my peace, even though I had a mind to give Gordon a tongue lashing he would never forget. I listened to him as he shouted that most Christians were phonies, the church was filled with hypocrites, and there were at least a hundred ways to God. On and on he went.

The more I listened, the more something began to happen inside me. After a while, I no longer saw a son whose head was clouded from the effects of pot. Instead, I began to hear him.

Even though I didn't—and don't—approve of anyone's ingesting drugs for recreational purposes, I knew that much of what Gordon had to say was true. There is a tremendous absence of love for each other within the body of Christ. Too often our lifestyles do bear little resemblance to that of the Man from Galilee. And yes, Christians are not perfect, and no, they don't all know how to be friends.

I can remember a hot tear falling on my cheek, then another and another as Gordon spoke. I knew in my heart of hearts he was also talking about me. I only tell you this story to say this: Although that winter evening in January 1968 was difficult, humiliating, and upsetting, I think it may have been the first night I really listened to Gordon. In a fresh, new way, I was establishing a real relationship with my son. It was something that changed my life—our lives. It was the beginning of what has now become a beautiful friendship.

Is There No One Who Will Listen?

It's been called a fine art, an uncommon personal skill that must be practiced, developed, and nurtured. It's also been referred to as the most difficult thing for most people to do. Yet, for meaningful, effective living—and to ensure lifelong friendships—it is something we neglect at our own peril.

I'm talking about the ability to listen. The French writer, Pascal, said, "We only consult the ear because the heart is waiting." Shakespeare wrote, "Give every man thine ear, but few thy voice." A modern sales representative reminds his sales staff: "When you're telling, you're not selling." Listening! How important! How very difficult! John Drakeford gives us these thoughts on listening.

- Poor listening is responsible for a tremendous waste in education, industry, and many other areas of life.
- Any capable democratic leader can immeasurably improve his effectiveness by cultivating a listening ear.
- Time spent in listening plays a vital part in building

good relationships with people.

- Marriages that are sick can often be strengthened when husbands and wives will learn to listen to each other.
- As we listen to people we help them break out of their skin–enclosed isolation and enter into the community of experience and discover their potential.
- All forms of psychotherapy emphasize that listening is probably the most simple and effective single technique for helping troubled people.[1]

All of these statements should tell us everyone is looking for a friendly ear. Therefore, an important principle of friendship can be stated:

COMMIT YOURSELF TO LEARNING HOW TO LISTEN

It may be a furrowed brow, a grimace that speaks volumes, a hard swallow, or a sigh that simply says "I hear you, I understand, and I think I know what you're going through"—all are part of what it means to listen. It's absolutely amazing what we can do without saying a word. Conversely, it can be devastating to everyone concerned when we hear only what we want to hear. A personal example will illustrate this fact.

A man well known in Christian circles was being accused of homosexuality. The rumors were flying of his sexual exploits both at home and abroad. No one had yet proved anything, but it seemed as if the allegations had every reason to be true. I believed them, and when I finally brought the man into my office, I unloaded both barrels. I judged him, I spoke harshly, I was so relentless in my attack that he quickly found himself painted into a corner from which there was no possible escape.

I was so certain I was right that I didn't bother to listen to him. I knew I was right, and I knew he had done wrong. That is, until the truth emerged some weeks later that every rumor had been untrue. He was not, nor had he ever been, a homosexual.

Those are the painful lessons that come with not listening. But there is a better way, and one of the great masters of the theater is our example.

THE POWER OF SILENCE

Perhaps you've had the privilege of seeing him perform. He is the amazing, renowned French mime, Marcel Marceau. He speaks four languages and could easily hold his own on just about any subject imaginable, but every year he chooses to perform before hundreds of thousands of awestruck fans in absolute silence.

Marceau's facial expression of anguish is more graphic than if he had taken ten minutes to tell you in words the pain he feels. When in his performance he accepts a loving gift from a friend, his whole body says thank you. Marceau can make you laugh, cry, and feel anger, pity, or remorse by the skillful display of simple, subtle facial and body movements.

He has often explained his phenomenal success by saying that people simply want to be communicated with, and his pantomimes never fail to break through barriers of culture, language, and what would otherwise be human misunderstanding.

When Marceau first came to the United States from France, would–be promoters who saw his act said, "No sex, no scenery and he doesn't say a word? It will never be commercial."[2] That just goes to show how wrong agents can be! For someone with the time–proven performing skills of a Marcel Marceau, the absence of sex and scenery and the presence of silence have hardly been detrimental to his career.

As I found myself reading story after story of this amazing showman (and I encourage you to see him perform whenever you have the opportunity), I couldn't help thinking about the untapped power of silence that could do so much good in our lives, if we would only let it. It's common knowledge that virtually every high school and college in the land has a course in public speaking, but we would be hard pressed to find in the curriculum many classes on how to listen or how to express our deepest feelings without saying a word. Yet, these are precisely the skills each of us must develop if we are to learn how to become a friend.

Marcel Marceau has nonverbal skills few of us will ever match. In fact, many of us speak more loudly with our bodies than with words. In his book, *More Communication Keys to Your Marriage*, H. Norman Wright, nationally known and respected lecturer, marriage counselor, and author, asks us to give two or three responses to a list of "non–verbal/non–voice behaviors." I found this exercise fascinating and helpful.

Take a few minutes and see what responses you come up with. Read each item on the following list and try to give two or three "meanings" to each behavior. "Listen" to what you see here:

    a. A child nods his head up and down.

    b. A person turns her head rapidly in a certain direction.

    c. A person smiles slightly.

    d. A person's lower lip quivers slightly.

    e. A person speaks in a loud, harsh voice.

    f. A person speaks in a low, monotonous voice.

    g. A person suddenly opens his eyes wide.

    h. A person keeps her eyes lowered as she speaks to you.

    i. A person speaks in a very halting or hesitant voice.

    j. A person yawns during a conversation.

    k. A person shrugs his shoulders.[3]

After you've done this exercise, give it to your spouse, your children, or a friend or colleague. See how your individual responses differ. I think you'll discover a whole new

117

communication awareness. At the same time you'll unearth another powerful way to respond to the needs of your friend as you develop your skills of observing and listening without ears.

HOW TO RUIN A FRIENDSHIP IN ONE EASY LESSON

It was a Friday. The time was 2:30 A.M. Two of our close friends I will call Pete and Joan Johnson were sleeping soundly when Joan heard a noise outside their window. She rose to check on the strange sounds only to discover the neighbor's cat sharpening her claws on their shake roof. Joan started to return to bed when she felt faint. Before she knew it, she had fallen to the floor, limp and immobilized. Somehow she was able to call to her husband, "Help me, help me." Pete woke up to find his wife lying shivering in the darkness, unable to move.

Pete took Joan in his arms and placed her on the bed. He turned on the light to discover his wife's body had by now gone completely limp and her eyes had rolled back up into her head. In panic, Pete rushed to the medicine cabinet and returned with a ten–year–old bottle of smelling salts he hoped still had some potency. They did. He slapped at Joan's face and gave her nostrils a hefty dose of pungent salts. Startled, she opened her eyes. After a few minutes it was apparent she would be all right. But for those few brief moments, Pete thought he had lost his dear wife.

Pete and Joan had been invited to dinner the next evening with very good friends, but they both felt it would be better if they stayed home. The trauma of the early morning was still too much to deal with. They knew that rest and relaxation were more appropriate than having to talk loudly for three hours in a noisy restaurant. Besides, they wanted to be sure Joan was all right.

Joan called and spoke to the woman who had invited them. Joan said she had fainted that morning and Pete was afraid she had died. They felt it would be best to take a rain check on the evening.

Without missing a beat, Joan's friend quipped, "Oh, that's nothing. I've fainted lots of times. Now, when can we get together? I mean I was really counting on you two coming. The Michaels will be there, and so will the Wilsons." Joan then said quietly, "But Pete was really afraid that I was gone." To which her friend said, "Oh, well, I've never had quite that experience. But I've fainted lots of times. Now let's get our datebooks out and set a new time for dinner."

To hear Joan tell it, it was one of the most devastating conversations she ever had with her friend. There were no listening, no compassion, no concerned silence—none of the responses you would expect from a true friend. At that moment a blow was struck at the friendship. Perhaps it will not be a fatal blow, at least I hope not. But it hurt. It cut deeply.

HEAR THE NEEDS OF YOUR FRIEND

For whatever reason, Joan's friend forgot that one of the most vital ingredients in a friendship is being there to listen at any time of the day or night. It's good for us to listen to stories such as these, because if we observe ourselves in our busy, day-to-day activities we may discover we are often overly preoccupied with our own concerns to hear the needs of a friend. I have one friend in particular who is never too busy to talk to me. And he is one of the busiest men in America.

During one of the more difficult early years of my association with World Vision, I made more than one attempt to extricate myself from the virtually unmanageable fiscal problems and personality conflicts that were daily dogging my steps. In short, I wanted to resign. I was determined to get out. I felt I could no longer cope with the problems.

I went to my friend Dick Halverson, chairman of the World Vision board—later to become chaplain of the United States Senate—and I was as direct as I've ever been in my entire life. I said I was through—finished. He looked me straight in the eye and said, "Oh, no, you're not. You've just begun. Besides, if you leave, it will be the death of World Vision."

I doubt the truth of that last statement, but one thing was certain. Dick did not approve of my decision. I listened, he listened, we cried, we prayed, and I stayed.

On yet another occasion Dorothy and I made plans for a long weekend with our dear friends Bette and Ned Vessey. I needed to get away just to think and pray—again about my future relationship with World Vision. I'm not normally one to walk away from a challenge, but the pressures, the uncertainties, the personality conflicts were becoming too much to bear.

I told Ned I wanted out, that I simply could not manage the affairs of World Vision any longer. Ned listened. He would nod his head, purse his lips, perhaps shift his feet a bit as he sat there. But he said nothing, not a single word. I just talked and talked. Ned listened and listened.

Hours later when I was all through talking, and when I figured Ned was probably through listening, an uncommon wave of peace came over my heart. I found myself not wanting to leave World Vision at all. If anything, my spirit was renewed, my faith was rekindled, hope was restored, and I was a new man. I resolved not to resign, and I was prepared to pour my very best into my work. All Ned had done was listen.

I'm not suggesting every outcome will be the same for you as it was for me during those critical hours. I do know the staying power of a friend's listening ear can help restore perspective to what may be little more than mass confusion.

"Smile and Let the Talk Wash Over"

As I started to write this chapter I noticed a copy of *Sports Illustrated* on my desk. I take a degree of pride in staying up–to–date with current theological books, missions articles, and a variety of magazines that help me to keep abreast of world events. I must confess, when *Sports Illustrated* arrives, I put many of those other journals aside to bury myself in that week's exploits of our nation's greatest athletes. Today was no different.

The headline on the cover read: "Sportswoman of the Year." One of the pictures below showed Mary Decker pressing the tape as she defeated—by inches—the Soviet champion, Zamira Zaitseva, in a 1500–meter world championship race. The article went on to describe her phenomenal performances in San Diego, Los Angeles, Gateshead (England), Stockholm, Paris, and Oslo.

I was particularly struck by one comment made about Mary by the writer of the article. He wrote, "She can be demanding. *She can sit all evening at the feet of a friend and not say anything, just smile and let the talk wash over her*" (italics mine).[4]

Those last words hit me between the eyes. What a wonderful way to put it. Have you ever done that—just let the "talk wash over"? If you have, you know the joy that comes from this kind of maximum friendship. After all, when you are with your best friend there is little need to rely on non–stop conversation. Often it will be enough to smile, listen, and let the talk wash over you. Ultimately, this quiet, intentional listening may even turn an adversary into a friend. It happened to me.

It's been said that experience is what you get when you were expecting something else. When we translate that into relationships, it reads something like: I thought we would always be friends. Never in my wildest dreams did I ever think this friendship would end. Yet the years prove to all of us that friends do come and go. People we worked with, played with, and even prayed with at some point are no longer close to us. Some even become adversaries. I experienced this in my up and down relationship with the founder of World Vision, Bob Pierce, and learned that there is a way to deal with this most difficult situation.

I first met Bob at a Youth for Christ Conference in Medicine Lake, Minnesota, at the second annual conference of YFC. I was taken to him immediately, and we began what would become a long friendship. I was next with him at the great World Congress on Evangelism in Beatenberg, Switzerland, in 1948. During that time he was carrying on his missionary activities and evangelism in China. It was also the time when he wrote in his Bible, "Let my heart be broken with the things that break

121

the heart of God," which became his life's slogan.

Bob and Dr. Frank C. Phillips then organized World Vision officially as an incorporated body in 1950. During those early years I was very close to Bob Pierce. I was a frequent guest in his home, and I often spoke on his Mutual Network radio broadcast in California. Bob also came to our home in Wheaton, Illinois, on numerous occasions. We would talk, pray, laugh, and enjoy each other to the point where our friendship fast became one of supreme importance to both of us.

In 1963 when I resigned as president of Youth for Christ International, Bob invited me to meet with the World Vision board of directors. I was invited to become vice-president of World Vision. Bob said the Lord had laid my name on his heart, and he asked me if I would be willing to consider coming with him in this new role. I told him I wasn't sure, but I would certainly pray about it. After meeting twice with the World Vision board, I accepted their invitation to become executive vice-president of the organization.

It was September 1963. When I came with World Vision, I knew there were obstacles and challenges to Bob Pierce's vision, but I was unaware just how great some of those obstacles were. I soon learned World Vision was in deep financial trouble. We had over $440,000 in debts hanging over our heads from the great Tokyo Crusade Bob had directed. We were also falling behind about $30,000 each month with Bob's radio broadcasts (which was a lot of money in those days—and still is!).

I revealed these realities to the board at a special meeting in Laguna Beach, California, in the fall of 1963. Bob was smitten, literally upended, at my report. He asked for a leave of absence, which was granted by the board. For the next year, I was instructed to do all I could to bring some order out of what I sensed was absolute chaos.

"A ROOT OF BITTERNESS"

Bob never forgave me for what he said was my "stealing" of his organization and for "taking him off the air." There were tremendous tensions, angry words, and unpleasant encounters for that entire one year—tensions that continued when Bob returned for his final two years as president of World Vision.

Later, Bob Pierce resigned, but he did so with what he said was "bitterness in his heart." He continued to hold me responsible for his leaving. Our friendship seemed to be on its last legs. That was in 1968.

In 1973, I was in Africa conducting World Vision business when I received a cable from Bob. He referred to his "root of bitterness" in the cable. He asked if we could meet together upon my return home: I cabled him immediately and said I would call him the hour I returned to Los Angeles, which I did.

The next day, Bob and I met at noon at the Derby Restaurant near the World Vision offices. We parted at five o'clock. We looked each other in the eye as we shared our hurts and fears, wept, and listened to each other as we had never listened before. We prayed until we could pray no more, and listened until we could listen no more, with the one theme of our prayer being that our hearts would be reunited. It was the most exhausting personal encounter I've ever known, but during those five hours Bob and I began to understand many of the problems basic to our separation.

I had thought, when I came to California, that I was coming as Bob Pierce's friend. He saw me coming as his employee and the person to assist him in running the organization. When we really started listening to each other, we discovered that each of us had an entirely different concept of what my role was to be.

As we sat across from each other for those five hours in that restaurant, we finally cleared the air and paved the way for reconciliation. Although our friendship was never again blessed with the openness and beauty of those earlier years, we had done what was necessary to restore the relationship. From that day forward Bob and I were able to be comfortable with each other right up to the day he went to be with the Lord.

I deeply loved Bob Pierce, and even though the hurts were on both sides of the friendship, I know in the end there was an equal amount of mutual affection. There is no question that

Bob was the most complex person I've ever known. But World Vision could never have become what it has become over the years without the drive, dream, and energy that Bob brought to everything he did.

For both Bob and me, turning an adversary into a friend took hours of praying and weeping. It took a mutual choosing to listen, to love, and to trust one another once again, but it was worth every single struggling minute of it.

The key word here is *choose*. The restoration of a friendship *never* comes about automatically, nor can it ever be unilateral. It takes the willingness to be uncompromisingly open. It requires total commitment on both sides that says, "We want our friendship to be all it can be." Above all, it demands the courtesy of unselfish listening.

Never pass up an opportunity to show affection with a smile and a kind word.

12

The Magic of Praise and Encouragement

How important is praise and encouragement?

My friend and colleague and best–selling author, Dr. James Dobson, tells a powerful story in the opening chapter of his book *Hide or Seek* that I want to share with you. I guarantee once you read the account of this young man's life, it will be a story you'll never forget!

He began his life with all the classic handicaps and disadvantages. His mother was a powerfully built, dominating woman who found it difficult to love anyone. She had been married three times, and her second husband divorced her because she beat him up regularly. The father of the child I'm describing was her third husband; he died of a heart attack a few months before the child's birth. As a consequence, the mother had to work long hours from his earliest childhood.

She gave him no affection, no love, no discipline, and no training during those early years. She even forbade him to call her at work. Other children had little to do with him, so he was alone most of the time. He was absolutely rejected from his earliest childhood. He was ugly and poor and untrained and unlovable. When he was thirteen years old a school psychologist commented that he probably didn't even know the meaning of the word "love." During adolescence, the girls would have nothing to do with him and he fought with the boys.

Despite a high IQ, he failed academically, and finally dropped out during his third year of high school. He thought he might find a new acceptance in the Marine Corps; they reportedly built men, and he wanted to be one. But his problems went with him. The other Marines laughed at him and ridiculed him. He fought back, resisted authority, and was court–martialed and thrown out of the Marines with an undesirable discharge. So there he was—a young man in his early twenties—absolutely friendless and shipwrecked. He was small and scrawny in stature. He had an adolescent squeak in his voice. He was balding. He had no talent, no skill, no sense of worthiness. He didn't even have a driver's license.

Once again he thought he could run from his problems so he went to live in a foreign country. But he was rejected there too. Nothing had changed. While there, he married a girl who herself had been an illegitimate child and brought her back to America with him. Soon, she began to develop the same contempt for him that everyone else displayed. She bore him two children, but he never enjoyed the status and respect that a father should have. His marriage continued to crumble. His wife demanded more and more things that he could not provide. Instead of being his ally against the bitter world, as he hoped, she became his most vicious opponent. She could outfight him, and she learned to bully him. On one occasion, she locked him in the bathroom as punishment. Finally, she forced him to leave.

He tried to make it on his own, but he was terribly lonely. After days of solitude, he went home and literally begged her to take him back. He surrendered all pride. He crawled. He accepted humiliation. He came on her terms. Despite his meager salary, he brought her seventy–eight dollars as a gift, asking her to take it and spend it any way she wished. But she laughed at him. She belittled his feeble attempts to supply the family's needs. She ridiculed his failure. She made fun of his sexual impotency in front of a friend who was there. At one point, he fell on his knees and wept bitterly, as the greater darkness of his private nightmare enveloped him.

Finally, in silence, he pleaded no more. No one wanted him. No one had ever wanted him. He was perhaps the most rejected man of our time. His ego lay shattered in fragmented dust! The next day, he was a strangely different man. He arose, went to the garage, and took down a rifle he had hidden there. He carried it with him to his newly acquired job at a book–storage building. And from a window on the third floor of that building, shortly after noon, November 22, 1963, he sent two shells crashing into the head of President John Fitzgerald Kennedy.[1]

Each time I read this brutal account of how Lee Harvey Oswald grew up friendless—without love, encouragement, praise, or discipline—a chill races down my spine. I'm reminded we often are guilty of treating people the same way, sometimes those we truly love most. Where we could have loved, we stubbornly withheld affection. When it would have been so easy to respond with a smile and a compliment, we criticized. When we were confronted with a molehill, we turned it into an emotional Mount Everest. When a single word of encouragement would have won the day, for whatever dark reasons we chose to remain silent.

In so doing, we probably did not begin the psychic programming of a killer, although there is no guarantee of that. We certainly did some killing of our own, because we aimed our rifle of rejection at that person's self–esteem and self–respect. We unloaded our shells; we called in the troops; we dropped the bomb; we won a little war.

Or did we? During that moment of unkindness, part of our friend, our spouse, our colleague, our child died a little inside. However, what we perhaps failed to notice was that we died a little too. This is what happens to us when we fail to remember another powerful principle of the fine art of friendship: Be generous with legitimate praise and encouragement.

THE ADVENTURES OF MEMO MAN!

Some members of my staff call me the "memo man." Others insist I'm hopelessly afflicted with memo madness and have fostered an organization–wide conspiracy that promotes memo mania. I'm told that words like *memo machine* and *management by memo* often hang over conversations where my name is mentioned. I cannot deny that the memo is for me what the seven–hundred–page novel is to James Michener.

I use memos to say a friendly hello, to say thank you, to encourage, to reprimand, to announce, to praise, and to express sincere appreciation. Most of my time at the dictaphone involves asking my secretaries and assistants to "take a memo." When all is said and done, I take all the ribbing about being "Mr. Memo" in the playful spirit in which it is intended.

On the day of her retirement, Dorothy Haskins, an employee of more than ten years, asked me to come down to her office. I did, not knowing what to expect. She reached over and picked up a gigantic book that was so heavy I had to help her lift it. It obviously held considerable value for Dorothy, because the book was beautifully bound. She asked mysteriously, "Well, what do you think this is?"

I said I didn't have the foggiest idea.

"Well, then," she went on, "let me show you." To my amazement, she leafed through page after page of every single one of the memos I had written her during her entire ten years at World Vision. I couldn't believe what I was seeing. They went on endlessly! At that moment I had to say to myself: *So that's what I've been doing with all my time!*

In Dorothy Haskins's case it was encouraging to note that most of the memos were of thanks, a compliment, or a word of encouragement. I don't say that in an attempt to ingratiate myself with you the reader. But I must say this: As I quickly scanned my ten years of dictation to Dorothy, I was truly grateful that God had given me the desire and, hopefully, the ability to be an encouragement to others. As I looked over that huge volume I felt good inside.

In fact, I was so moved by Dorothy's gesture that I could hardly wait to thank her in the manner to which she had become accustomed. Of course, I promptly thanked her with a memo!

THE OLD SWEDE WHO KNEW HOW TO LOVE

It was Valentine's Day, 1984. Robert Larson, my friend and colleague who has been of such immeasurable help in researching and writing this book, was shaken awake by the telephone at 4 A.M. It was his mother in South San Francisco. Choking through her tears, she told Bob that a team of paramedics had just arrived in the family living room, and at that very moment they were trying to save his dad's life. The seventy–four–year–old pastor and friend to so many lay pale and motionless on the floor, stricken by a massive heart attack. At 5 A.M. another call came. Bob's dad was dead.

For the next six days, Bob and his family were at Anna Larson's side, comforting, holding, and reminding her that Harry Larson had literally given his heart for the people he loved.

It had been my privilege to meet Dr. Larson on several occasions. I remember him as that "dear old Swede." He always had a kind word for everyone. He was an encourager and always a strong supporter of the work of World Vision and of missions throughout the world. For forty years he had touched the lives of the people of South San Francisco. For forty years he had loved and cared for them—and for some, in ways they had never known.

When Bob returned to Los Angeles after the funeral, he told me some of the stories he heard after his dad's death. One man, weeping over the open casket, told Bob how last Christmas he and his family had not received their Social Security checks. There was no money for food, the rent was due, and unpaid medical bills were stacking up. When Harry Larson heard about it, he bought several bags of groceries and took them to the home of his friends. He also gave them a generous check to help them along. He continued this week after week, until they were able to get back on their feet.

A former bank executive in town, a devout Roman Catholic, took Bob's hand after the service and said, "Your dad and I were so close. We'd meet downtown almost every day. He'd ask me what I learned at Mass that morning, and he listened as I told him. Then he'd give me his sermon outlines for the next few Sundays, and I would listen. He was my dear friend. I'll miss him. He always had a good word for me. He was such an encouragement."

The stories went on and on about this man's friendships. His friendships truly lasted a lifetime, and he enjoyed relationships built on praise and seeing the good in others.

Why is it often so difficult for us to say an encouraging word to those we love the most? Why do we tend to overlook the obvious good and dwell instead on the negative? What are the reasons for the roadblocks we set up that keep us from truly being a friend to those we love the most? What can we do to change our attitudes and behavior?

DISTINGUISH BETWEEN THE PERFORMANCE AND THE PERFORMER

Denis Waitley, in his magnificent book *Seeds of Greatness,* helps us address our dilemma on two specific fronts. I've found his insights especially helpful in handling conflicts both within my family and among my colleagues. Waitley suggests that "in communicating with others, always treat *behavior* and *performance* as being *distinctly separate* from the *personhood* or *character* of the individual you are trying to influence."

Here are some all–too–truthful communication examples from my own experience. Perhaps you will be able to identify with them!

> Bad: "Why do you never meet your deadlines?"
> Better: "When the work you're assigned isn't completed on time, it makes it difficult for many others involved in the project. Let's spend some time talking about it, OK?"

> Bad: "How many times have I told you I expect regular field reports from your department?"
> Better: "I need more help in knowing what's going on in your department, and I particularly need *your* input. By the way, I'm getting good feedback on your performance, and I

value your contribution."

Bad: "You're not telling me the truth!"
Better: "What you're telling me doesn't match up with what I've heard. Let's check it out together."

The message? Criticize the performance, praise the performer—a top priority item in learning the art of friendship. Every time I think or speak on the subject of encouragement and praise, a special poem comes to mind. Some people may consider it to be a bit corny. But I like it because its verses capture the essence of what it means to be a friend. Its message asks us to remember a great truth: *by denying love and happiness to others we lose our own wished-for happiness.* Conversely, the more we share, the more we possess. The more we praise and encourage, the greater the blessings that flood our own souls. See if these lines speak to your heart.

> There are hermit souls that live withdrawn
> In the peace of their self–content,
> There are souls, like stars, that dwell apart,
> In a fellowless firmament;
> There are pioneer souls that blaze their paths
> Where highways never ran—
> But let me live by the side of the road
> And be a friend to man.
>
> Let me live in a house by the side of the road,
> By the side of the highway of life,
> The men who press with the ardor of hope,
> The men who are faint with the strife.
> But I turn not away from their smiles nor their
>   tears—
> Let me live in my house by the side of the road
> And be a friend to man.
>
> I know there are brook–gladdened meadows ahead
> And mountains of wearisome height;
> And the road passes on through the long afternoon
> And stretches away to the night.
> But still I rejoice when the travelers rejoice,

And weep with the strangers that moan,
Nor live in my house by the side of the road
Like a man who dwells alone.

Let me live in my house by the side of the road
Where the race of men go by—
They are good, they are bad, they are weak, they are
    strong,
Wise, foolish—so am I.
Then why should I sit in the scorner's seat
Or hurl the cynic's ban?–
Let me live in my house by the side of the road
And be a friend to man.

—"The House by the Side of the Road"
by Sam Walter Foss[2]

What better time than now and what better person than
you to begin to become this kind of man or woman? Let your
friendship be genuine, your praise sincere, and your
encouragement generous to all you meet. Those whom you touch
with a word of kindness or deed of mercy—especially your
children—will long remember you, and they will thank you for
being a friend.

All of us who are parents have learned, more often than
not the hard way, how much more is accomplished when we
praise our children rather than constantly criticize them. Our
three children, now each happily married to wonderful mates
and each with their own families, were adopted as infants by
Dorothy and me. We told them from their earliest childhood that
we had selected them to join our family; they were our choice.
Often, as little ones, we would hear them tell their playmates,
"My Mom and Dad chose us; yours *had* to take you." We would
always tell them how grateful we were for the delight and joy
they were bringing to our lives and how proud we were of them.
This closeness, praise, and appreciation have knit our family in a
special way.

The three of them as adults have remained the closest of
friends as well as brothers and sisters in Christ. It is also a

source of great joy to Dorothy and me that they are our friends as adults as well as our sons and daughter.

Praising your child or grandchild costs you nothing, but what rich dividends it pays you in cementing relationships that endure the stress and difficulties of the years. Whether this encouragement is given to your children, your spouse, your neighbors, or the clerk at the local store, praise and encouragement will ultimately win the day. That is why spoken appreciation is so important in learning the art of friendship. Think about it. Do it!

Five crucial guidelines to help others feel valued.

13

Making Others Number One

William Blake, the great eighteenth–century English poet, once wrote about the sensitive, vulnerable butterfly. If we grab at it as it sits on our shoulder and think solely of our own selfish interests to possess it, we snuff out its tiny, fragile life. On the other hand, when we relax, enjoy its brief company, and allow it to be its own important self, it lives and flourishes. Here are Blake's words:

> He who binds to himself a joy
> Does the winged life destroy,
> But he who kisses the joy as it flies
> Lives in eternity's sunrise.

Blake's poetic sentiments remind me of what Martin Marty, theologian, writer, and critic, wrote in his book simply called *Friendship*, in which he says friendship, much like happiness, presents itself most readily when we don't seek it. Marty says, "There is no reason to make the search for friendship sound like an animal instinct. Friendship does not always come as a result of a search; it can come when we least look for it, just as it denies itself when we pursue it too earnestly and with pathetic eagerness."[1]

Friendship, then, can be just like the butterfly that lands on our shoulder. When it presents itself to us, we can seize it, smother it, and eventually kill it, or we can treat it with dignity, courtesy, and unfailing respect. That is why this next principle of the art of friendship is so important:

Make your friends Number One,
preferring them above yourself.

You may be saying, "Hold on a minute. That is not usually what is written on that subject these days. We are being told over and over again to 'look out for Number One,' to take care of ourselves and our own self–interests – at any cost! We're reminded it's a jungle out there, where only the fittest survive and the winner takes all."

How do we reconcile these two strains of thought? Of course we need to take care of ourselves. I brush my own teeth, of course, put on my own socks, and tie my own shoelaces. Those are my responsibilities to myself. Yes, we do need to be our own best friend. In fact, until we're a true friend to ourselves we're not going to possess a great deal of self–worth, nor will we enjoy much of a relationship with others. (To say nothing of how little they are going to enjoy us.)

FIRST, BEFRIEND YOURSELF

Of all the books and articles I've read on the critical subject of self–esteem, psychologist Dr. Neil C. Warren in his tremendously helpful book, *Make Anger Your Ally*, says it best. In a chapter entitled "And a Close Friendship with Yourself," he writes:

> No friendship you have is as crucial to your self–esteem as that friendship you maintain with yourself. In fact, all your other friendships combined are not as important to the way you feel about yourself as your internal friendship with you is.
>
> In support of this radical statement, consider the thousands of messages you send every day to your own self–assessment center. The content of these messages undoubtedly determines the way you evaluate your worth. And

the evaluation you make of your worth invariably sets your self–esteem level.

After suggesting we list what we like about ourselves as a part of an objective personal survey, Dr. Warren concludes:

> But in the final analysis your appreciation of yourself will not depend on the length of your list of positive attributes. Rather, it will be due to your having been created unique and loveable. The fact is, that no one in history can replace you. And the clear word from the Bible is that you are enormously worthy solely on the basis of the magnificence of the created you.[2]

I'm glad my friend Dr. Warren wrote those words because they put the issue of "friendship with ourselves" in proper perspective. Once having established a friendship with ourselves, we can then, and then only, promote the good in others, look for ways to be genuinely complimentary, and be willing to take a back seat. After all, sitting in the back seat still gets us to our destination.

When you find yourself more concerned with *giving* friendship than in simply *receiving* it, you will discover you are in a most enviable position: You will be one who has tapped one of the richest mines of human relationships. You will have discovered the fine art of friendship.

Don't be like the man who said to the old potbelly stove, "Come on, give me some warmth and then I'll add the wood." It doesn't work that way for stoves *or* people *or* friendship.

ONE WOMAN'S SELFLESSNESS

One of the most moving books I've ever read is called *Letters to an Unborn Child*, written by David Ireland who, as he writes, is dying from a crippling neurological disease. David writes these letters to the unborn child still in the womb of his wife—a child he may never see. He will be unable to take his child to either ball games or ballet lessons. There will be no romps in the park, no stories read on daddy's knee. Still, he wants that child to know that dead or alive, "Daddy loves his little boy or girl." Here are some of Dave Ireland's thoughts:

> Your mother is very special. Few men know what it's like to receive appreciation for taking their wives out to dinner when it entails what it does for us. It means that she has to dress me, shave me, brush my teeth, comb my hair, wheel me out of the house and down the steps, open the garage and put me in the car, take the pedals off the chair, stand me up, sit me in the seat of the car, twist me around so that I'm comfortable, fold the wheelchair, put it in the car, go around to the other side of the car, start it up, back it out, get out of the car, pull the garage door down, get back into the car, and drive off to the restaurant.
>
> And then, it starts all over again; she gets out of the car, unfolds the wheelchair, opens the door, spins me around, stands me up, seats me in the wheelchair, pushes the pedals out, closes and locks the car, wheels me into the restaurant, then takes the pedals off the wheelchair so I won't be uncomfortable. We sit down to have dinner, and she feeds me throughout the entire meal. And when it's over she pays the bill, pushes the wheelchair out to the car again, and reverses the same routine.
>
> And when it's over — finished — with real warmth she'll say, "Honey, thank you for taking me out to dinner." I never quite know what to answer.[3]

What an account of tough love, energy, caring, and friendship! David's wife, Joyce, has to be the epitome of what it means to be willing to be Number Two, Three, Four, or whatever for the sake of her husband. I think it's good for us to hear about people like David and Joyce once in a while. It does something to us at our very core. And that is good. But how do you and I go about being Number Two and *liking* it?

HOW TO MAKE OTHERS NUMBER ONE

My colleague, Ed Dayton, and I spend a large portion of our time giving time management seminars to pastors, teachers, leaders, and laypersons throughout the country. Because of our high profile in this subject and because we are so-called "experts," we are always being asked for our opinions, comments, and special insights.

After one exhausting session, I met privately for dinner with a small group of men who had been in the all–day conference. Because I had been the speaker all day, I had more or less assumed they wanted more "wisdom" from their leader.

Wrong! But it took me twenty minutes to realize it. I had continued to hold forth during the early part of dinner, taking the initiative, exercising leadership, motivating these fine men to do greater, more wonderful things, only to discover that was not what they wanted at this meal. Finally, one man said, "Ted, I think we have all had just about all the time management we can handle in one day. We just wanted to get together for fellowship."

Don't make the mistakes I made. To help you make others Number One, here are five important guidelines I've learned from real–life experience.

1. *Catch the drift of the conversation before you assume people have assembled to hear what you have to say.* Consider the overwhelming words of 1 Corinthians 13. In the J. B. Phillips rendering of one of those powerful verses, we read, "Love has good manners and does not pursue selfish advantage." For the time being let's substitute the words *a friend* for *love.* Now it reads, "A friend has good manners and does not pursue selfish advantage." Wouldn't you agree?

I saw a sign on a colleague's wall recently that said: "Too many people operate on the assumption you don't need road manners if you're a fifteen–ton truck." Psychologically, if you must always draw attention to yourself, you have a problem. If you must receive all the praise and credit and are immobilized when you are not leading each and every conversation then you don't know the first thing about how to be a friend. Psychologists refer to this malady as "performance anxiety." To counteract that problem, let's examine the next guideline.

2. *Learn to ask questions—and then wait for answers.* A young woman in your office comes by your desk. She points to a

letter in her hand and tearfully says, "My boyfriend has left with another girl. He's gone. Forever. He says he never wants to see me again." She breaks down and sobs some more.

If you are your own Number One, you might take her by the hand and say, "Now, now, that's not so bad. Let me tell you what happened to me. Let's see—was it two or three years ago? Yes, that's right, it was three years ago. You see, I was dating this guy who . . . "

What is the problem with this reaction? It says you are so concerned with your own three-year-old problem that you cannot hear the pain of your friend now. What if, instead, you take her hand and say, "I don't know what to say. I'm so sorry. Are you going to be all right?" Then, "You probably don't need to cook dinner tonight. Why don't we go out together and get a bite. We can talk more then." Or, "What can I do to help you walk through this tough time?"

What a difference! *That* is a friend. *That* is being willing to stand in a Number Two position and feel good about it. Why? Because there are times in our lives when the concerns of another merit more attention than our own. It's one of the most important factors in learning the fine art of friendship.

Here is an exercise for you. Make it a point in the next day or two to talk with two or three friends. Tell them something wonderful that has happened to you, and note their response. Do they stay with you and your excitement? Or do they use the occasion to talk about themselves?

An even better experiment will be the next time someone turns to you and relates a situation—good or bad—that is on his or her mind. Will you ask questions that draw out how this person feels? Will you be patient in listening? Will you affirm your friendship by making your friend feel he or she is the most important person in the world at that moment? When you do, you'll be practicing one of the most powerful, yet rarely understood, principles in learning how to be a friend. You'll find yourself in a perfect position to implement guideline number three.

3. *Take full responsibility for the pattern of growth you have experienced and encourage others to do the same.* The story is told of a trusted advisor of President Lincoln who recommended a candidate for Lincoln's cabinet. Lincoln declined and when he was asked why, he said, "I don't like the man's face."

"But the poor man is not responsible for his face," his advisor insisted.

"Every man over forty is responsible for his face," Lincoln replied, and the prospect was considered no more.

Just as you and I, according to Lincoln, are responsible for our "face," so are we responsible, with the patience and guidance of a loving God, for our own pattern of spiritual and emotional growth.

Dr. Wayne Dyer, lecturer and author of the best–selling book *The Sky's the Limit*, warns against our mindless conforming to the ideas and whims of the many influences that surround us. Dr. Dyer writes:

> In counseling I always think it is important to help anyone to resist automatic conformity to anything, because it detracts seriously from a person's basic human dignity by elevating other authority to a level higher than one's own. This is true for dominated children, wives, husbands, employees or anyone else: If you can't think for yourself, if you are unable to be other than conforming and submissive, then you are always going to be gullible, a slave to whatever any authority figure dictates.[4]

Those are good words to help us become our own persons, but they don't tell the whole story. In fact, there is great danger in becoming a law unto ourselves. The follower of Jesus has only one model, one standard, one mentor. If the gospel teaches anything, it teaches that the will of God for our lives is to be conformed, submissive, and molded into the image of His Son, Jesus Christ. Such a relationship is not slavery. It is ultimate freedom. It's the kind of 100 percent allegiance that does not detract from our basic human dignity; instead, it's the one relationship above all others that makes you and me truly human. It is a friendship beyond comparison. Furthermore, it is a relationship worth sharing with others. The world around you is waiting to know that such a friendship is possible.

This verse has been underlined in my Bible as long as I can remember: "Seek ye first the kingdom of God, and His righteousness; and all these things shall be added unto you" (Matthew 6:33, KJV). What things? Things like joy, peace, hope, faith, courage, and love.

Too often the people who insist on being Number One do so at tremendous cost. It is always precarious to have to be on top all the time, and still more risky if we're perched there because of irrational thinking and careless behavior. Even a fallen Humpty Dumpty discovered the best of the king's horses and men didn't have all the answers when it came to putting him back together.

Look closely at your motivation for ascending the ladder. Take a hard look at your friendships. Do you really need to be Number One? I hope you will come to the conclusion that you don't need to worry about being any number at all.

It's my prayer that you'll discover something strangely wonderful beginning to happen to you when you work at taking full responsibility for your own pattern of growth and encourage others to do the same. Enjoy who you are. Enjoy your friends for who they are. Suddenly you'll find you will no longer be threatened by the success of others. You'll discover yourself able to compliment the one who has done well, won the award, made a touchdown, or been given the promotion.

You'll also find you will be able to be a better friend than ever before. You'll be able to appreciate without pressure to compete, applaud without wishing you were in the limelight. You'll notice you are relaxed, warm, and spontaneous in your praise, because you have chosen to conform to a higher power, one who has given you the strength and courage to be the friend He meant you to be. You can be Number Two, Twenty-two, or Two Hundred Twenty-two and still enjoy it. The best news of all: This is not idle theory. It works! It also puts you on firm footing for guideline number four.

4. *Mention your own faults before you begin criticizing your friend.* If you want a sure–fire way to keep from usurping the Number One position in a relationship, this is it. How can you feel superior when you choose to take the initiative in admitting a mistake or misguided action you've made? This doesn't mean you are inferior or ignorant, but it does put your friend on notice that you are honest about yourself. This attitude of honesty creates a fresh, convincing atmosphere of trust and camaraderie, qualities lasting friendships thrive on.

I recall one day on an overseas trip being brutally curt and short with a committee that had worked diligently and long in preparation for a meeting we were to conduct in that city. It was my responsibility to make certain everything would be in order, and upon my arrival, I found that practically all my instructions had been either ignored or wrongly executed. Frustrated, I verbally tore into those people who had worked so hard in their own cultural milieu, which I did not fully understand.

I had great difficulty sleeping that night. The next day I called them together to apologize. Gratefully, they accepted my apology and carried out their responsibilities in their *own* right, good way, and the event was wonderfully blessed of God. From that experience of vulnerability developed a warm friendship that has lasted over the years.

My problem was simple. I saw it as "my show," and I wanted it done my way. I wanted to be Number One. I wanted it done the American Way, the Red, White and Blue Way, the way we do it at home! What a mistake! In spite of all my overseas experience, I had forgotten one of the most important principles of friendship. Be willing to stand back, and let your friends be Number One.

Someone has said that it is the weak who are cruel. Gentleness can only be expected from the strong. What a good word to motivate us to admit our errors. Learn to share your own errors with a friend before you are critical of his or her actions. It adds to your stature to admit you are fully human.

5. *Do your part to make this planet a friend-ship.* One of my favorite verses of Scripture reads, "And outdo one another in showing affection." Just think what would happen if you and I engaged in that happy activity for even five minutes a day every day. The change in us and in our friends would be revolutionary. Besides, is it really so difficult to say something nice to those around you?

What about the waitress who in spite of being harried and rushed gives you exceptional service? Be a friend and tell her so (and don't forget to leave a terrific tip!). What about the elderly woman who sits alone all day in the musty lobby of a retirement home with nothing to do and no one to care about her? Isn't there something you can do or be to demonstrate you care? If you regard yourself as Number One, chances are you'll just let her sit there growing old alone. But miracles begin to happen within you when your love exceeds your reach, when you make her and others Number One.

What about your children or your spouse? If you are going to learn how to be a friend, what better place to start than at home! You might be the father or the mother, but that doesn't mean you are a ruler whose divine right is to treat your family members as lesser servants. We all know how disparaging and unkind we can be to each other. Too often, we show the least amount of courtesy and friendship to the ones we say we love the most. We compliment the mailman, the milkman, our employees, and the people in the beauty salon, but we never compliment our own children, our own husband or wife. What a crime!

Don't let a day go by without seeing something good in your loved ones. Once you've seen it, then say something. Don't remain silent. Some days you might have to struggle a bit to find something, but you'll find it. When you do, don't be bashful. In a recent lecture, university professor Leo Buscaglia exhorted his listeners to do something about this: "I'm always telling teachers it's impossible for children to deal with a concept that out of fifty, they got forty-nine wrong. Why not tell them, 'Johnny, you got one right! Bravo! Tomorrow we're going to make it two!' "

He went on:

> Remember what Grandma used to say, "You catch many more flies with honey than you do with vinegar." So why do we concentrate on the negative all the time—what you should be—what you should do? And all under the guise, "I'm telling this because I love you" . . . Those people whom we should be reinforcing the most because we love them so much are often the people we tell the least. And that's a pity. So in your home is where you begin to set this atmosphere of personal dignity. Telling people they *are* beautiful.[5]

Buscaglia's words remind me of the late, great football coach, Paul "Bear" Bryant. Several years ago, he was quoted as saying this about himself and his team:

> I'm just a plowhand from Arkansas, but I have learned how to hold a team together. How to lift some men up, how to calm down others, until finally they've got one heartbeat together, a team. There's just three things I'd ever say:
>
> If anything goes bad, I did it.
> If anything goes semi-good, then we did it.
> If anything goes real good, then you did it.
>
> That's all it takes to get people to win football games for you.[6]

Not only football games. It's also the winning attitude that nourishes the kinds of friendships that last a lifetime. Bear Bryant worked at getting his team to function with "one heartbeat," and so it should, and can, be between us and our friends.

When you are willing to be Number Two or Three or Four or Five Hundred, you'll discover you possess an inexhaustible supply of love, compassion and friendship to share with those around you. It's your choice. Choose love, choose hope, choose caring, choose to believe in those around you. Look for the best in others. Make your friends Number One. It will revolutionize your world.

Work, Goals and Problem Solving

Mention *work* to some people and you'd think you had introduced them to a ghost. Mention *work* to others and they immediately roll up their sleeves, asking you how soon they can start. Why we respond so differently to work is something we simply must classify as another one of those mysteries of the mind.

Then there's the workaholic who thinks he or she must work excessively to keep "bringing home the bacon," when in fact such a person is really slowly sinking in a quicksand of misguided priorities. The result of the ensuing personal and business conflicts are strain and stress which can eat at that person much as termites attack a house. If you find yourself in such a trap, and if you want to be released from an unhealthy workaholic bondage to labor, I think you'll gather some important insights in these chapters from *The Workaholic I Love*.

Then move on to the chapters taken from *Strategy for Leadership* and allow yourself to be directed toward the challenge of meeting the priorities and goals set by the Lord Himself for your personal life, family or organization. When you finish these chapters I think you'll agree that one of the most enjoyable tasks in the world is "problem solving."

But don't take my word for it. Read on and experience it for yourself.

*Why work is so important to your
sense of fulfillment.*

14

What Good Is Work,
Anyway?

Probably the complaint we Americans make most often is in regard to the weather. Running a close second are our comments concerning work. "Oh, if only I didn't have to go to work today. What a drag!" "I'd quit work forever if it wasn't for my wife and family." "Work . . . what a necessary evil." How often we have heard or used these types of comments.

Almost as much has been written about work as about love. Many famous people have commented on it. Bismarck once said, "To youth I have but three words of counsel—work, work, work." Jerome K. Jerome said, "I like work; it fascinates me. I can sit and look at it for hours." "Any man who has a job has a chance," said Elbert Hubbard.

Others take a pessimistic view. That old cynic, Mark Twain, once said, "Let us be grateful to Adam, our benefactor. He cut us out of the 'blessing' of idleness and won for us the 'curse' of labor."

What is work, anyway? It is not easy to define. You hear many definitions ranging from "that activity which renders payment for service rendered, such as earning money, making a living," to "that activity which occupies one's time during most of his waking hours." It could also be "the activity for which one utilizes his skills in some employment situation."

We are using the term *work* in a sense broad enough to include the white–collar person, the blue–collar worker, the top manager, homemakers, and even volunteers. Obviously, there are many variations and types of work done, depending on educational and cultural factors. Despite the differences, there are enough similarities to provide a basic meaning which is common to all.

James Coleman and Constance Hammen, who have written a textbook on business psychology, define work as "an activity that produces something of value for other people."[1]

But, as Lloyd Lofquist points out, if work is truly the focal point for the development of one's way of life and a means to adjust to it, then these definitions are inadequate. He states that from the earliest of time, work was seen as a curse or form of punishment and it became a means of atoning for sin.[2]

We do know that the ancient Greeks used the word *ponos* for work, which connoted drudgery. They associated it with sorrow and a burdensome experience. The ancient Hebrews saw it as a heavy yoke but believed it had value. Rabbis, for example, were expected to have a trade of some kind.

Later, Christianity added a positive value. Work was seen as a means of charity which lifted the concept to mean that through it the Kingdom of God would be fashioned on earth.

With the passing of the centuries, a distinction developed between work that was intellectual, spiritual and contemplative, and work that was manual, physical and exertive. The medieval universities, for instance, distinguished between the liberal arts and the servile arts. The servile arts were undertaken for the satisfaction of basic human needs. The liberal arts could not be put at the disposal of such utilitarian, albeit necessary, ends. Performance of a liberal art could not, rightly speaking, be paid for. The honorarium was nothing more than a contribution given toward the liberal artist's living expenses. On the other hand, a wage meant payment earned for a servile art, that is, for a particular piece of work, and with no necessary reference to the cost–of–living needs of the worker.[3]

Through the Middle Ages and with the addition of the philosophy of the Protestant reformers, work had three basic meanings: (1) work was a hard necessity, painful and burdensome; (2) work was instrumental, a means toward ends, especially religious ends; and (3) work was the creative act of man, therefore intrinsically good.[4]

These three views appear to be the basic ideal still prevalent today although they are increasingly being undermined.

THE IMPORTANCE OF WORK

Well, whether we like it or not, work is a vital part of our lives. If you don't think so, consider this. Even though the study of the psychological aspects of the loss of work owing to retirement has not been thoroughly investigated, have you noticed what so often happens to individuals when they retire?

Many of them die shortly thereafter. Of many of those who live, their wives complain because "the ol' man" just doesn't know what to do with himself. Some wives have been distraught, not knowing how to handle having him around all day.

There is a drastic change of pace. One moment the man has authority, the next he is without any. The workaholic will particularly suffer in this readjustment setting. One of his penalties is that when the trauma of retirement faces him, he finds it extremely difficult to change because he doesn't have adequate emotional equipment to make the necessary adjustments. It is generally because he lacks the spontaneity and flexibility to make them.

Perhaps the primary reason for the adjustment difficulties of people entering the retirement years is the fact that work is such an important phase of life. In fact, it is an extension of oneself. You may have noticed that when people meet for the first time, so very often the first question asked is, "What do you do?" "I'm a lawyer. What do *you* do?" "I'm an accountant."

When a man loses his job, have you observed how he is

treated? It would seem it's almost like having leprosy! He's avoided like a plague. Suddenly, it seems that his friends drop him. He and his wife don't get invited out nearly as frequently as before. Often his old buddies drop him. He becomes a misfit. That's why if ever a man is out of work, he really needs his friends.

There's no escaping it: Work is an institution. In fact, it is most basic because it actually helps to maintain survival. Much has been written about the work ethic over the centuries from religious, philosophical, moral, political, and psychological backgrounds. In his work, a person probably expends more energy over a lifetime than in any other kind of activity, and with the increase of life expectancy in our society, we may easily expect a person to average fifty years of his life working.

For most people, work is something that must be done. Thus, to many, it has a negative ring to it. However, psychologists have concluded that work has a crucial psychological bearing on life, for work provides important personal and social functions and outlets for the one working. These would, of course, include the need for achievement, personal worth, and self–identity.

Increasingly, people in our society are coming to realize once again the value of work in their quest for meaningfulness. In the 1960s, there was a mass movement away from the idea of the dignity of work. There was a flight away from the realities of personal responsibility. The hippie mentality played down the important aspects of work. Now, we are coming full circle. The self–defining and potentially self–fulfilling aspects of work should be considered to be significant insights for today's expanding world, for money and wages are seen not merely as ends in themselves.

WORK DEVELOPS PERSONALITY

Let us consider the meaning of work in terms of the individual, for indeed work ought to be, and can be, a deeply fulfilling and meaningful part of man's existence.

What Good Is Work, Anyway?

There are many positive effects of work upon people. The first is that through work a person is able to expend energy in a wholesome and acceptable way. The psychologist calls this sublimation. Therefore, work constitutes an important factor providing for equilibrium and development of the personality. Through it, man comes in better contact with reality and the meaning of his own existence. This was acutely felt by Sigmund Freud in one of his last books, in which he explained the role played by work:

> Stressing the importance of work has a greater effect than any other technique of living in binding the individual more closely to reality; in his work, he is at least securely attached to a part of reality, the human community. Work is no less valuable for the opportunity which it, and the human relations connected with it, provide for a very considerable discharge of fundamental libidinal impulses, narcissistic, aggressive and even erotic, than because it is indispensable for subsistence and justifies existence in society. The daily work of earning a livelihood affords especial satisfaction. It enables us to be made of existing inclinations, of instinctual impulses, hitherto repressed or more intense than usual for constitutional reasons.[5]

Freud was right in this context because he saw work as a balancing factor in a person's life, fitting him into the sociological structure of the human family, and enhancing his ability to make some contribution to that very society. Work, for better or for worse, helps a person change his environment and yes, even himself. Georges Friedmann says:

> It is work that raises man, as soon as he produces his own means of subsistence, above biological time and gives character to human history, of whose movements it is at once the explanation and the underlying cause . . . It is not surprising that an activity which is essential as determinant of species as well in the history of human societies should be just as essential a determinant for the individual microcosm, enabling him to understand his successes and his failures, his own individual history.[6]

153

Certainly one way to ascertain the importance of work in a person's life is to observe how men and women act when they are deprived of it. Strong feelings of insecurity usually occur right after the initial shock, which creates intense anxiety in most people. If an individual finds it increasingly difficult to work, depression of varying degrees may result. A feeling of inadequacy may be a tag–along, too, because self–esteem is jarred. Indeed, the loss of the settled framework of a job is enormous. One can hardly imagine that his peace of mind and control over one's family are so dependent upon a steady job.

Freud was right. Work does connect a person with his community.

It may be a very long time before we can fully comprehend all the underlying unconscious motives involved in the various aspects of human labor. But one thing appears to be true. The energy of aggressive needs in work can be a good force. A destructive impulse drive can be modified through the constructive activity of work.

This can be illustrated in many ways. The doctor who fights malaria, the teacher who fights prejudice, the minister who fights sin, all use a refined type of aggression. This energy is directed toward destructive forces or enemies of mankind.

Such sublimated energy is good. In such activities the worker, by using his aggressive drives to help others, also helps himself. Thus we see first that work serves as a means of expressing the life force, helping one to balance out his life and to drain off energy in acceptable ways. As an extension of oneself, it helps to upgrade a person's self–esteem because it gives him a sense of worth and dignity, especially if he experiences some achievement.

WORK IS GOOD THERAPY

"Why do people work?" is an oft–asked question. People do need to support themselves, but that is not always the dominant inspiration. Many may work because they prefer to be doing something rather than nothing, and because they may fear the social censure which is directed against idlers and loafers. But the value of work lies deeper than this. Otherwise, why would people work diligently without being paid for their services? All about us there is a great deal of volunteer work. And what about the best example of all, the faithful uncomplaining homemaker who may spend as much time, and often more, working in her home than her husband does at the office or shop!

When there is stress, work can oftentimes be very therapeutic, particularly if taken in reasonable doses. A man can go through a painful divorce or experience much grief over the loss of a loved one. He can come back to work and immediately get absorbed in his activity. The work then serves a useful purpose. It can be a wonderful form of therapy. After a period of time, mental—and physical—health may be restored.

Of course a person should not be sent out on a job until he or she is emotionally and physically ready. Recovery usually accelerates when a person is able to hold down a responsible job. It restores to him a sense of dignity and worth.

Examples abound which reveal the therapeutic value of finding fulfillment in a job situation.

Greater Satisfaction

People who are contented with their working conditions are bound to be much more fulfilled. Where there are dissatisfactions over job conditions, the pay, the fellow workers, or the nature of the work, there may be many psychological consequences that will yield repercussions later on. For example, people who feel like they count for little on the job may develop psychosomatic illnesses. They may be afraid to react, to allow themselves to feel or be understood. Anxiety, worry, hypertension, and loss of self-esteem are often direct results.

Studies reveal that greater mental health problems exist in jobs that are dull, unchallenging, repetitive, and that allow for little advancement. A deadening effect is created where people find their jobs exerting heavy pressure and responsibility without the accompanying status, security, and salary rewards.

But where satisfaction exists in a job the person usually experiences greater meaning and fulfillment in his life. By fulfillment we mean that a person will be restless and discontented unless he is really doing what he is fitted for or capable of performing.

In a study by George Andrew Sargeant, it was found that individuals who perceive a relatively clear purpose and meaning in their lives are more work motivated. The study revealed that there were significant differences between individuals with high and low "Purpose in Life" scores in terms of their attitudes toward work (that is, the meaning of work).[7] There is, then, a relationship between the perception of meaning in life and the perceived meaning of work and other major life concepts.

When discussing the subject of need satisfaction, we must include Abraham Maslow's views. He basically sought to determine the basic drives of the human personality and how they are satisfied and what these findings mean to each of us.

His theory about needs has application in all areas of life even though it has been challenged. Maslow assumes that all individuals have a basic set of needs which they strive to fulfill. His theory looks like this:

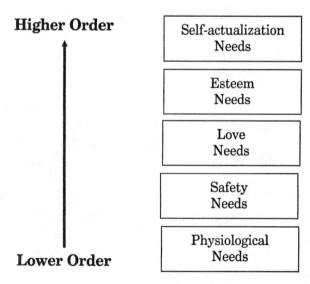

Higher Order

Self-actualization Needs

Esteem Needs

Love Needs

Safety Needs

Physiological Needs

Lower Order

What Good Is Work, Anyway?

Maslow states that all individuals will always strive to satisfy basic needs before higher–order needs and they will move up the hierarchy in a systematic manner, satisfying the lower needs before moving upward.

This theory has been a popular one in management circles because Maslow's theory is related to industrial behavior, since individuals will strive to fulfill all these needs in a work setting.

A person's philosophy about work will affect his outlook and the fulfillment needs which he deems necessary for meaningful living. This theory tells us that it is essential to know what needs the individual is trying to satisfy, since this will provide clues about an employee's motivation toward satisfaction. This implies, then, that a person will instigate, direct, and sustain activity at work to satisfy certain needs. Thus, it is helpful for a person to know which of his needs have the highest priority.

Reflecting on Maslow's views, it should be noted that human satisfaction is brief and is never complete. It is difficult to accurately measure the degree of satisfaction or dissatisfaction of a worker with his job because there are no absolute values which can be used to measure job satisfaction.

Debate exists today among management theoreticians and industrial psychologists concerning the problem of whether human satisfaction can be achieved on the job or outside the job: Is human motivation an integral part of the mental makeup of man or can outside factors motivate man toward greater effort?

Maslow regards the satisfaction of human needs as the key motivator in human economic activity. As noted, once a need is satisfied, it ceases to serve as a motivator. This role is then taken over by the successive need in the hierarchy.

As a result of this chain reaction, human satisfaction is always of a short duration. Thus, man cannot reach total satisfaction except, perhaps, for a short duration.

But Maslow overlooks the fact that the unsatisfied craving of man may be a product of our civilization. Culture will be

157

important in pronouncing the value placed on work. Also, it is true that aspirations of men may vary greatly from one group to another or from one individual to another. Drives within people will be determined by social or cultural backgrounds. Also, it must be remembered that men are driven by both rational and irrational motives. Maslow overemphasizes the importance of the rational. People may not have the desire to satisfy needs at the higher level of the hierarchy. They may also be prevented from moving upward because their perception of the degrees of satisfaction may vary.

FIND THE SIGNIFICANT MOTIVATOR

That is why it is important for management, for example, to try to determine whether at a given point physical or social needs are the most significant when it comes to motivating a person on the job. In other words, at which stage is it more important to pat a person on the back or provide extra dollars in wages?

There does often seem to be a tendency within management to overemphasize the on–the–job problems without probing for underlying problems which decrease job satisfaction.

There is also the question of whether it is possible to make all jobs equally interesting to all people, and if so, how to match up each worker with a suitable job. What is regarded by one person as desirable may be completely undesirable for another.

Studies reveal another insight. The common assumption is that a happy worker is a good producer. This is not always true. High morale is a positive factor in human motivation, but it does not necessarily follow that it will in every case increase productivity. There is no substitute for proper managerial leadership and planned coordination among the workers.

But one thing does appear certain. A person who achieves higher satisfaction on the job has a higher degree of capability to cope with outside problems and interests.

It is unfortunate that so many people see their work as

meaningless. They will so often try to relieve the emptiness by joking, idling, or seeking to outwit management.

When it's all said, it can hardly be assumed that for the most part people do not value their work. Though many today "goof off" or refuse to work, other responsible people, in fact, may consider their work as an end in itself. Especially is this true for the professional who sees work as a focal center for his self–identification. His work may become a central life interest, giving his living a great deal of meaning and purpose.

Most business and professional people view their work in terms of a career rather than a job. They depend on their work not only to structure their day but to provide some sense of adequacy which gives them a sense that they are living up to their potential as well as their education.

In contradistinction, the unemployed prove the significance and meaning of work when they talk about a sense of lostness without work. Others find such idleness as almost unbearable, sometimes worse than being without food and clothing. Often a sense of hopelessness prevails with them.

Work done for its own sake, enjoyed for its own intrinsic value, is within the reach of anyone who wants it by virtue of the freedom man has to choose his lot in life. Through it a person develops self–worth, resolution of conflicts, and greater satisfaction.

Scriptural principles to help you understand God's perspective.

15

What Does the Bible Say About Work?

A graduate engineering student was placed in a good job. After five years he surprised one of his companions by stating, "I would quit tomorrow if I had a chance. If only I had the money to retire. The only reason I work is to give me something to do and to keep my family in food and clothes."

What does the church have to say to this young man who is obviously unfulfilled and bored with his job? Does theology have anything to offer? Admittedly, millions of Americans are churchgoers. Religious fervor of every type is on the increase. Christian literature sells more rapidly than ever before. The Christian market has top priority, not only with Christian publishing houses but with secular publishers as well.

Yet it seems that fewer people "live close to God" in a truly meaningful way. Fewer still seem able to make the application of divine truth to their personal lives. Perhaps it is due to the forces of secularization, scientific rationalism, and the socialistic schemes found today.

Our workaday world is a very different matter than was the case centuries ago. Distinctions that once existed between the Christian and non–Christian worker are becoming blurred. The church may be partly to blame for this. Its emphasis often appears to be mainly upon subjective experience and personal piety. Of course, this is important. But where is the emphasis on personal application in the great bastions of our society as well as in one's own private affairs?

The man in the pew is told to go out and take the world for God. But how?

In a study of business ethics by Raymond Baumhart, a number of business managers were asked, "How much guidance did your church and clergymen provide for the ethical problems you and your business acquaintances faced in the last five years?" Here are the tabulated questionnaire results: About the right amount—16 percent; some, but not enough—25 percent; none—35 percent; can't say—23 percent; too much—1 percent. Baumhart concluded that about four out of every five businessmen were dissatisfied with what organized religion had to offer or say regarding the problems facing businessmen.[1]

This is a sad tale. Few ministers have had much economic training or study. They are sorely ignorant concerning business matters. This is not always by choice, but sometimes by design. Theological leaders see very little purpose in such an educational pursuit for clergy.

One of Baumhart's respondents, a young New York stockbroker, stated, "The average clergyman has such a scant understanding of the U.S. economy that his intervention in this area would be a mistake." A Louisiana insurance broker said, "I don't believe the clergy should be permitted to preach to businessmen." And the vice–president of a large cement plant in the East recently stated, "In the natural cycle of life—birth, marriage and death—the church is doing a fine job, but it is non-existent when decisions are being made in a man's line of work."

Baumhart did conclude that most business people do welcome the assistance of theologians who are educated in business concerns.

When they do speak out responsibly, far too few Christians make the transition of practical Christianity from the Sunday school classroom or sanctuary to their workaday world.

There is a need for theologians and social scientists to work together to help in the application process. Theology can make a significant contribution to the working world, as it has in the past two decades in the areas of race relations and civil rights.

By *theology* we mean an understanding of God and His work through history. It is not faith. Faith is subjective; theology is objective. It needs to be incorporated by faith to affect change. Theology then is an understanding of faith, especially regarding God's revelation of Himself and of His great and indescribable love for man.

There is a Christian way of life that must be applied. There are Christian principles that can help us in our daily economic actions. Faith and reason blended together can be of great incentive to men to labor with proper attitudes. It is self-evident that in all our labors we should choose the most efficient, the most economical methods. All Christians should seek to provide for the legitimate wants and needs of their fellow men as they provide for their own through work. This requires what economists call "the division of labor." All Christians should exchange the fruits of their specialized, and therefore more proficient, labors for the profit of their neighbors as well as themselves. Christians should refrain from envy, force, or fraud.

But where do such ideals originate? The greatest textbook for life is the Bible—both the Old and New Testaments. And issuing from the Holy Scriptures is our Judeo–Christian heritage.

The Bible has a great deal to say about work. Ruth gleaned in the fields when romance caught up with her. Gideon was working on the threshing floor when the angel of the Lord spoke to him about another kind of work. How about Moses the sheepherder? Just remember the personalities we meet in the Bible. It is a book written to workers. It is a book that is vitally relevant for today's world. Every aspect of life comes under its scrutiny. This includes our work philosophy, attitudes, and habits.

Here is a practical list of familiar Bible personalities who were cited in their work:

Noah, Boaz—farmers	Naaman—soldier
Moses—shepherd	Jonathan—warrior
Peter, James, John—fishermen	Ezra—reformer
Gideon, Samson, Samuel—judges	Amos—herdsman
Eli—priest	Matthew—tax collector
David—musician, king	Luke—physician
Solomon—lyric poet	Titus—social worker
Hiram—artisan	Naboth—grape grower
Paul—writer, missionary	Elijah, Jonah—prophets
Joseph, Daniel—prime ministers	Lydia—saleswoman

Can you add to this list? There are many others. It is interesting to note how often God spoke to men when they were faithfully at work and not in a state of idleness. It is as though God were blessing their labor.

For example, when did God call Moses? When he was tending his flocks. What were the shepherds doing in the Christmas story when they were told by an angel of the birth of the Savior? "Keeping watch over their flocks by night." When did Jesus call Peter? When Peter looked up from his fishing nets. Matthew was called while counting money as a tax collector.

When Jesus taught the multitudes, He often alluded to work situations. His illustrations often centered around vinedressers, farmers, builders, and magistrates. He told of managers and farmhands. And, He spoke of them in a favorable manner.

WORK IS INSTITUTED BY GOD

The first significant statement about work in the Bible is its relationship to man's fallen condition: "In the sweat of thy face shalt thou eat bread, till thou return into the ground . . ." (Genesis 3:19). First, we must bear in mind that work was ordained by God. Because man was told after our first father sinned that he would have to work by the sweat of his brow does not mean that labor is a penalty for sin. The Bible never considers work a curse.

Adam had the job of caring for the Garden of Eden before he ate of the forbidden fruit. Work was thus instituted and blessed by God. People in the world may adopt theft as a way of life, but the biblically inspired individual knows that it is not a shame to be caught working.

God Himself was a worker. Numerous times in the Scriptures this point is made.

> Thus the heavens and the earth were finished, and all the host of them. And on the seventh day God ended his work which he had made; and he rested on the seventh day from all his work which he had made. And God blessed the seventh day, and sanctified it; because that in it he had rested from all his work which God created and made (Genesis 2:1–3).

The emphasis is on ceasing rather than on resting. The associated word in English is the word *pause,* the word *rest* being used in something of the same sense as it is today in the technical language of music.

GOD COMMANDS WORK

The Bible frequently records the fact that God has commanded work to specific people. Hence, it must be deduced that work has a profitable purpose.

In the Ten Commandments God says, "Six days shalt thou labour, and do all thy work" (Exodus 20:9).

The Lord spoke to Moses on one occasion, citing Bezaleel to be a craftsman to help build the tabernacle during Israel's wilderness wanderings after they left Egypt.

> And I have filled him with the spirit of God, in wisdom, and in understanding, and in knowledge, and in all manner of workmanship, to devise cunning works, to work in gold, and in silver, and in brass, And in cutting of stones, to set them, and in carving of timber, to work in all manner of workmanship (Exodus 31:3–5).

When the Jews were defeated by Nebuchadnezzar in 586 B.C., thousands were carried off to Babylonia. During the seventy-year captivity, God inspired some of their leaders to go back to Jerusalem and rebuild the city walls and the sacred temple. Cyrus, the king of Babylon, gave his consent. One of the leaders given this tremendous assignment by God was Nehemiah. He indicated that the work was initiated by God:

> And it came to pass, that when all our enemies heard thereof, and all the heathen that were about us saw these things, they were much cast down in their own eyes; for they perceived that this work was wrought of our God (Nehemiah 6:16).

Haggai, one of the Jewish prophets living during this period of rehabilitation, speaks the Word of God:

> Yet now be strong, O Zerubbabel, saith the Lord; and be strong, O Joshua . . . all ye people of the land, saith the Lord, and work; for I am with you . . . (Haggai 2:4).

WORK IS HONORABLE

Work in the Old Testament, whether related to the ancient walls or the Temple in Jerusalem or secular employment, was seen as honorable. The following passages disclose the blessedness and dignity of work.

> And the Levite (because he hath no part nor inheritance with thee), and the [sojourner], and the fatherless, and the widow, which are within thy gates, shall come, and shall eat and be satisfied; that the Lord thy God may bless thee in all the work of thine hand which thou doest (Deuteronomy 14:29).

> When thou cuttest down thine harvest in thy field, and hast forgot a sheaf in the field, thou shalt not go again to fetch it; it shall be for the [sojourner], for the fatherless, and for the widow; that the Lord thy God may bless thee in all the work of thine hands (Deuteronomy 24:19).

How to understand workaholic behavior in yourself and others.

16

Don't Get Caught on the Treadmill

The devil made me do it," comedian Flip Wilson would say. That was his standard response when he would be caught in some sort of trouble. The causes of human behavior are multiple, and Flip had his answer. The reasons why people get caught in the work trap are likewise numerous. Let's look at some of them.

On the surface it appears that the real motivation for excessive work is so often the need for more money. Thus, the need to stay at the office longer or bring the work home, or the need to get that extra job. However, beneath the surface lie other very subtle factors that should be viewed to more fully understand the problem.

These factors make for some nice little rationalizations. "I surely don't want my wife to have to work." "I want the kids to have it easier than I had it." "I have to make sure my kids get a college education." "Of course, our family needs two cars. My wife can't stay stuck at home all the time—there are too many errands to be run." They all sound so good, but the vise gets noticeably tighter and tighter.

What many people do not realize is that a great deal of what we do or think comes from unconscious associations with our past. Emotional problems often exist because people were

167

deprived of or thwarted from having close, loving relationships.

To remain mentally healthy, one has to give vent to the disturbing influences of his existence. Every day our bodies cleanse themselves of harmful toxins through processes of waste elimination. If these toxins were allowed to accumulate, they would cause us to sicken and would eventually kill us.

MENTAL TOXINS

Our minds, too, become filled with toxins—the disturbing residue of assorted hurts, worries, fears, and traumas. Tucked away in the corners and recesses of our subconscious, they may surface to bother us occasionally, but their toxic influence is usually minimal, causing, at most, vague anxieties and now-and–then sadness.

But at other times these mental toxins build up to the point where they become disruptive to our emotional and psychological functioning. Symptoms of this psychological poisoning can show up as severe stress, nervousness, anxiety, and stress–related physical problems such as colitis, migraines, and tinnitus (ear noise) or, more seriously, as deep depression and even psychosis.

Take the true experience of Glen. He was so busy working continuously that he had no close friends. He was so bound to his desk at work that management failed to take him into their confidence because they hardly knew him. He deeply desired recognition, but never allowed his resentful feelings to surface.

Later his company shifted him to a new job. Intellectually he approved, but he was angry because he was not consulted prior to the decision. He interpreted this to mean that he was not appreciated. He supported the view by reminding himself that he had received only minimal salary increases for several years.

Later, he came to learn that he was a victim of his own silence, because management assumed that he was satisfied with his role. His overwork actually militated against him because he gave little of himself emotionally to others.

His feelings of not being appreciated had their roots in his childhood. He had had a stormy upbringing. He learned to sublimate his feelings in more positive areas. This worked for a time, but ultimately his bitterness became too strong and the protective barrier began to break down. Emergency defenses were set in motion: depression, self-depreciation, and psychosomatic illnesses.

We've all read success stories of how hard work brought men to great wealth, power, and prestige. But shortly after they reached the pinnacle, they collapsed—physically or mentally. Others work hard, not for economic reasons, but for purely psychological needs.

HOW WORKAHOLICS DEFEND THEIR BEHAVIOR

There is little question that many workaholics use their work as a defense against some form of anxiety, either from without or from within. Anxiety is both a painful experience and a warning of impending danger. This forces a person to do something about it. Either the person will cope and deal with the anxiety, or his ego will resort to some irrational protective measure known as a *defense mechanism.*

To defend itself, the ego will respond to trauma, conflict, or hurt either by attacking, withdrawing, compromising, or accommodating it. One psychologist says that the ego will either be put to *fight* or *flight.* We all use defenses to sustain our identity. The problem comes when they are used in unhealthy ways to avoid conflict which should be dealt with. What we don't realize is that these mechanisms usually operate on the unconscious level and they become habitual. Therefore they may lead to a measure of self-deception and reality distortion. We too often do not realistically cope with a stressful situation.

To understand better what is meant by defense mechanism, consider the complaint by a wife who, whenever her husband lost an article, would ask, "Why did you lose it?" or "Where did you lose it, dear?" He would invariably reply, "I

169

didn't lose it; it just disappeared." Rather amusing, but how sad. Here is a man who is unable to handle criticism or to admit wrong. His way of dealing with the issue is to deny that he had any part in the problem. The lost article in question just suddenly picked up and took off! And, it got to the point where, by a trick of the mind, he began to at least half believe it.

Everyone tries to deal with anxiety on the basis of how he has learned to cope, usually very early in childhood. It is then we begin to learn how to rationalize our behavior. That becomes reality even though to others it may seem to be irrational. Reality is therefore not the same for everyone. It is easy to forget that different people see things in different ways.

How often do you see a person do something that appears to you to be a stupid form of behavior? "How could they do such a dumb thing?" we ask ourselves. "Facts are facts." But we must remember that people deal with facts from the background of their own experience and perception.

That's why the alcoholic drinks. Drinking works for him; it kills emotional pain. "Better living through chemistry," is his motto. Let's not forget that the work addict has his own framework of reality and people respond to him according to their own perceptions.

Needed: Love and Sensitivity

That is why we must be sensitive to the workaholic. He is living in what to him is reality. It may be highly destructive, but he has reasoned it out for himself. We must, then, be careful to be as nonjudgmental as possible. Sensitivity and caring love must be communicated to such a person who has deliberately chosen, whether on a conscious or unconscious level, to use work as a means of cutting himself off from others.

One may manipulate someone to get the affection he thinks he needs, drink excessively to drown sorrow or stress, or act like a bully when he feels inferior. These actions have the same general effect; they make us less aware of the pain.

Because conflict can promote such defensive actions as

drinking, boasting, or working harder, it reveals that everyone has some anxieties and some defenses. Some, however, are more destructive than others.

> The world approves and rewards men who sacrifice to get ahead but generally disapproves of drinking and boasting as acceptable behavior. The braggart and the hard–charger may have the same psychological problems (feelings of inadequacy) but very different objective problems. The braggart alienates people, harms his career, and feels even more inadequate, whereas the hard–charger gains respect, advances his career, and may feel more adequate.
> The amount of anxiety a man feels may therefore be less important than the way he handles it. Defenses are a part of everyone's "psychic economy." They control anxiety and keep this economy functioning. Sometimes they are too costly and don't provide very good protection against anxiety; they may create other problems or fail to preserve comfort.[1]

Defenses, therefore, contribute to one's well–being by letting one express his feelings in less costly ways.

As stated, certain defenses are useful because they can help a person attain economic and other kinds of success. Many individuals have used defenses to achieve, when deep within themselves they felt inferior or inadequate. Even though there may be some cost in sacrificing social relationships, an obsession with money and profit can drive a person to control his anxiety over having been reared in a ghetto or in an impoverished home.

But, as Alan Schoonmaker points out, defenses can be "self–defeating because they can work only if a person deceives himself, and self–deception becomes more difficult and exhausting as time goes on."[2]

When it comes to work, the true workaholic uses it as a rebuttal to the trauma or psychic pain experienced earlier in life. But the harnessing of aggressive energy in work can break down and create untold havoc. We recognize these defense mechanisms as symptoms of illness. The greater illness awaits ahead—the inability to work and the inability to control the excess of hostility—which is behind the whole pattern.

Consider some of the basic defenses the workaholic may use in order to deal with some aspects of his or her life.

DEFENSE #1: REPRESSION

By definition, *repression* is the active process of keeping out, ejecting, and banishing from consciousness ideas or impulses that are unacceptable to it. It is quite simply an avoidance technique. The unfortunate thing about it is that it prevents a person from discovering who he really is, because it blocks feelings and pushes them out of his focus of awareness.

A good illustration of repression might be an individual who has suffered through a natural catastrophe, such as a flood or an earthquake. He goes to a first–aid station but remembers nothing about what happened. Repression is not a simple psychic function. One psychiatrist says that it is more than just forgetting something. It is forgetting that we have forgotten.[3]

Repression is probably the defense most used by workaholics. It helps to keep unpleasant memories and feelings out of consciousness. We try to forget the grief over the loss of a loved one. A woman forgets the intense pain of childbirth. When recalling experiences of the past, we tend to remember only the happy memories and forget the unpleasantries.

Repression is often more than forgetting. We repress the things we consider to be unpleasant or avoid the things we consider unimportant.

Usually we do not consciously choose to repress. We do it automatically in those areas where we may be hurt by someone or some stimulus in our environment. At this point, a distinction should be made between forgetting and repressing:

> . . . repression is much more complete and permanent. If we forget something, we can easily be reminded of it. A service station, a radio commercial, or an oil truck can remind us to buy gasoline. Thinking about dinner or our children can remind us to buy a quart of milk. When something is repressed, reminders usually do not work. We resist being reminded of our repressed feelings or memories even if they are obvious to other people.[4]

Repression as a defense may help us in time to overcome anxiety and to live with ourselves, but sometimes it is not strong enough to completely protect us. We may, for example, push down deep hatred for a person, but will express that intense feeling indirectly in overly criticizing him. We may repress our strong hate for authority figures, but get sadistic joy out of watching a boxer get pummeled into a knockout in the seventh round.

One thing we should know about repression is that it can become a means of blocking all feelings. A person who consistently blocks negative or bad feelings, such as anger and fear, will also automatically block good feelings as well.

One workaholic admitted while in therapy, "I need to work constantly because I just lose myself in my job. I'd go crazy if I couldn't work all the time. It's great to be able to forget my troubles."

Many workaholics use overwork to eliminate threatening thoughts, beliefs, and memories by blocking awareness of what's going on around them. It is their way of helping to reduce anxiety.

We should realize that when feelings are repressed they do not go out of existence. Science has told us for years that matter cannot be destroyed, it just changes form. We now know that neither can energy be destroyed. It must go someplace. Repressed material does not die within. It remains in our mind and often will come back to haunt us with tremendous force. For example, unexpressed anger may later lead to severe depression and then psychosomatic conditions. It may also lead to morbid thoughts and bizarre behavior.

Work used as a repressive defense measure conceals the true factors that direct a person's behavior. The likely result is that he will choose misguided goals. Because they turn out in the long run to be dissatisfying, such choices may lead to failure and feelings of self–contempt and the use of other destructive defense mechanisms.

DEFENSE #2: ISOLATION

Escape is one of the major defenses of the isolated workaholic. He would rather stay on the job than go home. A college student related an experience which occurred during his school days. He had gone home with a friend for a weekend. When they arrived near his buddy's home, they drove past his father's place of business before going to his house. His friend predicted a hundred miles before their arrival, "I bet my ol' man will still be working when we pull in." Sure enough. It was 11 P.M. The light in his office was still on. The friend reported with disappointment that it was not uncommon for his father to sleep at his place of work.

A number of reasons may exist for such an escape. It may be the dread of facing conflict in close relationships, or a difficult marriage, or the fact that work is more pleasurable than what happens at home.

One man, in being counseled, confessed that he liked the people on the job more than those in his own family. He thus chose isolation, staying at his work as much as he could. Psychology teaches us that there are people who possess *schizoid* tendencies in their personality. This term must be differentiated from schizophrenia, which is a form of psychosis. The workaholic who uses work to isolate himself for whatever reason may use this as a defense against anxiety.

Workaholics who are schizoid without question use work as an escape mechanism to avoid close personal relationships. The symptoms of their emotional problems are detachment, aloofness, and noninvolvement. At times they can get involved, but they would rather not. When they do, they have little interest because they are cut off, out of touch. Since they are so preoccupied with themselves, this leaves them oblivious to other people's feelings. Their tendency is not to hear quiet expressions or low-key criticism. They just are not in tune with others on a feeling level.

The loner workaholic, being isolated, uses other various psychological defenses which make it safer for him to deny the

174

real world of people. He enjoys his fantasy world because he does not have to face confrontation. Worse still, in such retreat he seldom sees how other people react to his behavior.

This is most unfortunate because we grow emotionally by getting feedback from others. The isolated workaholic is immature because his noninvolvement with people blocks growth. He can't stand losing an argument because it upsets the safe, fantasy world he has created. Anxiety is created because it is impossible for him to totally shut people out. They are always a threat to him. He has not learned to deal with them. This means that he has difficulty working or playing with them for any length of time, because of the fear that they will manipulate him to their own advantage, just as his parents did.

This kind of approach to the real world means loss of contact. The possibility of keeping or gaining friends is remote because the loner drives them away.

Workaholics who use work as an escape inhibit themselves from expressing anger through repressed isolation. They will often, therefore, express an overabundance of kindness, not wanting to create waves. They will attempt to avoid confrontation and arguments. They need constant reassurance that everything is moving along satisfactorily.

The isolated workaholic cannot be forced into a prescribed mold. There are varying gradations of the problem, depending upon the extent or the depth of the neurosis. All of them, however, appear to answer narcissistic hurts with simple denials and a protective covering. The person who is more severely disturbed emotionally may tend to react to frustrations with the loss of objective relationships.

One of the characteristics noted in schizoid persons is that, lacking contact with people, they become void of emotional expressions and generally appear to be emotionally inadequate.

Frequently, emotions are entirely lacking in situations where they are to be expected. A lack of emotions which is due not to mere repressions but to real loss of contact with the objective world gives the observer a specific impression of

175

"queerness." [5]

The workaholic as an isolate has a decided deficiency in spontaneity. Martin Haskell, in his excellent work which he considers an alternative to psychoanalysis, defines spontaneity as "the variable degree of adequate response to a situation with a variable degree of novelty." [6] In other words, the spontaneous person is able to respond by bringing into a given situation appropriate roles. However, indifference, apathy, coldness, and isolation toward people are certainly symptoms indicating varying degrees of deficiency in spontaneity. Haskell states:

> The more spontaneous a man is the better is he able to deal effectively with problems arising in the course of any of his relationships, personal or societal. He demonstrates an increased awareness of the many alternatives available to him. This awareness of alternatives makes him free to choose and free to act. Increased spontaneity enables man to improve his relationships with his wife or move to an alternative solution of his marital problems. He is also better able to derive satisfaction in his occupation or choose another. [7]

DEFENSE #3: RATIONALIZATION

Another common defense used by the workaholic is to accept superficially plausible explanations to justify his behavior or feelings that may be believed to be wrong. This can be illustrated in many ways. Take for example the fox in Aesop's Fable, who was unable to reach the grapes. He rationalized that they were perhaps sour anyway. Then consider the politician who justifies his shady political deals by rationalizing that it would be unfortunate for society to elect his opponent. Or, people who steal commodities from their employer, rationalizing that they are underpaid. Or, students who attribute low grades to unfair teachers.

The attempt to prove one's behavior as rational and justifiable is a means of proving to oneself that he is worthy of the approval of himself and others.

This defense is common to us all, but the true workaholic

really gets tangled up with this one. He must constantly find ways to rationalize the need to work or to keep people in his life thinking he is indispensable. Furthermore, he has to schedule his time to be able to work long hours. So he must always bear in mind the situation and the kind of behavior (isolation) that it requires. Justifying their thoughts and behavior, many workaholics thus ignore the real causes of their anxieties.

The person who is rationalizing his workaholic tendencies needs to deal with the basics of his problem. As long as his thoughts are isolated from his emotions he will continue to be alienated from himself and others.

The workaholic with this problem must forever shift from action back to thinking. Watch how meticulous he becomes. He is involved with reams and reams of details. Even before carrying out a simple act, great mounds of preparation must precede it. Otto Fenichel effectively describes this evasive process when he writes:

> Thinking is preparation for action. Persons who are afraid of actions increase the preparation. In the same way as compulsion neurotics think rather than act, they also prepare constantly for the future and never experience the present.[8]

How true! People who don't live in the NOW but always for the THEN have a severe problem.

The individual who lives primarily inside of his head does not express feelings because he has a fear of expressing them. He is not sure how they will come out because he is not used to dealing with them.

The reactive individual, who is attempting to hide from some deep fear or conflict through his work, does not usually have a great love for his work. Since work serves as a cover–up for feelings, his blocking of them prevents him from feeling at all. Therefore, he enjoys little. He often is a *frigid* person. Observers usually report this characterization of those who fall into the workaholic category.

The avoidance factor against feelings manifests itself in

yet another way. Workaholics, more often than not, will develop cold intellects. Through the intellect they develop a counterattack against feared emotions. Instead of letting go emotionally in a situation calling for laughter, this workaholic type may sit in the corner with his arms folded and a scowl on his face. He is defiantly saying, "Just try to make me laugh."

In therapy these people, hiding behind their intellectual defenses, will at times produce or reveal emotional material, but they lack the ability to relax in order to consider it objectively. They are usually poor subjects because they resist therapy. They have all the rational answers. They lack the spontaneity to feel. Their feelings are dammed up. All that is left is jargon. They want to argue with the therapist.

An individual of this type, unaware of his insufficiencies, many times must prove to himself that he is very much in control. "I am an efficient person." "I have a lot on the ball; just look at the amount of work I turn out." This is the rationale with which he defends his overwork. But deep within, such a person is cold and unable to show sympathy toward others. He is an empty shell emotionally.

Fantasy Rationalization: Quantity = Quality

Rationalization leads to fantasy. The workaholic has created his own fantasies which keep him going. The first fantasy rationalization has to do with the *quantity of work required*. He operates under a delusional system that rationalizes: "The solution to any problem is to work harder and harder at it." "If there is a financial problem, the solution is to get out there and roll up your sleeves and work harder." This is, of course, very faulty thinking.

Jim was a professed workaholic. He learned when he was a child that the most important thing in life was being a responsible person. His parents made him work constantly. In order for him to play baseball with the neighborhood boys he would have to sneak out to do so. In Jim's thinking, work was a virtue, play was a sin. At least that's the message that got through to him from his parents.

Wayne Oates, who quotes Robert Neale from *In Praise of Play,* writes an insightful paragraph on the magical thinking of the typical workaholic in answer to the question: "Why do reasonable men and women become addicted to perpetual work?"

> Robert Neale gives an excellent lead toward an answer; it is because we rely on the "magic" of our own clever efforts. He says that the spiritual creativity of life follows a pattern of "new discharge and new design." The response of faith and religion is one of rest and playfulness. Neale says the "magic is the work response" to the spiritual realm of life. By our own clever efforts and works, we seek to outwit our basic nature and that of the universe. Thus magic replaces creativity.

The workaholic assumes that everything happens as a result of his efforts and therefore he must work incessantly. His attitude reminds us of that of the rooster who proudly reminds God each day: "It is I whose crow causes the sun to rise!" With such vain fantasy, the workaholic becomes isolated and overloaded with a false sense of responsibility. "Nobody Knows the Troubles I've Seen" is the frenetic maneuvering of someone temporarily at a loss without his "work magic." [9]

Rationalization is mythical ("magical") thinking and it can upset the balance that leads toward a more fulfilled life. The constant need to work harder may, and often does, become self-defeating.

Fantasy Rationalization: The Need to Perform

The second fantasy rationalization which many workaholics use to a great extent is the *need to perform.* One of his underlying rationales is the formula, "What you *do* is more important than who you *are.*"

Where does that idea come from? The following may give us a clue.

One recognized workaholic said that the most important event in his household while he was growing up was the bringing home of report cards. A big thing was always made of it. He reported that for days before the grades were to come out he had diarrhea. If he was down in one subject, he would be sorely punished, perhaps by being grounded for some weeks. His parents were never satisfied with average or even above–average grades. He remembers well the time he brought home four A's on his report card. The only grade his father commented about was the one B. His father, a civil engineer, and his mother, a socialite, were success driven. Consequently, this man grew up believing that performance was the only thing that counted. He was continually at his studies or using what little leisure time he had to do something that would contribute to the furthering of his education.

We are geared for competition. The losing football team does not generate many fans to watch it play. The company that fails to gain contracts in competition with others is likely to go bankrupt. It is the students with superior records who win the competition for college entrance and graduate schools.

At the occupational level a person may be under considerable pressure to advance and make the increased income often needed to support a family. In general, most of us are encouraged to be ambitious and to think big.

We are told at every level that strict competition leads to greater productivity, an increased sense of purpose, and higher standards of excellence. In many cases this is true. However, inappropriate or indiscriminate competition can ruthlessly destroy a person or hurtfully divide a family or group. It can constantly overload a person's capacities and rob him of vitality and health.

Fantasy Rationalization: The Need to Be Perfect

A third fantasy rationalization for many is the *need to be perfect*, growing out of the need for approval.

Many workaholics fear that even the slightest mistake will completely crumble their entire structure of past achievements. Each thing that is done is too important to risk any kind of failure. So one really has to work at it. The risk exists in delegating work to others, because if they fail to carry out the perfected standards, this, too, represents personal failure. Trusting an associate is too great a risk. Nothing can be delegated. This chronic refusal grows out of a basic insecurity which feeds an obsessive fear of failure.

The wish to please one's parents, or to live up to their ideal or ambition, often determines a person's career. One day in a seminary classroom the professor asked members of the class why they had chosen the ministry. Almost one–third said it was because their parents or relatives wanted them to become ministers.

Unless a person develops maturity, the need for approval may become the deepest motivation in choosing a career. The father who wants his son to follow in his footsteps is a common occurrence. In the old world this was the rule, not the exception. In our world presently, this kind of parental hope may cause greater problems, because culturally it is not expected. The son has the freedom not to comply. If there is not any psychological maturity he may be ruled by a deep fear of displeasing his father. Dr. Karl Menninger speaks about this problem:

> But we know that beneath the conscious . . . there are unconscious motives which strongly influence any decision. Among these, in the case of vocational choice, one must undoubtedly include the unconscious reaction of the son to his father's attitudes.
>
> Where the conscious identification with the father in the selection the father's profession will appear to be positive, there will be negative valences in the unconscious and vice versa. In other words, a son may select his father's profession, or one that the father wishes him to follow, ostensibly because it flatters and pleases the father; but unconsciously such a son will often be motivated strongly by the repressed impulse to compete with, eclipse, or supersede his father. Similarly many a son who disappoints his father by what appears to be an aggressive rejection of the parental hopes is unconsciously deterred by love of the father, or by the fear of entering into competition with him. It reminds one of that parable of Jesus about the two sons, one of whom said quickly and politely, "I go sir. I do your bidding," but went not; while the other said, "I will not, I refuse to obey," but did.[10]

Perfectionist drives can have a ruthless effect upon one's personality. They allow little freedom or flexibility. Worst of all, they leave one with strong delusions, because those standards are seldom ever achieved.

The workaholic who simply rationalizes in a land of fantasy cuts himself off from a vast part of life. Wayne Oates puts it well:

> The work addict may be said to have a poverty of objects of attention. He is bound to the automatic perceptions, feelings, and centers of awareness of his job. He cannot see the whole architecture of life because he has his eye on one brick. Nor can he feel anything except that it is he who holds that brick in place, and that if he did not the whole structure would collapse. Furthermore, he acts as if the whole structure upholds the universe. None of this is so.[11]

DEFENSE #4: REACTION-FORMATION

If repressed feelings threaten to come into our conscious mind from the subconscious, we may try to keep them down by overreacting, opposite to what we truly feel about them. This can be a healthy way of dealing with reality by compensating for weakness in one area by achieving success in another. A person, for example, who is unable to have an active life in sports because he is physically handicapped, may have an unusually strong drive to excel in the field of music.

Again, reaction-formation may be manifested by people who crusade militantly against loose sexual morals or the evils of alcohol. Often such people have a background of earlier difficulties with such problems themselves, and their zealous crusading appears to be a means of safeguarding themselves against a recurrence of such behavior.

The deception lies in the fact that a person does not have the ability to accept himself as he is. Preventing an accurate self-picture, it also keeps him from realistically working through his problems and leads to rigidity and harshness in dealing with others.

This defense, used in an unhealthy manner, can be most destructive. Highly exaggerated attempts to overcompensate for strong feelings of self–contempt have made some people into dictators, causing untold suffering for millions as that hate is externalized.

Workaholics may use this reaction–formation defense in an unhealthy way as well. If they are fearful of getting involved with people they may compensate by directing their energies into work situations. Thus, many managers, to overcome strong feelings of inadequacy, will come on very strong at work, attempting to hide or repress such feelings by appearing to be independent and aggressive. Otto Fenichel discloses how this defense is related to the workaholic:

> Examples of the rigidity of reactive traits are the "hard workers" who are under the necessity of working constantly to keep from feeling their unbearable inner tension . . . It is obvious why work under these conditions necessarily is less effective. In this connection certain "Sunday Neuroses" should be mentioned; the patients become neurotic on Sunday because on workdays they avoid neuroses by a neurotic, that is, reactive type of work. Such people do not flee from something in the objective world that for them means temptation or punishment toward fantasy; they flee rather from instinctual fantasies toward some reactive external reality.[12]

Work as a reaction–formation against some instinctual impulses has other deeper meanings as well. Overwork may also be directly related to the conflicts about self–esteem. Many so–called ambitious people may present this side because they despise themselves for their deep–seated inferiority feelings. Overwork then becomes a need to contradict feelings of inferiority.

DEFENSE #5: SUBLIMATION

This defense allows us to take our unacceptable feelings and redirect them in useful ways. This lets us drain off some of the tension produced by these frustrated desires, but does not cause the guilt and anxiety that we would feel if we expressed them more directly. We would feel guilty if we yielded to our hostile impulses and hurt someone seriously, but we don't feel guilty about playing football or watching boxing matches and violent TV shows.

Sublimation is a defense that is felt to be socially acceptable. For instance, a Catholic nun who is unable to marry may have a strong desire to bear children. She will sublimate these feelings through great dedication when she teaches children in a parochial school.

This defense, however, can be destructive if it conceals reality by preventing confrontation with the real world thus denying the true satisfaction that comes through dealing with people in a warm, loving manner.

Many workaholics profess the view that they genuinely and thoroughly enjoy their work. But when their work drive is done by compulsion, external or internal, it actually gives them no pleasure at all. It becomes a bore, sheer drudgery. The sublimation may have a way of turning back upon itself.

This can be illustrated by the compulsive housewife. She cleans the home to make things pleasant for others and for herself. In this she is manifesting love for others. But at the same time she can, by her aggressive cleaning, attempt to get rid of *all* dirt, which comes to stand for *bad* things. Her continued desire to keep things clean may drive her family "up the wall." What started out to be a pleasurable act now makes everyone miserable because of her compulsive tidying up. The sublimation breaks down and hatred is actually turned against the people she loves. The same is true of the workaholic who uses work as a defense against intimacy or other necessary life responsibilities.

Over the long haul these mechanisms, when used for excessive work, are nonproductive. They serve to block a person from squarely facing problems and people in a warm and loving manner, and thus, emotional growth is thwarted. On the other hand, it can be one of the most rewarding experiences when the workaholic gives up misusing these defenses.

*How the right kind of goals can help you
achieve your dreams.*

17

The Awesome Power
of Goals

What we are about to discuss can do more to change
the future of your organization, church, family, and personal life
than anything else we will say in this book.

Many people tend to use the words *purpose* and *goal* in-
terchangeably, so before moving further we need to come to
more specific terms. It is not as important that you agree with
our definitions as it is that you understand what we mean.

Too often, Christians spend time arguing about the
meaning of words rather than attempting to understand one
another. This is quite natural when one considers how important words are to us. After all, we are people of The Book. We
assume that we have a revelation that has been given to us, an
inspired Word from God. Therefore, the words *justification, sal-
vation, sanctification,* and so on have a great deal of importance
to us. We are disturbed when people take words that we believe
mean one thing and pour a different content into them. But
when we use words that are part of the everyday coinage of
living, it is less important that we agree on the exact meaning of
the word than it is that we understand what the other person
means when he uses that word. We need to have fellowship
around the facts.

This is why it is important that we clearly distinguish between what we will call a "purpose" and a "goal." You may have different definitions for these words, but try to understand what we mean by them. Where we use the word *purpose,* you may be used to thinking about an "aim," a "mandate," or perhaps a "mission." Perhaps you are used to calling "goal" what we define as a "purpose." On the other hand, where we use the word *goal,* you may be used to calling such a concept an "objective," a "milestone," or a "task." These words are used in different ways by different people in different kinds of organizations. We purposely limit ourselves to the two words *purpose* and *goal.* For us, the basic distinction between the two pertains to our ability to measure.

WHAT IS A PURPOSE?

A purpose is something for which we ultimately hope. It is not necessarily measurable in itself, but it is a clear direction toward which we wish to move. "To give glory to God" is a purpose. "To have a God–honoring church" is a purpose. "To be a good Christian" or a good father or mother is a purpose. These are all very desirable. No one would argue that they are not something toward which we should move.

We need purposes. They set directions for our individual and corporate lives. But we also need to put some content into these purposes, to state what we think is likely to happen if we move in a given direction—what the outcomes will be. Unfortunately, Christian organizations have a great tendency to define their purposes and never get around to stating clearly what they intend to *do.* They suffer from "fuzzability thinking." They state things in such broad terms that it is often difficult to tell whether they have accomplished what they set out to do.

Take the case of a youth meeting that is being planned. The scheduled church hall could hold well over a hundred people. There are about sixty in the youth group normally. The youth leaders have the purpose of "having an inspiring and exciting evening," but that's as far as they have gone in their thinking. Different people have been given assignments for lead-

186

ing a Bible study, designing games, or bringing the refreshments. In the back of the leader's mind is the idea that there will be about fifty or sixty people at the meeting, which is scheduled for eight o'clock. By eight–thirty it is obvious that there are not going to be more than thirty–five young people present. The next day the pastor may ask the youth leader, "How did it go last night?"—and "Well, the Lord was really present!" may be the reply.

That *is* true. The Lord really was present. But what happened? Sixty young people were expected (there was room for more), and only about half showed up. We effectively "spiritualize" away our intentions so that it won't appear that we have failed.

This leads us quite naturally to the need to come up with some *definable* and *measurable* statements of purpose. We call these "goals."

WHAT IS A GOAL?

A goal, by our definition, is first an image or a picture of the future. We are not very much concerned with setting goals for two months ago! Goals are future events. Therefore, for the Christian individual or organization, a goal—this picture of the future—is *a statement of faith*. Don't miss that one! We need to recognize this when we begin to be concerned about "failure."

The next quality of a goal is that we believe it can be accomplished. The people who set the goal believe that it is practical, or at least possible. They have a clear picture of what the world will be like when this future event is accomplished.

Another characteristic of a goal—over and against a purpose—is that it can be measured in two ways. It is here that our definition clearly differentiates between goals and purposes. First, a goal can be measured by *time*. We will know the date by which it will be accomplished or when it will be put into effect. We also should be able to measure it by *performance*. We will be able to establish the fact that the goal has been reached, the event has happened. In other words, it will become a past event.

In his delightful book, *Goal Analysis,* Robert Mager presents us with the "Hey, Dad, watch me" test. If you want to find out whether you have a real goal (one which can be measured by time and performance), put that phrase in front of the goal statement. You might say, "I want to become a self–actualized person." Is that a goal? If we try it with the test—"Hey, Dad, watch me *become a self–actualized person!*"—we find that we don't really know what is going to be *done.* Dad may say, "Okay, Son, go ahead!"—but how will he know when you have become a "self–actualized person"?

Another way of saying this is that *a goal is a future event toward which we can measure progress.* Although a goal may change or be modified by future circumstances, it is—as best we know at a point in time—what we believe we should accomplish. It is important to see that the goals are not ends in themselves, but merely steps along the way in your life. Just as purposes without goals can be discouraging, so goals without purposes can be hopeless. There must be some ultimate purpose toward which the Christian is moving.

WHY ARE WE AFRAID OF GOALS?

Why is it that many Christian individuals and organizations never get around to expressing their goals—stating those future events that they hope will occur as a result of their service before the Lord? There are a number of reasons, but two appear to be paramount:

Fear of failure. Many times we are afraid of failure. After all, if we say that we will do such–and–such a thing by such–and–such a time, and it does not come about, we will feel that we have "failed." A number of things can be said at this point. The first observation has already been made: Life seems to many more chances for failure than for success. It is interesting to note that when a major–league ball player goes to bat, he fails more times than he succeeds. Indeed, the individual who hits three times out of ten (bats .300) is considered to be quite a success!

But perhaps we are afraid to fail because we have taken upon ourselves too much responsibility for the task we are about. Remember that, as a Christian, your business is supposed to be God's business! If goals are statements of faith, we expect that God is going to honor our faith by using what we have done for His glory. Think of it this way: When we set goals for ourselves, our families, or our organization, we are essentially saying, "Lord, here is our understanding of what You would have us do. This is our statement about the way we think the world should be in the future, based on our belief about what would be pleasing to You. Where we are wrong, give us insight. Where we are right, strengthen our hand."

God's sovereignty vs. man's responsibility. Another major reason we fear goals is that we are afraid people may think we are trying to "do the work of the Holy Spirit." They picture any attempt to describe the future as trying to take over what they consider to be God's domain. We realize that there is an age–old theological tension here between the sovereignty of God and the responsibility of man. In our view, we do well to accept the biblical paradox that although God is completely in charge, we are totally responsible for the world. Of course, we are doing the work of the Holy Spirit! If that is not what we are about, then we are not involved in a *Christian* endeavor!

THE POWER OF GOALS

1. Goals give a sense of direction and purpose. They tell workers where the organization is going and help them to see where they fit. "If you don't know where you're going, any road will take you there." Perhaps it is better said in the words of the prophet Amos: "Can two walk together, except they be agreed?" (Amos 3:3, KJV).

2. Goals give us the power to live in the present. We can't really make any decisions about the future. We are not even sure who will be alive at any given time in the future. But if we know the kind of desirable future that we want, we can make decisions *today* which are more likely to bring us into that future. Goals— statements of faith about the future—help us to do that.

3. Goals promote enthusiasm and strong organizational life. When people know that they are working together for the common good, there is an increased sense of fellowship. It is much easier to build fellowship around a task that people are accomplishing together than it is to build fellowship for fellowship's sake. How many times have you had the experience of trying to get together to "have fellowship," only to discover that there was little to have fellowship about? On the other hand, remember the excitement of accomplishing a common goal with other people!

4. Goals help us operate more effectively. They don't necessarily help us operate more *efficiently,* since we may change our goals and therefore have to change the way we work. But they do emphasize *effectiveness.* One definition of a problem is "a deviation from a goal." The assumption is that if there is no goal from which to deviate, we really don't have a problem. Goals tell us where to put our energies.

5. Goals help us to evaluate our progress. This also increases our effectiveness. If we don't know how far we have come, how can we know whether we have arrived?

6. Goals force us to plan ahead. They help us to look at the future and not focus our attention on the past.

7. Goals help us to communicate within the organization. They tell us where we are going and how we are doing. Have you ever said to yourself, "I wonder who's responsible for *that!*"? Evidently you didn't have a clear picture of who was assigned responsibility for that particular goal. This is why it's important that different departments and sections be organized around goals rather than around tasks.

8. Goals give people a clear understanding of what is expected. This helps the individual to see how he or she is doing. This is the whole concept behind "management by objectives" (MBO). The exciting thing about having a goal is seeing ourselves moving toward it. If the members of an organization are not given specific goals, they have no way of knowing whether they are being "successful."

9. Goals help to reduce needless conflict and duplication of effort. Too often, when goals are unclear, two people may be doing the same thing without knowing it. We have also run into the response of "Oh, I thought that was *your* responsibility!" Goals therefore reduce the needless misunderstanding which results from having unclear aims.

10. Goals take the emphasis off activity and place it on output. It is not how much we do (activity) that counts, but what we get done (output). The organization which focuses on all the good things it does, rather than on the goals it accomplishes, is on the road to failure.

GOAL RELATIONSHIPS

In any organization there is (or should be) a relationship between all of the goals. There are a number of different kinds of relationships, but the two most important are (1) the dependency of some goals upon others; and (2) the relationship of goals to one another in time.

In Figure 1, we have shown a series of goals represented by boxes. The arrows are intended to show that in order to accomplish the highest goal—our *primary* goal—it is necessary to achieve the three goals below it—our *secondary* goals. You have seen situations like this many times. Suppose, for example, you wanted to begin a special series of programs by June 1, perhaps a group of evangelistic meetings. To meet the goal of "beginning," there are a number of things which must be done. Someone has to have a goal of having the facility prepared. Someone else has to have a goal of having the various participants briefed. Still another may have a goal of making sure that people are invited. These three goals all have to be met before the higher goal of being ready to start is accomplished. These lower goals will be supported by other goals that might have to do with the everyday things of life—such things as making sure that the buildings are heated, that the weekly communication bulletin is issued, that the needs of the staff are met, and so on.

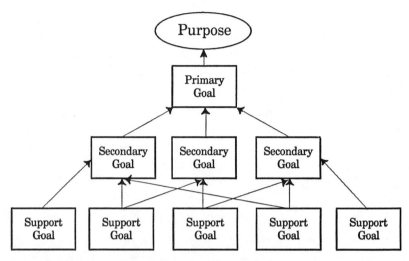

GOAL DEPENDENCIES
Figure 1

What names or titles are given to the different goal levels are not important. Some people might call the goal at the top a "primary" goal and the ones underneath the "secondary" goals. Others might wish to use such terms as "subgoals," "milestones," or "objectives." The important thing is to see the relationship. Whatever terms you use to describe your goals, make sure that everyone is using the same language.

We have already indicated that a number of different people may be the "goal owners." One person's primary goal may be another person's secondary goal. If I am the person ultimately responsible for starting the program, I may view the goal of "having the facility ready" as a secondary goal. If on the other hand, I am the person responsible for that facility goal, this will be *my* primary goal. Thus we see that goals help people relate to one another. It is important that I understand what *your* goals are, so that I can see how *my* goals relate to yours. Strong organizational life is built upon such an understanding.

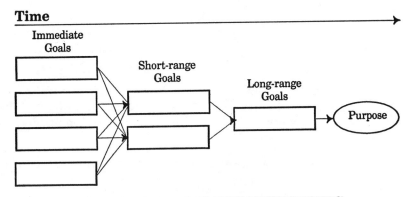

GOALS AND TIME DEPENDENCIES
Figure 2

The second relationship that goals have to one another is contingent on time. In Figure 2, we have shown the same diagram as in Figure 1—this time turned on its side, with the time direction from left to right. The goals at the extreme left might be called immediate goals, things that have to be done right now. The ones in the middle might be called short-range goals, while the ultimate goals might be the long-range ones.

Note that these are relative terms. The long-range goal of one activity may be different from the long-range goal of another activity. For instance, the long-range goal of a baseball game is to win the ball game, perhaps two or three hours from now. The long-range ten-year goal of the space program was to get a man on the moon and return him safely.

So we see that goals are not only related to one another but are related in time. The goals of an organization impact upon one another in the same way as do the events of history. It turns out that plans are nothing more than a series of goals. When we talk about taking steps toward a goal, we are really talking about a subgoal (a step) which really moves us toward another goal. When we note that we had better do "this" thing before we do "that" thing, we are recognizing that one goal is time-dependent upon another.

CLEAR GOALS VS. FUZZY GOALS

Sometimes we have difficulty stating goals that accurately communicate what we want to do. The two relationships that we have just discussed—dependency and time—can help us here. If you are having difficulty stating a goal, attempt to state what things must happen before the goal is reached—or attempt to state first the general purpose and then what goals are needed to make this purpose a reality.

For example, suppose that you serve on your church Christian education committee. About the best you can state a Christian education goal is that you "would like to have adults know more about the Bible." What are some of the things that might have to happen before adults have better knowledge of the Bible? Here are some goals that might support such a general "fuzzy" idea:

1. Twenty–five adults will complete a ten-week survey course of the Bible by June 30.

2. Four Sunday evenings will be given over to one hour of Bible exposition during the month of May.

3. A new translation of the Bible will be placed in the pew racks in the church—with one Bible for every two people—by June 22.

You can't *prove* that any of these goals will actually give adults better knowledge of the Bible. They are your statements of faith about what you believe you should do in order to see this accomplished.

This leads us to the question of stating or writing goals accurately.

Well–written goals are:

1. Stated in terms of end results, as past events.

2. Achievable in a definite time. We know when they will become past events.

3. Definite as to what is expected.

4. Practical and feasible. We believe we know how to reach them.

5. Precisely stated in terms of quantities, where possible.

6. Limited to one important goal per statement.

Poorly written goals tend to be:

1. Stated in terms of process or activity. They emphasize *doing* things.

2. Never fully achievable, no specific target dates set.

3. Ambiguous as to what is expected.

4. Theoretical or idealistic.

5. Too brief and indefinite, or too long and complex.

6. Written with two or more goals per statement.

GOAL SETTING AS A PROCESS

It is very easy to think that once we have clearly stated our goals, our job is done. We imagine that now all we need to do is get on with the business of reaching our goals. One tends to believe that if one just really knew what the future should be like, one could press on toward it without turning to the left or to the right. But the future that lies before us will be quite different from the future we expect. Change will come —individually and organizationally. Others will change; the needs of the world will change; situations will change. This means that the review and reestablishment of our goals is a process which must go on continually. That is why we show "management for mission" as a cycle, and why we say that goals point direction, rather than define precisely where we will eventually arrive.

OPERATIONAL GOALS

It is one thing to write down or state a goal. It is quite another to carry it out. Because organizations are comprised of

195

many individuals, the possibility for failure is increased as the number of relationships increases. When an individual has a personal goal, he can often be the goal setter, planner, and executor all wrapped up in one. If he changes his mind, he knows exactly to whom to give instructions — himself.

But organizations are dependent upon individuals' working together. Before a goal can become operational and put into effect, it must have some additional characteristics.

1. A goal should be related in some way to the organization's purposes. What is your overall mission? For goals to be meaningful to yourself and others, your mission — the organization's purpose for existing — must be crystal clear.

2. We must believe we can do it. Goals are often set so high that they are unrealistic. People are not really convinced that the organization can accomplish the goal. In fact, they may believe it is just a dream put up there as a "target" by the leadership. For example, suppose a growth-minded pastor challenges each member of his congregation to bring five new people "next Sunday." That 2 or 3 percent of the people might be able to do this is believable, but not that all of the congregation will be able to do it — particularly when the church could seat only one-quarter of them if they all came. This goal is unrealistic and thus fails to challenge. On the other hand, if the goal were for each to bring *one,* that would be believable.

3. A goal should have a date when it will be accomplished. We should know when we want it done. It ultimately should be in the past tense. If people do not have a clear picture as to the time frame within which a goal lies, they have entirely different assumptions as to how urgent it is. For a pastor to say, "Let's get in there and double our giving!" doesn't mean very much until someone says *when* (and, of course, how).

4. A goal must be measurable. Everyone must be able to tell that it has happened, that it has become a past event. If we don't make goals measurable, we will take away from people their sense of accomplishment. If the goal is to "double the giving," we had better decide how much money this will produce.

5. A goal needs to be supported by a plan. The point here is that we must know *how* we plan to reach the goal. We must believe we can get "there" from "here," and have some understanding of which way the path will lead.

6. A goal needs to be claimed by someone. Someone must believe that he owns it. We must all know *who* will take the steps to reach the goal. What is everyone's business is *no one's* business. The question is not whether we all believe in the goal, but who believes in it enough to make it happen.

7. A goal must be supported by the necessary resources. We must have an understanding of what it is going to cost in money, facilities, and other types of "energy," and we must have these resources available. Too often, Christian organizations begin with money when they should begin with goals. But the fact remains that if the people do not have the energy to carry it off, the goal will not become operational.

These characteristics of an operational goal are shown in worksheet form in Figure 3. You may want to make a copy of this and use it with groups in your own organization. It may be too short for many goals. On the other hand, it has the ability to communicate what we are saying here. If you present this form without going through all the explanations, you may be able to communicate the concepts by doing, rather than explaining (a much better way to learn).

GUIDELINES FOR GOAL SETTING

Limit goals to major objectives. These should be accomplished during a given time. In other words, don't clutter up the future with goals that are so far in the future that they don't seem real to the participants.

Assign goals to people and then hold them accountable for them. At the same time, allow room for flexibility and change. Things will be different from what we expected. There may be legitimate reasons for modifying a goal as we go along. The important thing here is to make sure that such a goal is restated in different terms, rather than just abandoned.

WORK, GOALS AND PROBLEM SOLVING

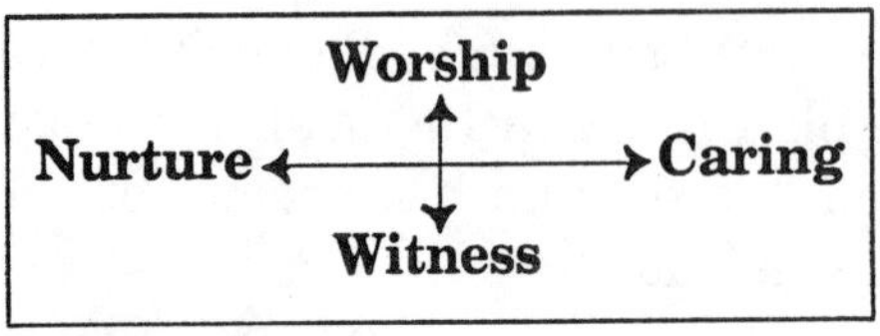

Worship
Nurture ←————→ Caring
Witness

Operational Goal For:

_____

PURPOSE

For this reason: _____

_____

_____

GOAL

We plan to
accomplish this: _____

_____

_____

by this date: _____

We will know it
has happened
because: _____

_____

_____

STEPS

We plan to take
these steps: _____

_____

_____

PEOPLE

These people
are responsible: _____

_____

_____

COST

It will cost
this amount: _____

Figure 3

198

Keep the goal–setting process simple and flexible. Avoid too many rigid forms, overdocumentation, and things which tend to confuse people. Remember, *you* may understand the process, but it is not going to work unless the people who have to put it into operation understand it.

Take people into account in setting and assigning organizational goals. Some goals will have to be tailored to the gifts, skills, and potential contribution of an individual. Too often we set up idealized goals which demand such an outstanding person that they become just that — unattainable ideals.

Provide guidance in helping individuals set realistic goals for themselves. If allowed to set their own goals, most people will set them too high. This is good, but it can be discouraging if the people consistently fail to reach their own goals.

Don't set goals in a vacuum. Get people involved. It may seem trite, but good goals are *our* goals and bad goals are *their* goals.

FINAL ASSUMPTIONS ABOUT GOALS

As we conclude this chapter on goals and goal setting, it might be useful to state some additional assumptions . . .

Goal setting assumes that *people are more willing to commit themselves to goals which they participated in setting* and are less likely to commit themselves to goals that originated with others. We are much more likely to want to work on something that has been our own idea.

Goal setting assumes that *people perform better if they can measure their progress.* If I know where I am going and can see how I am doing, I can see whether I have to work harder and more carefully, or perhaps even slow down.

Goal setting assumes that *most people desire to make a significant contribution* to the organization if they are given the opportunity. Time and time again this has proven so in practice.

Goal setting *utilizes the concept of delegation and mutual agreement* on what has been delegated. By announcing that "this is *your* goal," we are in a sense telling a person that he is responsible, and he can know clearly where the limits of the delegation lie.

Goal setting *emphasizes results rather than means.* This cannot be overemphasized.

Goal setting assumes that *people perform better when they have some control over their future.* Goals (statements of faith) help us to define together what we think the future should be like, and therefore help us to relax in these statements of faith, trusting in God's good will for us.

Good goals and bad goals. One final word about goals. Good goals are *our* goals and bad goals are *their* goals. The goals we appreciate most and to which we are committed are *our* goals, those which we have shared in defining.

*Here's a step–by–step approach that will help
you turn problems into progress.*

18
Problem Solving

The future seldom conforms to our plans. We live in times in which it is impossible to take into account many of the future events that will face us. For an enterprise of any size, there will always be the need to take corrective action as we act upon our plans and to a large degree, this is what "management" is all about. In this section we focus on the need for problem solving—the need to overcome the obstacles that are bound to lie in our path as we try to go through this process of goals, priorities, planning, and managing.

PLANNING VS. PROBLEM SOLVING

There is a close relationship between planning and problem solving. In each case, there is recognition that action is required and that there are a variety of approaches to carry out that action. There is an element of doubt about the outcome, since we cannot predict what the future will be like. There is also the element of time needed to carry out the action. Finally, there is the recognition that there are a number of steps necessary for a successful action.

What, then, is the difference between planning and problem solving? Basically, planning has to do with deciding on a course of action to reach a goal. It is an attempt to write future history. Problem solving is an attempt to understand what keeps us from reaching a goal and what step (or new steps) we have to take in order to reach it. Another way of saying this is that when we think about "planning," we are assuming that we have a great deal of the future still before us. Problem solving has a "nowness" about it. There is a need *right now* to overcome an obstacle that lies in our path. It is probably this factor of timeliness that basically differentiates problem solving from planning, although the steps to both are quite similar.

The basic steps of problem solving are:

1. Understand what needs to be done.

2. Compare the task or problem with known experience.

3. Devise an overall strategy or approach.

4. Make a plan to solve the problem.

5. Gather resources to carry out the plan.

6. Carry out the plan.

7. Use the results.

1. Understand what needs to be done. There is an adage that "Understanding what needs to be done is half the solution." (There is another adage that "Knowing it *can* be done is half the solution." With those two it looks like we're almost home!) This understanding of what needs to be done is not as simple as it may seem. Problems usually arrive well disguised as something quite different. Many times you first become aware of them when someone comes rushing into your office with a statement that "something has to be done about . . . !" That "something" may be too many cars in the parking lot, the morning service not starting on time, missionaries on the field not receiving their monthly allowances on schedule—or even a major war in Africa. But how does that problem relate to you and your organization? Is it really *your* problem, and is it really the problem? How do you find out?

Attempt to state the problem as a deviation from a goal. This is the first step. After all, if the situation is not keeping you from reaching one of your goals, is it really *your* problem? Many times this leads you to state some new subgoal that you did not realize you had or needed. It was just something that you had not taken into account in your planning. In other words, it is not very worthwhile to identify what you wanted to happen that is *not* happening—or what *is* happening that you did not want to happen!

State the problem in writing. Now, there are many problems that the manager's experience permits him to handle quickly and without a great deal of detailed planning. However, we cannot overemphasize the value of framing the problem in words that will communicate meaningfully to others and yourself. Another helpful factor involved here is that you need to *take time*—to slow down and really understand what is going on. We usually have more time to solve a problem than we lead ourselves to believe. The more thought you can give before acting, the more likely you will deal with the problem as effectively as you can.

What are some of the factors that you need to note down? Ask yourself some questions: How did we first learn about this problem? How accurate is our information? How serious is the problem? How much time do we have to solve the problem? (This is probably the most important question.)

Break the problem down into its logical elements. For example, suppose that your problem is one of parking. Let us assume that you are working in a local church. You have planned a new outreach which is attracting a number of additional people to the Sunday morning service, but you forgot to take into account the problem of where these people would park. The situation is that on Sunday morning the thirty parking spaces are being overwhelmed with sixty automobiles, carrying a hundred and sixty people. What are the elements of this problem?

First, there is the element of space. (You have thirty spaces on the church grounds.) Second, there is the element of the number of cars. (You have thirty spaces, but sixty cars.) Third, there is the element of the number of people riding in those cars. (As best as you can tell, there are a hundred and sixty people arriving in sixty cars — less than three per car.) Fourth is the element of time. (These people are all arriving between 10:50 and 11:00 A.M. There is only one church service.)

Now go further into your analysis of each of these elements, doing your best to try to describe the components of each. Is there a possibility of getting more parking space on the grounds? Is there some way that we can get people to come at different times? What is the major cause of the problem? What would the situation be like if the problem did not exist? Would this be a desirable situation? These and many other questions — with answers written down — will really help you and others to understand the problem. In all of this writing down, many things are going on. You are not only helping yourself and others to understand, but at the same time you are giving yourself and others training in problem solving, while providing some kind of record of your thought processes. At the end of this chapter is a suggested form which might be of help in understanding and organizing the approach to problem solving. It can be adapted to the specific needs of any problem at hand.

2. Compare the task with known experience. Our entire perception of the future is and must be based upon our perception of the past. When we talk about "using our experience" to solve a problem, we are talking about using past happenings to help us in the future. It may be somebody else's experience that has been written down in a book or that we have heard about in some other way. The main thing to remember is to begin by assuming that somebody else has had this problem and probably has solved it. Surprisingly, much can be done with a few phone calls to ask other people whether they (or someone they know) have had a similar problem.

Ask yourself such questions as: "Do we know of an approach that has worked before?" or "Has someone else had a problem which was close enough to ours that we think using their approach might be a good way to go?" On the other hand, do we know of some approaches that we (or others) have tried and found to be harmful, that not only have not worked, but that have set us back further than we were before? As an example, in our parking problem, somebody might have once attempted to start charging people to park in the church parking lot on Sunday morning—only to discover that although the parking spaces were not filled, the number of people in church dropped dramatically!

A third kind of experience from the past is one which is neither helpful nor harmful. It is useless and neither advances us nor puts us back. For example, someone might once have suggested a set of car pools, only to discover that this just did not fit the lifestyle of our congregation. Nobody got angry about it, but it didn't help our problem either.

Gather as much information as you can. Most of the time, in the very business of understanding the problem, the solution will become obvious. As we have said before, what appears to be a step–by–step, logical process on paper does not usually go on inside our heads in the same "logical" way.

If we have no previous experience at hand for this particular problem, we may have to do research. A simple definition of research is "an attempt to supply missing experience." Most research is carried out to learn something that will further mankind and may be either very formal or informal. Thus, when we start calling other local churches to ask them about *their* parking problems, we are involved in research.

3. Devise an overall strategy or approach. A strategy is an overview of how we will go about something. In one sense, it defines the things that we are not going to do and the approaches that we are not going to take. It is not a detailed plan in itself, but is rather a description of how we are going to go about solving the problem.

Let us say that for our parking problem our overall strategy was to have the regular members of the church not use the parking lot. The steps that we would take to get them to leave the parking spaces for visitors would be part of our detailed plan.

If we have a complicated problem, our strategy will be correspondingly more complicated. The usefulness of a strategy statement is to communicate to one another what our general approach is going to be and to help people understand those things which we have decided not to do.

4. Make a plan to solve the problem. Having decided upon an overall strategy and selected an approach based on previous experience or research, the time has come to make a decision to move ahead. This is not always as easy as it sounds. Many times we will be faced with the need to make a very difficult decision. As we mentioned when we discussed long–range planning, there is an element of risk involved. In our example, just about the time we are ready to execute our plan, we may begin to wonder whether some of the old–timers in the church will really go along with it. Don't let such feelings immobilize you. Use them to help you foresee other obstacles that you may need to overcome before you can move ahead.

Once the decision is made, the next step is to try to set subgoals for the different elements involved. In our example, we have already broken down the problem into elements of parking spaces, automobiles, people, and time. It is obvious that we must set a goal so that people either leave their cars home or are provided with other suitable parking places. We may have to set some goals for *when* we expect these people to arrive at church. For example, if we are going to ask the regular members to park some distance from the church, we must set a goal to try to have them leave home earlier.

At this point, people very often leave out a key part of the planning process by forgetting to plan on how they will evaluate success. In our example, this evaluation is pretty straightforward. We can stand by the parking lot and notice how many cars arrive! However, even in this simple situation, we may need somebody on subsequent Sundays to determine if the solution is working or if some new problem is arising. In other words, there are two evaluations to be made. We first evaluate whether our approach to the problem is working. Second, we evaluate whether we have actually met the goal. By building in the evaluation as one of the planned elements, we insure that we will not continue along a course of action that is either useless or harmful.

Having made a plan, we need to go through the regular steps of estimating the time needed for each step, the money (budget), the facilities for each step (resources), and the people (organization). If one of our estimates indicates that our plan will not work, we then need to replan or seek another solution, which may eventually mean modifying the goal. A lot of people get hung up at this point. They wonder about the sense of writing all these things down—only to discover that they won't work. What's the point?

A story is told about Thomas Edison, who invented (among other things) the electric light bulb. As we know, the principle of the light bulb is that when a current is passed through a resistant material the material gets very hot and glows, creating a light. The difficulty is that certain materials quickly burn up, even if kept in a vacuum where there is no oxygen. It took Thomas Edison a long time to discover this, and along the way he experimented with many different materials. One night, so the story goes, he returned home and announced to his wife that he "just finished the ten thousandth experiment!"

"Did it work?" she queried.

"Nope."

"Aren't you discouraged?" she asked.

"Discouraged? We now know ten thousand ways that won't work!"

Well, Edison's way is one way—but maybe it is easier to fail on paper than through thousands of experiments.

5. *Gather resources.* It is useful to remember that everything that has taken so long to describe may happen very quickly. You may have arrived at the plan to solve your parking

problem within fifteen minutes after it was first announced to you. On the other hand, a week longer may have gone by while you discussed it with different people. Again, this will depend on the seriousness of the problem with respect to time.

Now comes the moment to begin to put the plan into action. The same cycle we saw before in the total organization begins to take effect. We now need to gather the resources and organize them for action. There will be finances to be appropriated, tasks to be assigned, and facilities to be allocated.

For example, let us assume we decided to have signs painted at the two entrances of our parking lot, indicating that the lot was reserved for handicapped persons, senior citizens, or visitors to the church—and announcing that others are asked to park elsewhere. There also might have been a need to print up a flyer to be given out to church members a week or two ahead of time, identifying the location of other places where friendly merchants would allow church parking on Sunday mornings. There were probably some staff people who were involved. Perhaps a task force was appointed to pull all this together and to be there on Sunday mornings to direct people to the proper place. There had been the merchants to be contacted for permission to use their parking lots—as well as some kind of program to encourage people to walk that extra five minutes as part of their contribution toward the outreach of the church.

6. Carry out the plan. As we begin to put the plan into action, we need to measure results continually, starting at the beginning. It may be too late to wait until Sunday morning to find out that people are not paying any attention to our signs. We may have to take some earlier action within the congregation to find out if people will accept this. We may be able to discover how many people plan to use the outlying parking facilities rather than the church facility on the following Sunday.

No doubt we will run into problems. Perhaps the merchant who has made available his lot forgets that he has planned a Sunday sale that particular day. Somebody had better be ready with a contingency plan! Perhaps we discover that the instructions we thought were so clear have turned out to be obscure and in need of correction. Perhaps we discover that people who have been coming to the church for two or three Sundays don't consider themselves "visitors" anymore—and now *everybody* is parking outside the church parking lot, giving it a very empty look!

Another factor that we need to take into account as we carry out the plan is to consolidate our gains. Too often in Christian work we fail to plan for success. We plan an evangelistic campaign and expect to have a hundred people make a decision for Christ, but provide only two counselors. When people are performing according to our hopes and expectations, they need to be affirmed in what they are doing. We need to congratulate those people who have parked in the outlying parking lots, even while we assure visitors that they are welcome to use the main lot. Be ready for success. It does come!

Finally, when the results match the definition of our goal—when the number of empty spaces on Sunday morning is what we hoped for—we have reached our goal and have solved our problem.

7. *Use the results.* It is surprising how often, after we solve the problem, we do not continue to take advantage of the gains we have made. It may take six months before church members get in the habit of parking outside the parking lot. There is probably going to be a need for continuing reminders and affirmation of people who cooperate. In other words, we need to remind people that the goal is part of a larger task—the parking problem is really not the basic one. Our basic problem was that not enough people were coming to church. What we were trying to do was alleviate one of the conditions that kept them from coming. What else can we do to foster church growth?

We need to make sure to remember what we have learned. Once we have done something well, we need to celebrate that victory and use it to give us the confidence to take on new problems.

To help you see the whole process in action, here is a suggested *Guide for Problem Solvers.* Adapted to individual needs and situations, it can be an invaluable tool. Italicized "answers" illustrate its use on one specific problem, broadly stated as the need for adequate parking space (to encourage new–member church attendance).

1. Understand the Problem

What seems to be the situation? *We don't have enough parking spaces.*

What goal is this problem keeping us from achieving? *Our desire to have new members come to our church.*

How do we know that this is really the situation? *We can see the parking lot on Sunday morning.*

How accurate is our information? *Quite accurate.*

How much time do we have to solve the problem? *One to two months.*

How serious is it? *Very serious if we really want to see our church grow.*

Can we break it down into different components? *(1) Parking spaces; (2) number of cars; (3) number of people; (4) time.*

Who are the people involved? *The congregation and the church board.*

Whose mind, attitude, or behavior has to be changed to solve the problem? *The congregation and the church board.*

2. Compare the Task With Known Experience

Have we ever seen a problem like this before? *No. Our recent church growth is a new phenomenon to us.*

Who else might have or has had the same problem? *Other churches who are growing as we are.*

Is there a solution to another problem that might work for this one? *Not that we can think of.*

Do we know of attempted solutions to this problem that have been useless or harmful? *(1) Trying to make parking spaces smaller; (2) spending a lot of money on parking.*

How can we go about getting more information on possible solutions? *Telephone the three other growing churches in our area.*

3. Devise an Overall Strategy

What is our general approach to solving the problem? *Find alternate parking and convince the congregation to use it.*

What are we *not* going to do? *Add another service.*

4. Make a Plan to Solve the Problem

What are the different elements of the problem and the goal for solving each one? *(1) Ten empty spaces on Sunday morning; (2) most of the congregation using different lots.*

What steps need to be taken to reach each of these goals? *(1) Find alternate parking; (2) motivate the congregation to use the alternate parking.*

When will each step need to be accomplished? *Four weeks from now.*

Who will be responsible for the overall supervision and each step? *Chairman: Bill Brown. Committee: Burns, Rogers, and Stearn.*

How much will it cost? *$39 for leaflets and signs.*

How will we measure progress against our solution? *Observation each Sunday.*

Do we have the people, resources and courage to carry out this approach? *Yes.*

5. Carry Out the Plan

How are we doing against each phase? *First Sunday: 2 empty spaces; second Sunday: 5 empty spaces; third Sunday: 15 empty spaces.*

What corrective action needs to be taken? *First Sunday: additional encouragement to the congregation and information on alternate lots.*

How can we consolidate the gains we have made? *Keep affirming those who are walking from some distance.*

6. Use the Results

Who needs to be congratulated? *The committee and the congregation.*

Now that we have solved the problem, how is our program really better? *New members are coming to our church.*

Has the real problem been solved? *Yes.*

What have we learned to keep us from repeating the problem? *As new members join the church, they need to be encouraged to park in the alternate lots provided by friendly merchants.*

What have we learned that will help us solve other problems? *People will cooperate if they see a real need and it is adequately communicated.*

How can we communicate what we have learned to ourselves and others? *Call the other churches that we asked information from and tell them how we solved the problem.*

Managing Your Time

Time is the great leveler. The same amount of this indispensable commodity is assigned to all. The rich, the poor, the weak, the strong—all have equal shares in this most marvelous of all gifts. You cannot delay the clock or hasten it. You cannot buy time, nor can you give it away. But you *can* manage your activities—and indeed your life—so that you make time work for you.

In these chapters from *Managing Your Time,* you will learn who the real "time bandit" is. And the answer may surprise you. Ted will also help you unravel some of the misconceptions about time that will help free you to use your hours more wisely and profitably. So if you have decided to make your days more productive, and if you wish to become a better steward of your gift of time, these two brief chapters may be just what you are looking for.

Is time the problem, or are YOU?

19

The Key to Getting Things Done

Robert MacIver notes that time, like space, is a dimension rather than a force. He discerningly observes that time as measured by the clock or calendar is not adequate to many of man's needs. Man may be victimized by clock time, but the real difference, according to the author, is between time *measured* and time *lived.*[1]

Time as measured is the enemy of time as lived. Of the various ways in which we become victims of time, perhaps the most obvious is when the work we do is denuded of interest for us. How important our view of work becomes at this point! At once comes to mind the picture of the schoolboy squirming for the closing bell, the office worker with thoughts only for the evening's coming activities, the machine operator listlessly pursuing prescribed routine, the lawyer dutifully preparing a dull brief for a case that leaves him cold.

Having seen how much our use of time may depend upon our view of our work, let us consider a few of the common misconceptions about time.

In the lives of busy executives there is no question asked more often than "Where has the time gone?" Does it seem strange that the question most often asked, rhetorically to be sure, should so misstate the case? Does time depart the scene, as the question suggests? Or has it simply passed at the rate it always has while we accomplished far less than we should? Or, perhaps, are we really asking, "How could I have planned so poorly and left so much to be done in so little time?"

"Time is money and must be spent wisely," we have been told all our lives. But have we any choice *not* to spend it? Of course we do not. The hands of the clock move onward inexorably. We have no control over their speed of flight. We may "stop the clock" on a basketball court or on a football field—but never in the game of life.

The sundial's shadow and the sands in the hourglass mean something more than a commodity to be controlled or dispensed at will. So we speak of the ravages of time . . . a hand that cannot be stayed . . . a scythe with which an old man levels all. But is time really a force to be so dreaded, or does it in fact create nothing . . . destroy nothing?

Faith Baldwin called time a seamstress specializing in alterations. But we know that rocks wear down and stars grow dim, men age and empires decay, *not* because time works on them but because of the ebb and flow of energy systems operating within the physical laws of the universe established by God. If space is the dimension in which things exist, why not accept time, as Robert MacIver suggests, as the dimension in which things change?

"Time flies!" we exclaim—when we mean that we have not accomplished the results expected within the time available.

"Time will take care of it," we say—instead of asserting that the condition will undoubtedly rectify itself, given adequate time.

"I don't have the time," we protest—instead of admitting that the proposal is not sufficiently important in our priorities to warrant *taking* the time for it. We always make time for things that are important enough.

We talk about "the tyranny of time," ascribing to it a capability of acting instead of recognizing it as a measurement of too large a number of tasks to be performed within the time available.

After all, time isn't money or even a commodity; it's not going anywhere . . . can't be speeded up or slowed down; it can't be bought or bartered; it's not a ravaging force of evil or an inscrutable judge or an omniscient healer. It is, as Webster put it simply, "the period during which action or process continues." Like sands in the hourglass, so are the days of our lives.

RESPONSIBLE STEWARDSHIP

Surprised by our lack of perception as to the true nature of time, we may well be startled as we contemplate the significance of its equal distribution. When God chose to create us, along with life itself came His gift to all the world. We have the same amount of time in every day as everyone else has. Whether paperboy or president . . . author or housewife . . . farmer or financier . . . the clocks we buy run at the same rate. We have . . . whoever we are and wherever we be . . . the same number of minutes in our hours as everyone everywhere has. *No one has any more time than you!*

With a clear philosophy of work as a foundation, and a view of time and its management that is closely related to our view of work, our focus on the "stewardship of time" sharpens. We are here to work within God's divine purpose. Among the resources granted for the task, whatever it be, is a fixed amount of time. A biblical injunction regarding its use is found in Colossians 4:5: "Make the best possible use of your time" (Phillips).

Much is said regarding the stewardship of wealth and possessions. Less is said about stewardship of talent. Little is said concerning stewardship of time. Perhaps even less is understood. What do we mean by being "stewards of our time"? Is it really our time we're talking about, or is it God's time? Has it been granted to us, along with the gift of life itself, to be disposed according to our own purposes . . . with only a portion of our own determining going back to Him from whence it came? Or, as Charles Shedd suggests, since God fashioned the world and all that is in it, does *all* our time *belong to Him?*

Shedd proposes "Ten Affirmations for Christian Use of Time."[2] Appropriately, he begins with purpose: "Life's Single Holy Assignment." From Luke 10:41–42 he draws the parallel of Christ's gentle reminder to Martha that "but one thing is needful." Rather than all her lavish attentions, a simple, quiet chat on heavenly things would have been preferred. A truly effective life, according to Shedd, does not result from getting God to help us. Our lives assume maximum worth when we "turn our wills over to Him and ask that we might be of assistance to His purposes."

Management of time thus becomes, for the Christian, management of His time. And this brings us to what may appear to be a slightly revolutionary thought. When things get out of joint . . . when tasks pile up . . . and when things go wrong . . . how often do we stop to ask God if we're doing what *He* wants us to do? It is *His* time we're managing. Isn't *this* where we should begin?

Colleen Townsend Evans has described how this works for her. When life gets just too harried she tries to stop the merry-go-round with the question, "Have I pushed Christ out of the center of my life?"[3]

Bruce Larson suggests that "getting our marching orders" can make the difference.[4] Settling the question of whether what we are doing is what *God wants* us to be doing could be the greatest single key to our management of time!

And isn't this scriptural from yet another perspective— God's promise to supply our every need (Philippians 4:19)? Surely this must include *time* to *do* the things we ought. Thus the quest for a solution to the problem of better management of time becomes a simple query—"Am I in the center of God's will for my life?"—since He has promised to provide the time to do the things I must for Him!

IS TIME THE PROBLEM . . . OR ARE YOU?

Stripped of high-sounding phrases—"a measured piece of eternity"—and common misconceptions—"I had some time on my hands"—we arrive at the conclusion that time is but a measurement . . . a dimension. Hence, *it* can scarcely be our problem. In any query into the matter of time and its management, all roads ultimately lead back to management of ourselves. The entire science of personal management deals with the way you allocate your time.

Should this be so startling? Note the similarity in the complaints about time. There just doesn't seem to be enough of it. More precisely, of course, we try to do too much in the time we have available. Remember . . . we have, and always have had, all the time there is!

So the problem is, has been, and will be, not time—but ourselves. And, fortunately, we can do something about this.

Before we attack the matter of self–management, let us beware of stumbling over the first hurdle—God's will. We have already observed that our most basic problem with lack of time may well be that we have pushed God away from the center of our lives. We have seen that His promise to provide for all our needs certainly must extend to this most basic element—time. Now, however, we find ourselves in the human arena where God, despite our frailties, has chosen to work. He has endowed us with certain talents and capabilities, each unique, then given each of us the right to choose his own path.

Out of this divinely created relationship, open to whoever would have it, comes the question, "How do I know when the path I choose is the one God would have me take?" How do we know when the resources God has placed in our care are being used as He wills them to be?

We approach the matter of managing ourselves, then, from the perspective of being in God's perfect will for our lives, of committing our wills to Him, of harnessing all our faculties and all the resources He has entrusted to our care to the ultimate purpose He may have for our lives.

*How wise planning will help you accomplish
the most important tasks.*

20

Where Are You Heading?

It is time to take a look at your job. What results are you expected to achieve? Is your assignment spelled out in terms of activities or results? If the former, can you make the conversion to results?

Christian psychologist Henry Brandt asks the questions: "Where do you want to go in life? How do you want to get there? Do the roles you fill contribute to your goal? What is really important that you do? What merely fills up time?"

He says further, "In determining your best roles you ought to keep those that advance you toward your goal – perhaps even expand one or more if you can and eliminate those that are useless and a drag. Your trouble may be too many good roles. You cannot afford to take on more than you can handle well."

In his classic presentation of *Managing a Manager's Time,* William Oncken divides a leader's duties into three categories: job–imposed; system (organization)–imposed; and self–imposed. He suggests that what sets apart or distinguishes the effective or successful leaders is the number, significance and rate of completion of their self–imposed tasks. These are those tasks not called for in the job description . . . not required by the organization . . . but voluntarily assumed by the executive who sees a need and a means of fulfilling it on his own. The manager who thinks in this area—Oncken calls it the "area of ambiguity" due to the lack of guidelines—will be an "opportunity–oriented" manager. Concentration on such areas may offer great potential gains as opposed to concentration on problem areas alone.[1]

In considering what *could* be accomplished in your job, again think in terms of results, not activities . . . of accomplishments, not stated duties. If things went right . . . if events transpired in a favorable sequence . . . if resources could be marshalled at the opportune place and moment . . . what *might* be possible? One head of an international Christian organization has found this very question to be of significant help in orienting and directing his entire organizational effort.

In a recent *Guideposts* piece, Dr. Dorothy L. Brown wrote, "Just as God gives each one of us our special talent, so does He give us our dreams to make us aware of the talent."

THE ACCEPTANCE OF CHANGE

Today's executives have developed a keen appreciation for change . . . that is, in matters other than their own jobs. Gaining acceptance of change in organizational policies has become a common subject for executive seminars and management publications. New insights from the behavioral sciences have reinforced what may have been long suspected by some: whatever gets done is done through people; to do things better means change; people resist change. Hence the emphasis on winning acceptance of change.

The change in a manager's own job may be so gradual, and so continual, that it is scarcely discernable. Even when sought in any but the most thorough and systematic way, such change may go unrecognized.

From time to time, it is important to compare your own job requirements with your organization's objectives. If these over–all objectives are in writing, the task is simple. If they are not, write them down, and then compare. If there are aspects of your job which do not coincide with any stated organizational objectives, take a second look at that particular aspect of your job. Why are you doing it? Because your predecessor did it? Because things in the organization have always been done this way? Did an influential member of the board inaugurate the procedure—and is he pretty sticky about suggestions for change?

Hopefully, this process will result in redefining, modifying, and especially eliminating many activities done previously without questioning. Then, when your own objectives and job requirements have been trimmed to coincide precisely with the organization's objectives, *concentrate* your efforts *on the essentials.* Ray Josephs refers to this as the "instinct for the jugular."[2] No characteristic better describes the critical activity of the successful Christian leader than his conscious application of effort to the strategic requirements of the job.

PLAN YOUR WORK

It has been said that time is on the manager's side the moment he organizes it. While the time an executive should spend planning ahead may vary depending on a number of factors, the consensus among consultants is that almost no executives spend *enough* time on this critical area. The higher up the executive ladder one goes, the smaller is the proportion of his time which should be spent on present problems and the greater is the proportion which ought to be spent on future considerations.

Long–Range Planning

In developing the planning function, logic favors starting long–range. Until you know where you want to be at the journey's end, it is difficult to plot the course on a daily or weekly basis. Just as long–range objectives are the most important of all objectives . . . so with planning. While some industries plan up to twenty years ahead, consensus holds that planning for five years ahead is practical for most endeavors.

A realistic approach to developing plans five years ahead is to request from each department or division their five–year expectations of accomplishment. The composite of these divisional goals, discussed and modified as they certainly should be, will provide the basic structure for your long–range plan. General experience has shown that goals set by managers or supervisors for themselves tend to be too high. There appears to be a tendency to want to set the objectives or goals at the highest possible level. Managers and executives face the problem of applying a realistic yardstick to goals which have been set in such a way. That this tendency should almost uniformly result from participative goal-setting is reason enough to practice this method. Other benefits include the increased tendency to feel highly motivated to accomplish goals which you have had a part in establishing.

Intermediate–Range Planning

While planning from one to five years ahead may conveniently be termed long–range, that from one month to one year may be termed intermediate–range planning. Once the long–range plans are set, the question is put: "Where must we be in three months . . . or six . . . or nine . . . in order to achieve the long–range objectives in one year?" Thus, by starting with the longest–range objectives, intermediate requirements which must be met in each division or department, when grouped together, become the intermediate objectives or plans.

Short–Range Planning

We must also consider those requirements which, in order to achieve the intermediate goals, must be accomplished in one day to one month. Whatever must be accomplished within this short span of time in order to achieve the intermediate objectives become the short–range plans or objectives.

But, you ask, what happens to the longer–range plans when something goes wrong short–range? A good question. It puts the finger on a point often neglected . . . that of flexibility or adjustability of planning. The Critical Path Method tells planners in space and electronics industries what happens "down the line" when a delay is encountered at any point along the path. As actual progress of your plan is plotted against short– and intermediate–range plans, and the deviations between planned and actual performance are visible, these discrepancies should be transferred to the longer-range plans, unless other action is possible to compensate for the loss.

Similarly, every year that passes converts all plans to a minus-one-year basis. Thus the former five-year plan is now the four-year plan, with corrections to accommodate actual performance over the past year. A new five-year plan must be created, based on the best information available at the time.

When to Plan

The most successful Christian planners in Christian service seem to find that a few moments of prayerful, relative quiet at the end of a given period (a day . . . or a week) provide the best opportunity for planning the next period.

For instance, at the end of the afternoon you can write up a calendar page consisting simply of the items to be accomplished. As they are completed, cross them off. As new tasks arise, simply add them to the list. On a good day you may cross off nearly all the items. On a poor day, planning-wise, you may cross off only one or two. But the list is there . . . directly in front of you . . . a constant reminder of the things to be done *that day.* By stopping at the end of one day to consider what needs to be done the next you are more likely to think of what really must be accomplished because you are still geared to thinking about the job. Further, once you have written your list for tomorrow, you stand a better chance of being able to leave your problems in the office when you go home, without fear of forgetting them.

Remember that you set long-range objectives first, then intermediate, then short. Thus, in setting daily tasks, you really must know what you planned to accomplish in a given week. These subgoals, those which must be accomplished if the week's goals are to be met, added to the new goals which arise in the course of everyday business, make up the daily targets confronting the conscientious worker.

It is common to misjudge by as much as 50 percent . . . or for a job to require twice as long for completion as originally thought necessary.

This discovery frequently leads to another even more disconcerting: that in terms of results accomplished, far less is done in the typical workday than we ever dreamed. Thus another benefit of the entire planning procedure arises . . . that of resolving to set priorities since so much less is accomplished than we thought . . . and that of concentrating on the essentials since we will then be accomplishing the greatest possible results with the effort expended.

Many benefits have been cited by managers who plan ahead for the things they want to accomplish the following day. One perhaps less apparent than others is the avoiding of indecision. Upon arrival at the office and a cluttered desk, what executive has not shrugged his shoulders and wondered where to begin? What executive has not found himself beginning at the top of the stack . . . with whatever item happened, by pure chance, to be on top? Though each of us has, at one time or another, done precisely this, we would not welcome the conclusion that at this very point our job was running us. Yet such a conclusion is inescapable. By writing down the things to be accomplished, and in order of priority, the indecision which may be one of the manager's more deadly enemies, and certainly one of his greatest timewasters, can be reduced considerably.

THE $25,000 IDEA

Most students of management are familiar with the incident regarding the remarkable payment of twenty–five thousand dollars for essentially the suggestions presented thus far in this chapter. For the reader who may not have chanced upon the story, it is well worth repeating.

When Charles M. Schwab was president of Bethlehem Steel, he confronted Ivy Lee, a management consultant, with an unusual challenge: "Show me a way to get more things done," he demanded. "If it works, I'll pay anything within reason."

Lee handed Schwab a piece of paper. "Write down the things you have to do tomorrow," he said. Schwab did it. "Now number these items in the order of their real importance," Lee continued. Schwab did that. "The first thing tomorrow morning," Lee added, "start working on number one and stay with it until it is completed. Next take number two and don't go any further until it is completed. Then proceed to number three, and so on. If you can't complete everything on schedule, don't worry. At least you will have taken care of the most important things before getting distracted by items of lesser consequence.

"The secret is to do this daily," continued Lee. "Evaluate the relative importance of the things you have to get done . . . establish priorities . . . record your plan of action . . . and stick with it. Do this every working day. After you have convinced yourself of the value of this system, have your men try it. Test it as long as you like. Then send me a check for whatever you think the idea is worth."

In a few weeks, Charles Schwab sent Ivy Lee a check for twenty–five thousand dollars. Schwab later said that this lesson was the most profitable one he had ever learned in his business career.

Developing Your Leadership Style

Dynamic, effective leadership is the key to growth and success in any organization — secular or religious. Therefore it should come as no surprise that within all groups of organized working units there is a desperate need for leadership that manifests a clear understanding of tested principles of management and human relations.

In these chapters taken from *The Making of A Christian Leader* and *The Christian Leader's 60–Second Management Guide*, you will be encouraged to capture the essence of practicing and developing those qualities and personal traits that make good leaders and managers. The following pages were written to help you get a clearer picture of *how to think about the development of your own leadership style* and then *how to make that style work best for you.*

As Ted Engstrom has told thousands of seminar attendees over the years, there's only one way to know if you are a leader . . . and that's *to step out and LEAD.* Allow these chapters to get under your skin and into your heart as you continue to develop your leadership and management skills.

What every leader should know about the important role he plays.

21

What Is Leadership?

A friend of mine once visited a friend of his in a little church in Connecticut. He had been there for many years, preaching to a handful of people. When my friend saw the minister washing the church windows, he asked "What in the world are you doing?"

The minister was occupied with every menial task in the church—many tasks that could have been turned over to high-school students or men and women in the church. His answer appeared pious and commendable—actually it was tragic. He said, "I do everything myself [to demonstrate his self-sacrificing]. I run off my own bulletins. I wash the windows in the church, as you can see. I put out the hymnbooks. I do everything . . . this way I know it's done properly."

Was that minister a leader in the best sense?

Well, what is leadership? Everyone knows what it is. Or do they? No one seems really to be sure. We are able to define what managers do, but the closest we seem able to come to a broadly acceptable definition of leadership is, "it is what leaders do." Then when we try to define leaders, about all the agreement we get is that leaders lead.

Frankly, leadership is an elusive quality, if in fact it is a quality at all. Sociologists and psychologists have examined individuals for leadership traits, far too often with meager results. The fairly recent enthusiasm for group sociometrics has proved to be somewhat more rewarding, but still leaves much in doubt.

Why should we be concerned? Because leadership development is the key to meaningful development of modern society and the effective future of the Christian family and church in the world. We must take a closer look, because true leadership is a quality found in far too few individuals.

MAKES THINGS HAPPEN

Nicholas Murray Butler, a former president of Columbia University, said, "There are three kinds of people in the world—those who don't know what's happening, those who watch what's happening, and those who make things happen."

Though leadership may be hard to define, the one characteristic common to all leaders is the ability to make things happen—to act in order to stimulate and encourage others to realize their fullest potential to contribute meaningfully.

Outstanding results cannot be forced out of people. They occur only when individuals collaborate under a leader's stimulation and inspiration in striving toward a worthy common goal. Action is the key, because the leader and manager types are not mutually exclusive. The leader usually is a good manager, but a good manager is not necessarily a good leader because he may be weak in terms of motivating action in others.

When all the facts are in, swift and clear decision is a mark of true leadership. Leaders will resist the temptation to procrastinate in reaching a decision, and they will not vacillate after it has been made.

We might say, then, that leadership is an *act* or behavior required by a group to meet its goals, rather than a condition. It is an act by either word or deed to influence behavior toward a desired end. A leader usually leads in many directions. We often identify people as leaders by virtue of their occupying a position;

possessing recognized skill, knowledge, or prestige; holding a certain social status; or having certain compelling personal characteristics. However, they still may not be included in our definition because of the inability to motivate people and act decisively to accomplish this. Complete is the man who can meet *every* action requirement in all situations. Few there are.

NOT A PASSIVE PUPPET

Men of faith have always been men of action. It is an impossibility for active men to serve in a passive role. This implies that such people are decisive in nature. Leadership action demands faith. The setting of and striving for goals is an act of faith.

In his excellent book, *Man at the Top,* Richard Wolfe points out that when God creates a leader he or she is given a volition for action. It is in this way that God works in people (Philippians 2:13). Wolfe further states that prayer is not a substitute for action which flows from decision.[1]

That Christ motivates leaders for action does not mean that human beings are merely passive puppets. This is unbiblical. Paul admitted that God worked in him (1 Corinthians 15:10), but he never disclaimed his active part in getting results in his ministry. This is a part of the tension always evident in leadership action. The apostle was able toward the end of his life to say, "I have fought a good fight . . . " (2 Timothy 2:7), meaning that he recognized the need and effectiveness of grace, but he did not underestimate the attributes that made him an active agent in leadership.

PERFORMS COMPETENTLY

It used to be that the main difference between a professional and an amateur was that professionals earn their living or are paid for what they do; amateurs do it for free.

We need to enlarge the definition of leadership to mean that professionals are also the best at what they do and get results. This means they are professionals because of their ability not only to act, but to perform at a high efficiency level. Such would be true of all fields and vocations. Persons are where they are because of prescribed study and credentials. But more than that, they perform competently. If not, they soon lose their right to practice through competition.

PRINCIPLES FOR DECISIVE ACTION

If a leader is to act decisively to get results, he must follow certain principles. Here are some of the major considerations to help you achieve the best results:

1. *Determining your objectives:* Determine the important end results you want to attain and when. State them in writing—accurately, briefly, and clearly.

2. *Planning necessary activities:* Decide what major activities must be performed in order to achieve your general objectives; specific objectives; long–range, intermediate, and immediate. Question every proposed activity: Is it necessary? Is it important? Why?

3. *Organizing your program*: Make a checklist of all *important* things that must be done. Remember that urgent things are not necessarily important. Dwight D. Eisenhower said, "The important is seldom urgent, and the urgent is seldom important." Arrange these in an order of priorities. Make a breakdown of each activity. Identify essential steps in sequence of importance. Question every step: *What* is its purpose? *Why* is it necessary? *Where* should it be done? *When* should it be done? *Who* should do it? *How* should it be done?

4. *Preparing a timetable:* Prepare a work schedule. Set a time limit for the completion of each step in your program. Stick to your schedule—or reset it. Don't let time slip by without definite action. Follow through.

5. *Establishing control points:* Determine where and when you will review progress in relation to objectives. Establish bench marks. Make necessary adjustments. Determine remedial action as required.

6. *Clarifying responsibilities and accountability*: Clarify

all delegated responsibilities, authorities, and relationships, and see to it that they are *coordinated and controlled.*

7. *Maintaining channels of communication:* Keep your associates (superiors, assistants, subordinates, and others affected) fully informed. Make it easy for them to keep you advised on all pertinent matters essential to successful operations.

8. *Developing cooperation*: Successful achievement largely depends upon groups of people working together. Clarify results to be accomplished; identify what is expected of every individual affected. Otherwise lost motion, misunderstandings, and frictions are almost certain to delay progress.

9. *Resolving problems:* Group thinking multiplies individual thinking and coordinates capacities of members of the group. Build morale through participation. An operating problem is any interference with desired end results.

> a. Spot the problem: clarify it. Tackle one specific problem at a time. Analyze underlying causes, contributing conditions.
>
> b. Develop possible solution: Select the best solution.
>
> c. Determine a plan of action: Put it into effect.
>
> d. Check results in terms of improvements and objectives.

10. *Giving credit where credit is due:* Recognize and give due acknowledgment and credit to all who assist in the successful attainment of your objectives. The *law of recognition* is as fundamental as the *law of action and reaction.*

LEADING VS. MANAGING

Because leadership is an attitude as well as an action it must be distinguished from management. While there are certain functional similarities in both leadership and management, leadership has distinctive characteristics. It is unfortunate that so often little attention is given to these distinctives in developing organizational philosophy and in training an organization's executive personnel. Christian organizations are no exception.

What then are some of these distinctives? Comparison may be helpful at this point. My friend Olan Hendrix has made the following distinctions (with some personal modifications):

1. Leadership is a quality; management is a science and an art.

2. Leadership provides vision; management supplies realistic perspectives.

3. Leadership deals with concepts; management relates to functions.

4. Leadership exercises faith; management has to do with fact.

5. Leadership seeks for effectiveness; management strives for efficiency.

6. Leadership is an influence for good among potential resources; management is the coordination of available resources organized for maximum accomplishment.

7. Leadership provides direction; management is concerned about control.

8. Leadership thrives on finding opportunity; management succeeds on accomplishment.

NOT AS EASY AS IT LOOKS

Sometimes one might see a leader effectively managing a group of people and he is apt to think, "That looks easy. Let me at it. I can do that."

A friend of mine told me about friends who visited him in the East. My friend took two sons and two of his visitor's sons water skiing. One was about fifteen years old; he said, "I'd like to ski, too."

"Do you know how, Jim?"

"Oh, yeh, yeh, sure."

My friend agreed to let him try it. As the pilot pulled the rope taut, the boy's skis were very unsteady. When it seemed the boy was ready, the pilot raced the engine and began to pull the skis; legs and arms went all over the place! The pilot pulled back around, harnessed the boy again, and tried once more. Again legs and arms and skis went in all directions. After the fourth time my friend asked, "Jim, are you sure you know how to ski?"

"Sure, I know how to ski."

My friend thought better of the question and asked, "Jim, have you ever skied?"

"Well, maybe not, but it looks so easy."

That's the way it is with leaders. We stand a few feet back and watch a person leading effectively and think, "Oh, that's easy." So we smile, say a few words, write letters, and lead meetings. We can give orders and receive reports, and it's great . . . until we really try. Then we discover that the leadership function is not that simple. Most fail because they do not possess the inherent capacity to take the necessary and right actions.

Summary Definition

To summarize, a *leader* is one who guides the activities of others and who himself acts and performs to bring those activities about. He is capable of performing acts which will guide a group in achieving objectives. He takes the capacities of vision and faith, has the ability to be concerned and to comprehend, and exercises action through effective and personal influence in the direction of an enterprise and the development of the potential into the practical and/or profitable means.

To accomplish this, a true leader must have a strong drive to take the initiative to act—a kind of initial stirring that causes people and an organization to use their best abilities to accomplish a desired end.

These examples from the Old Testament show that the key principles of good leadership are timeless.

22
Profiles in Effective Leadership

Christian leadership represents action, but it is also a set of tools for spiritual men and women. It is not moral or immoral—it is amoral. Effective leadership methods can be used for ulterior and worldly purposes by people who are not spiritual at all. By the same token spiritual men and women can take these tools and use them for the glory of God, whether or not all the tools in the leader's arsenal are spiritual. The issue is the spirituality of the person and how he can better use leadership tools for the glory of God.

But where should the spiritual person look for the tools? Is it enough to borrow from the secular world and its literature?

Legitimate questions may be asked: "Is the subject of leadership biblical? Are there valid principles for organization and spiritual leadership? Can we study the Bible and find methods to guide our thinking?"

Yes, on all counts—if we have an open mind to perceive the Bible's insight. I believe that every basic, honorable principle in leadership and management has its root and foundation in the Word of God.

The Bible is filled with examples of God's searching for

239

leaders, and when He found them He used them to accomplish His purpose, despite their human failings.

Close scrutiny of leaders mentioned in the Bible indicates that most experienced failure at one time or another. Many failed at some point in their lives in a marked way, but the key to their success was that they never groveled in the dust. They learned from the hand of failure, repented, and then were used in even mightier ways.

EGYPT'S TOP ADMINISTRATOR

First consider Joseph. Is there in all of history a more magnificent example of leadership skill than his? Remember, he was placed in a high administrative position in Egypt not long after his jealous brothers had sold him to a passing caravan. He was given charge over the monumental harvest in Egypt. Then came the horrible years of famine, the delegation of the work, planning the whole operation, distribution of the materials and the foodstuffs, satisfying the complaints, and handling the grievances. The people he had to work with no doubt helped little (Genesis 41:14–57).

What a magnificent example of organization in Scripture! But God did not simply plant the skills in Joseph's brain so that he did it instinctively without thinking. I do not believe God works that way with men; generally I believe He will guide us to the subjects we need to study and learn if we show and exercise leadership qualities.

In the book I co–authored with my friend, Alec Mackenzie, *Managing Your Time*, I develop a biblical perspective regarding leadership.

> One's view of leadership must be based upon one's view of man. The Bible gives us a clear view of man: "All we like sheep have gone astray; we have turned every one to his own way ... " (Isaiah 53:6). Thus, as sheep must be directed to move the entire flock along a single path, so groups of people need direction so that their efforts and energies will be directed toward a common goal.
> This direction which people need must come from the top.

God has ordained this and Scripture teaches it in many ways. Moses set up lines of authority following Jethro's advice which we shall examine more closely (Exodus 18:13–27). The Aaronic priesthood was set up with a high priest and orders of priests under him in varying ranks (1 Chronicles 24). The husband is head of the home and a parallel relationship exists in the Church (1 Timothy 3:4–5). It is important to recognize that authority flows from the higher levels to the lower in God's plan.

In Christian organizations there appears to be a recurring tendency to forget this, confusing equality before the Lord with organizational equality. Christian workers may do themselves and their organizations a great disservice by refusing to accept duly constituted authority. We are admonished, "Let every person be subject to the governing authorities" (Romans 13:1). We recall the Roman soldier who asked the Lord to come to his home to heal his servant, saying, "For I also am a man set under authority, having under me soldiers, and I say unto one, Go, and he goeth; and to another, Come, and he cometh; and to my servant, Do this, and he doeth it." When Jesus heard these things, he marvelled at him, and turned him about, and said unto the people that followed him, "I say unto you, I have not found so great faith, no, not in Israel" (Luke 7:6–9).

PLACE FOR RESPONSIBLE AUTHORITY

None of this is to imply that all authority, of whatever character, is to be condoned. Authority carries with it great responsibility. Desirable authority is not viewed as being unwillingly imposed, all–powerful, insensitive and unenlightened. Those entrusted with authority are divinely ordained to use it responsibly for His purposes. His ultimate purposes and those of the organization – hopefully one – must be paramount. Sensitivity to the needs of those who are serving as well as those being served is essential.

The nature of authority may be far more complex than is commonly recognized even by those in management. The probability of this seems clear from the comment of Chester I. Barnard, the noted authority on management:

A person can and will accept a communication as authoritative only when four conditions simultaneously obtain: (a) he can and does understand the communication; (b) at the time of his decision he believes that it is not inconsistent with the purpose of the organization: (c) at the time of his decision, he believes it to be compatible with his personal interest as a whole; and (d) he is able mentally and physically to comply with it.[1]

Barnard reminds us of not only the complex nature of authority, but also how much it does, in fact, depend upon the attitude with which it is received by those reporting to the person exercising it. Of the forces at work in leadership situations, we must identify those within the leader, those within the followers, and those within the situation.

The life of Winston Churchill, who may not be seriously challenged for the title "Man of the Century," bears graphic evidence of these three kinds of forces. Recall that after marshalling the morale and the forces of the British Empire in her darkest hour during World War II, he was rejected by his own constituency and replaced as prime minister by Clement Atlee. He returned as prime minister at the age of seventy-seven, but never forgot the bitter lessons learned at the hands of fickle followers and history.

How to Manage a Multitude

Turning again to *Managing Your Time:*

The Bible has been quoted in numerous instances for its demonstration of management principles. One of the most outstanding examples is the instruction of Moses by Jethro some fifteen hundred years before the birth of Christ (Exodus 18:13–27). Noted below, from the Amplified Version, are these verses along with some of the management ideas and principles they suggest.

13. Next day Moses sat to judge the people, and the people stood around Moses from morning till evening.

(Observation and Personal Inspection)

242

14. When Moses' father–in–law saw all that he was doing for the people, he said, What is this that you do for the people? Why do you sit alone, and all the people stand around you from morning till evening?

(Questioning — Discerning Inquiry)

15. Moses said to his father–in–law, Because the people come to me to inquire of God.

16. When they have a dispute they come to me, and I judge between a man and his neighbor, and I make them know the statutes of God and His laws.

(Conflict Resolution, Correction)

17. Moses' father–in–law said to him, The thing that you are doing is not good.

(Judgment)

18. You will surely wear out both yourself and this people with you, for the thing is too heavy for you; you are not able to perform it all by yourself.

(Evaluation — of Effect on Leader and People)

19. Listen now to me, I will counsel you, and God will be with you. You shall represent the people before God, bringing their cases to Him.

(Coaching–Counseling, Representation, Establishing Procedures)

20. Teaching them the decrees and laws, showing them the way they must walk, and the work they must do.

(Teaching, Demonstration, Job Specification, Delegation)

21. Moreover you shall choose able men from all the people, God–fearing men of truth, who hate unjust gain, and place them over thousands, hundreds, fifties, and tens, to be their rulers.

(Selection, Establish Qualification, Assign Responsibilities)

(Chain of Command)

22. And let them judge the people at all times; every great matter they shall bring to you, but every small matter they shall judge. So it will be easier

(Span of Control, Judging-Evaluation-Appraisal; Limits of Decision–Making;

243

for you, and they will bear the burden with you. *(Management by Exception)*

23. If you will do this, and God so commands you, you will be able to endure the strain, and all these people also will go to their tents in peace. *(Explanation of Benefits)*

24. So Moses listened to and heeded the voice of his father–in–law, and did all that he had said. *(Listening, Implementation)*

25. Moses chose able men out of all Israel, and made them heads over the people, rulers of thousands, of hundreds, of fifties, and of tens. *(Choosing–Selecting, Assign Responsibility, Span of Control)*

26. And they judged the people at all times; the hard cases they brought to Moses, but every small matter they decided themselves. *(Judging–Evaluating, Management by Exception)*

27. Then Moses let his father–in–law depart, and he went his way into his own land.²

FACING THE IMPOSSIBLE

It is clear from this passage that Moses received much direction and encouragement for the great tasks which lay before him. On numerous occasions he demonstrated great qualities of leadership even though his career as a statesman actually did not begin until he was eighty. At the outset, after God had called him, the people did not understand his role in their midst (cf. Acts 7:23–25). They asked, "Who made you a ruler and a judge over us?" Note that he never lost sight of his calling in life which made it possible for him to emancipate his people from the oppression of Egypt. His steadfast heart and consuming drive to achieve made him an outstanding example for all potential Christian leaders.

Moses' experience at the Red Sea showed how well he had passed the test for would–be leaders when he faced an utterly impossible situation. Who would not have shrunk from the task? Before him lay the Red Sea; behind, the legions of Pharaoh. The people, faced with certain annihilation, were complaining bitterly. But Moses, with a resolute spirit, focused on God's promises and exclaimed to the people, "Fear not." They all had every reason to fear. And because of Moses' faithfulness, God was able to demonstrate His power through one man, and it became a rallying point to assist the Israelites in their march toward the Promised Land. Superb leadership and implicit faith had won the day!

Later in the wilderness, Moses had the right attitude when he knew it was time to train someone else for leadership. He was fearful of being a paternal leader and pleaded with God to give the Israelites a successor. Thus, he did not indulge in self–pity, knowing that he would not lead the people into the land of promise. He was more concerned about the right kind of direction and future leadership.

WELL SPOKEN OF

The New Testament provides a rather comprehensive commentary on the outstanding leadership qualities that Moses possessed, enabling him to succeed (Hebrews 11).

1. Faith (verse 24; "By faith Moses, when he was come to years, refused to be called the son of Pharaoh's daughter.")

2. Integrity (verse 25; "Choosing rather to suffer affliction with the people of God, than to enjoy the pleasures of sin for a season.")

3. Vision (verse 26; "Esteeming the reproach of Christ greater riches than the treasure in Egypt; for he had respect unto the recompence of the reward.")

4. Decisiveness (verse 27; "By faith he forsook Egypt, not fearing the wrath of the king; for he endured, as seeing him who is invisible.")

5. Obedience (verse 28; "Through faith he kept the passover, and the sprinkling of blood, lest he that destroyed the firstborn should touch them.")

6. Responsibility (verse 29; "By faith they passed through the Red Sea as by dry land; which the Egyptians assaying to do were drowned.")

It is no wonder that to this day, nearly all Jews — Orthodox, Reformed, and Conservative — consider Moses the greatest of all the prophets and leaders in the long history of Israel.

A STRONG SPIRITUAL LEADER

David, the second king of Israel, was a striking contrast to Saul, the first king. Whereas David was noble, generous, and admirable, Saul was ignoble and lacked most of the fine qualities one expects in leadership.

David came to the throne about 1000 B.C. and reigned for approximately forty years. He conducted many wars of conquest, laid the foundation of the Solomonic empire, and initiated a period of splendor and power for the Israelite nation that has never been equaled. Behind David's accomplishments was the blessing of God. The reasons for his success are not difficult to find.

When David was approached by the elders of Israel (2 Samuel 5:1–3) they recognized his many sterling qualities and strong traits of leadership.

The nation had been torn by civil war, and the people were weary of strife. The happiness and prosperity of Judah under David motivated the rest of the tribes to desire the administration of David's kingship.

But in addition, the relation of all the tribes to David was an inducement: "We are thy bone and thy flesh." They would have him know that their feelings toward him were warm and tender. David was no foreigner, unqualified by the Mosaic law to be king over the Lord's people (Deuteronomy 17:15).

The Israelite tribes through their representatives advanced another good reason for desiring David as their king. They referred to his former valuable service to the nation: "When Saul was king over us, thou wast he that leddest out and broughtest in Israel."

They were telling David that he was the real power in Saul's government. Saul was only a figurehead. It was David who led Israel against their enemies and returned with the spoils of victory. Who then was more qualified to fill the vacant throne?

The strongest reason of all that the Israelite tribes offered for wanting David to rule was that he was God's choice. "The Lord said to thee, Thou shalt feed my people Israel." Christian leaders serve better when they are convinced they are in the will of God, for then they know they will be equipped for their tasks by God's power.

As a leader, David possessed qualities which attracted others. The elders came to him (2 Samuel 5:3a); he did not go to them. He had ruled Judah well for seven years, and there was every reason to believe he would rule all the tribes as skillfully. David took a loyalty oath with the people to protect them as their judge in peace and their captain in war. They in turn obliged themselves to loyalty and obedience to David as their sovereign under God. Such a sacred pact and solemn inauguration inspired much confidence in the people.

Valiant conquest and wise administration were important elements in the glory of David's reign. His very first exploit after he became king over all Israel was to capture Jerusalem from the Jebusites and make it the capital of the twelve tribes. He showed his valor by storming and taking the city. He displayed his political and administrative sagacity as well when he made the city the capital. Jerusalem was not so centrally located as Shechem, but he must have thought through the decision well. Jerusalem was a natural fortress, and it had a high elevation on the central highland ridge in Palestine that made the city a delightfully cool spot through the torrid summer.

SECRETS TO DAVID'S SUCCESS

There were several secrets to the glory of David's leadership. First, wise diplomacy distinguished his reign (2 Samuel 5:11). The king's generosity and attractive traits of personality won him many allies. He knew how to placate enemies as well as win friends. He was lovable. He made friends readily, while Saul had the strange ability to alienate people. These traits made

David a successful diplomat. Those who did not respond to his generous nature he dealt with by force. But the wise, like Hiram of Tyre, cultivated his friendship and sent representatives to offer him favors.

Hiram I of Tyre (c. 969–936 B.C.) was a contemporary of both David and Solomon. He presided over a commercial kingdom with his capital in Tyre. His people dealt mainly in commerce and were skilled artisans, shipbuilders, and technicians. Hiram had access to the Lebanon forest of cedar in Syria and helped David with skilled labor and building materials for the construction of a palace and, doubtless, other major construction projects.

Thus we see David possessing the ability to reach out and strategically build his own empire. Leaders must have this quality—to treat and lead others in such a way that their contributions may be used to good advantage.

Second, David's recognition of the Lord God in all his blessings made his rule outstanding (2 Samuel 5:12). He did not take credit to himself for all his success and prosperity. He was not boastful and self–assuming, as are so many who become power hungry. He humbly attributed his rise to power to the Lord and saw Israel as the Lord's people and himself as the leader under God, responsible to the Lord for leadership. Christian leaders who would lead people in this manner need never worry about success. When they recognize their highest responsibility is to the Lord, it makes all the difference in the world.

Third, David constantly sought the Lord's blessing (2 Samuel 6:12–15). This is the occasion of the ark's being brought to Jerusalem. There had been an earlier attempt to get the ark but a Levite named Uzzah put out his hand to support the ark in defiance to a command of the law (Numbers 4:15).

The ark was left in the care of Obed–edom the Gittite. Those who watched the ark saw that the entire household of Obed–edom was blessed because of its presence in his house. They told David the news. When David heard it he proceeded to bring the ark into the city. He knew the absolute necessity of having God's blessing upon his work and administration. The Christian leader today needs no less desire for his life and work.

Fourth, as a leader David was not ashamed to be involved in spiritual exercises. He was able to acknowledge the need for sacrifice for sin (2 Samuel 6:13). This time every precaution was taken to insure the proper conduct of the ark to the city. He rectified the former mistake. He did not place the ark in a cart now, but ordered those whose business it was to carry it on their shoulders to do so.

At the outset, when the Levites "had gone six paces," David offered sacrifices of "oxen and fatlings" as atonement for former errors. When the Levites finished their task in safety, a thank offering of seven bullocks and seven rams was brought (1 Chronicles 15:26).

David was also unashamed to praise and thank the Lord (2 Samuel 6:14). He "danced before the Lord with all his might." He leaped for joy because his heart was so filled with gladness, and he was so taken up with the Lord's glory that he became almost oblivious of the fact that he was, after all, a dignified king. This more than anything else gives us insight into the heart of a man who loved the Lord so much that he did not concern himself about what people thought.

Lastly, David, as a strong leader, led his people in praising the Lord (2 Samuel 6:15). The great king thought it no disparagement to his dignity to lay aside his royal purple and put on the simple garb (a linen ephod) in order to minister better to his people. Such a garb was used in religious exercises by those who were not priests, as in the case of Samuel (1 Samuel 2:18).

The result was that the people brought the ark to Jerusalem with loud acclamation; they were demonstrative and joyful. They brought the ark to the city of David and put it in the place that the king had provided (cf. 1 Chronicles 15:1; 16:1). In the presence of the ark, God was in the midst of His people.

David illustrated clearly that the Christian leader, too, must be willing to exercise spiritual means to mold, stimulate, and continually challenge his colleagues and subordinates. In spiritual work we rather expect it; in the secular world many shy away from it. However, the principles abide: God will always bless those who highly regard Him, no matter what the endeavor.

THE GREAT BUILDER/LEADER

Another striking example of strong leadership is Nehemiah, who along with Ezra and Zerubbabel was instrumental in rebuilding Jerusalem's temple and wall. Talk about organization! He possessed many qualities prerequisite for leadership excellence. His character was beyond reproach; he was a praying man; he displayed great courage in the face of much opposition; he had a deep concern for his people exhibited by his insight, tact, impartiality, and decisiveness. Furthermore, he did not shirk responsibility given to him.

Nehemiah had a tremendous ability to encourage his countrymen and then express appreciation when it was in order. He quickly dealt with problems before they became too severe. Thus he was a strong leader who was able to inspire his people to great heights.

His organizational ability, disclosed by his skillful strategy and detailed plans, is a challenge to every would–be leader. I encourage you to read the entire Book of Nehemiah, looking for every leadership and management principle.

The books of Ezra and Nehemiah tell of the returning exiles from Babylon and how they were absorbed into the Jewish community at the time. The accounts are a grand illustration of the importance of planning. Ezra stated that in all, 42,360 exiles returned with 7,337 slaves and 200 singing men and women. The priests numbered 4,289, there were 74 Levites, 128 singers of the children of Asaph, 139 porters, and 392 Nethinim and children of Solomon's servants.

COMPLETE REORGANIZATION

At this time some of the social and religious traditions were changed, especially in music. During the days of reconstruction there were more singing guilds, and the temple ministry was reorganized. The musical staff was enlarged (1 Chronicles 6:33–37). Details are preserved of the organization of the Levites as well as the porters who were distributed among the different gates. The Levites were divided into various areas of responsibility such as work in the chambers and the treasuries (cf. 1 Chronicles 9:26–32; 23:24–32). These accounts were no doubt referring to the period of Nehemiah.

THREE MAJOR ACCOMPLISHMENTS

In summarizing this great leader, we can say that Nehemiah is known in Bible history as the great builder. In Nehemiah 3:1–6:16 three facts stand out. First, see how great he was as an administrator. He knew what he wanted to do, how it had to be done, and who was to do it. The what, how, and who are tremendously important. They spell the difference between success and failure. Nehemiah had a clear objective or goal, a sound technique, and a good enlistment program. His function as an administrator included the ability to *analyze*.

Second, he also succeeded in a program of total mobilization after he determined the plan. Everyone in and about Jerusalem was involved, from the high priest and his fellow priests to the goldsmith and the merchants (Nehemiah 3:1–31). The two rulers of Jerusalem as well as the common citizens were involved. At first some nobles did not feel it was proper for them to do such work, but apparently they changed their minds (cf. 3:5; 4:14). Thus Nehemiah mobilized the entire population, revealing his ability to *deputize* and *delegate*.

Third we see how Nehemiah achieved perfect coordination. In Nehemiah 3 it is almost tedious to read the phrase "next unto him [or them]." It appears over a dozen times, and "after him" another dozen or more times. Every man had his work and his place. Such perfect coordination enabled the wall to be finished in record time. We clearly see Nehemiah's ability to *supervise*.

Indeed, Nehemiah stands forever as a model for all would–be leaders who aspire to the heights of success, because he organized the whole nation and fulfilled his role as leader.

GOD ORDAINS PEOPLE TO LEAD

The ancient Wisdom Literature of the Israelites, such as Psalms and Proverbs, addresses itself a great deal to leadership principles. One of the Proverbs says that the hand of the diligent shall rule. The *Living Bible* reads, "Work hard and become a leader" (Proverbs 12:24). A true leader will use his imagination to improve his work and anticipate the next task.

That God ordains people to serve is clear from Psalm 75:6,7: "Promotion cometh neither from the east, nor from the west, nor from the south. But God . . . putteth down one, and setteth up another."

The Bible constantly discloses the fact that God searches for people whom He can count on as leaders. Note the following examples:

1. 1 Samuel 13:14: "The Lord hath sought him a man after his own heart."

2. Jeremiah 4:25: "I beheld, and lo, there was no man."

3. Jeremiah 5:1: "Run ye to and fro through the streets of Jerusalem, and see . . . if ye can find a man. . . that executeth judgment, that seeketh the truth; and I will pardon it."

God's plea for stable and effective leadership is probably best epitomized by the prophet Ezekiel, who said, "I sought for a man . . . that should . . . stand in the gap" (Ezekiel 22:30).

The five styles of leadership: What is most effective—and when?

23

Styles of Leadership

The great American entrepreneur John D. Rockefeller stated, "I will pay more for the ability to deal with people than any other ability under the sun." According to a report by the American Management Association, an overwhelming majority of the two hundred managers who participated in a survey agreed that the most important single skill of an executive is his ability to get along with people. In the survey, management rated this ability more vital than intelligence, decisiveness, knowledge, or job skills.

Leadership style, by definition, is the way a leader carries out his functions and how he is perceived by those he attempts to lead.

The more a leader adapts his style of leadership behavior to meet the particular situation and the needs of his followers, the more effective he becomes in reaching personal and organizational goals.

The concept of leadership behavior questions the existence of a "best" style of leadership; it is a matter not of the best style, but of the most effective style for a particular situation. A number of leader–behavior styles may be effective or ineffective depending on the important elements of the situation, as we will note in this chapter.

Empirical studies tend to show that there is no normative (best) style of leadership. Successful leaders adapt their leader behavior to meet the needs of the group and the particular situation.

From student body president to President of the United States, from preschool teacher to college professor, leadership relates to every aspect of human endeavor. Everyone is interested in style as much as the person's philosophy or purpose in leadership. So the issue is more than academic—it is intensely practical.

YOUR STYLE SHOULD DEPEND ON THE SITUATION

The style of leadership depends upon several factors: the personality, the character or needs of the group to be supervised, and the immediate situation (which the German rationalists called the *Sitz in Leben*—"the seat in life," or life setting).

Whether we talk of government, business, or the church, moods or conditions at the time often dictate the kind of leader who emerges to meet the situational demands. Church history abounds with illustrations of people who became leaders because of an existing condition. Whenever the church found itself at a low ebb spiritually or morally, God raised up men like Athanasis, Tertullian, Augustine, Bernard of Clarivaux, Anselm, Luther, Calvin, Knox, Wesley.

In our day the success of Billy Graham is due at least in part to the pressures of modern life, the secularization of the church, and the impersonal philosophy of collectivism. Man is viewed as a machine to be controlled or manipulated. True to the authority of Scripture, Graham's message emphasizes God's continuing interest in the individual, thereby bringing meaning and purpose to the hungry and longing soul who searches for meaning and an adequate philosophy of life. The times determined his style.

The Bible provides a graphic illustration of styles, displaying the emergence of men who were uniquely fitted for the task of leadership. The effective leader must always consider the present existential consideration. This does not mean that a person must capitalize or be an opportunist to gain advantage over his confreres, but it does mean he must be alert to the needs people have, to their attitudes in face of crisis and decision, and to the best methodology for getting the best results for the most people possible. He must know the crucial point, the decisive moment for action. Solomon illustrated this point when he built the temple; he seized upon the opportunity and the need of the moment to unify the Israelites with a national purpose.

The existing condition usually cannot be manufactured — it does not emerge from a vacuum. A leader cannot create a condition; he has to keep in step with the times and make the best of the situation.

The Christian leader must also recognize his personality and gifts, the needs of the people, and the given condition. He cannot be driven by the thirst for power.

A leader who discerns the times is able to clarify and suggest the best course of action. He has flexibility, for should the existing conditions change, he is able to adjust and be equally effective. Many organizations lose ground or become less effective because their leadership is not imaginative or creative enough to keep up with the times. "We've always done it this way in the past, why change?" is the prevailing mood. Maintaining the status quo is lethal.

Not only must the situation dictate the best style, but also the challenge of the task. This means the leader must be in tune with himself—his character and personality structure and his motivational level. He has to know the style most comfortable for himself, and he must analyze the group for whom he is responsible. Do they know the goals? What is their past performance? Have we prepared them to accept delegated responsibility and authority?

It is important to distinguish between management and leadership. In essence, leadership is a broader concept than management. Management is thought of as a special kind of leadership in which the accomplishment of organizational goals is paramount. While leadership also involves working with and through people to accomplish goals, these are not necessarily organizational goals.

YOUR STYLE IS CRITICAL TO SUCCESS

Not long ago a report was submitted by the Northwest Friends churches which presented a study made of growth patterns of churches.[1] Sixty churches were studied, showing statistics for attendance, age, and average income of each. Also, questions were asked to disclose the attitudes and thinking of the various leaders.

Unsurprisingly the findings showed that different styles determined whether a church was static or growing. The leaders in the dynamic situations were characterized as positive, confident, cheerful, and goal–oriented. They always tried to involve as many people in the congregation as possible.

The static churches, on the other hand, had leaders with little vision and little creative imagination. Goal setting, the report said, is unquestionably the most important ingredient needed for growth. Leaders who are not visionary enough stifle church growth. Usually they are inflexible as well, without the ability to delegate work because they do not trust others.

This study can be a model for churches everywhere. Style is critical.

WHAT LEADERSHIP STYLES ARE THERE?

Because leadership style includes how a person functions or operates within the context of his group or organization, it is perhaps easiest to discuss the subject by describing the kind of situation that either results from or is appropriate to a particular style. My focus now is on those aspiring to it. It is, therefore, vital for them to examine their own methods of managing and/or leading people.

There may be as many different leadership styles as there

are types of people, but they fall into several main categories. The styles could also be thought of as methods of management. Much has been written on this subject. Contributions range from the "autocrat–bureaucrat–demand" grouping to the "managerial grid" based on a vertical coordinate of concern for people and a horizontal coordinate of concern for production.

Several modern views reject the idea that firm and tightly structured styles of leadership are effective. Rather, there are combinations of styles leaders use as required by the demands of the position, the composition of the personnel being led, the individual leader's personality, and the expectation of the company.

In *Managing Your Time* I briefly discuss five basic categories from which all the other combinations emanate:

(1) *Laissez–Faire:* No structure or supervision given; members set own goals and standards of performance; leader is "first among equals," without authority, a resource man;

(2) *Democratic–Participative:* Provides some structure and framework within which members still largely set own goals and standards; leader and advisor with minimum authority;

(3) *Manipulative–Inspirational:* Some structure, usually confused and ambiguous; goals set by management with little participation but employees' acceptance sought by hard sell;

(4) *Benevolent–Autocratic:* Activities of group largely structured; relatively close supervision; however, employees encouraged to make suggestions concerning their goals, working conditions, etc.;

(5) *Autocratic–Bureaucratic:* Activities of group totally and arbitrarily structured; participation by group in any context totally discouraged; supervision is authoritarian and autocratic; questioning of orders regarded as insubordinate.[2]

Laissez–Faire

Using this list as a guide, let us describe various types in more detail and look at them in terms of how the leader operates within the organization.

The laissez-faire kind of a leader gives minimum direction and provides maximum freedom for group decisions. He recedes into the background, allowing others to express themselves. He establishes rapport and remains silent until his specific direction or opinion is called for. His role is similar to the non-directive approach in psychological therapy. This view operates on the assumption that man himself and society contain remedial forces to allow a strong, healthy relationship between the leader and the group. This permits growth through group decision.

Actually we could say that this style is practically no leadership at all and allows everything to run its own course. The leader simply performs a maintenance function. For example, a pastor may act as a figurehead and concern himself only with his pulpit ministry while others are left to work out the details of how the church is to function.

This style lends itself best to those leaders who are away a lot or who have been temporarily put in charge.

Democratic–Participative

The democratic concept is a relatively new idea in world history. Previously, control was in the hands of one person or a distinct elite. But democracy describes a form of government or leadership where decisions are made for the people through representation. It follows that a leader carries out the needs of the group and helps to define more sharply their aspirations.

The emphasis is upon the group through participation of the collective. Policies become the group decision. The leader in this kind of structure is there to assist, suggest, and allow adequate communication to flow so the entire group is alerted to problems and so the people can resolve them.

This style is used by those who believe the way to motivate others is to involve them in decision making. This hopefully creates goal ownership and a feeling of shared purpose.

Studies involving thousands of supervisors at all levels have proved that leadership style in any organization is a major determinant of employee productivity. For example, the best records of performance are found where the primary attention of the leaders is on the human aspect of their subordinates; sharing concern for their problems, allowing them to help make decisions.

Certainly one way to accomplish a high level of production is by letting people do the job the way they want to as long as they accomplish the objective. This may mean letting them take time out from the monotony. They should also be made to feel they are something special and not just run–of–the–mill. If employees are kept from feeling put upon, they are far more apt to expend the needed effort to get the work completed on time.

By contrast, the less successful leader is one who probably has an interest in people but considers it a type of luxury. The attitude is, "I've just got to keep the pressure on for production sake, and when I get production up, then I can afford to take more time to show an interest in my people."

Studies made at many large corporations conclude that motivation is strongly related to the supervisory style of the immediate boss. This would be equally true in Christian organizations. People are people no matter where you find them. Strong supervisors stimulate motivation; weak supervisors inhibit it. Interviews with all kinds of people show that practically everyone prefers a developmental, people–oriented supervisor regardless of their own values or the style they themselves practice.

Some time ago an excellent article set forth the necessary qualities needed in groups if they are to be led by a free, democratic leader or administration:

> If the subordinates have relatively high needs for independence.
> If the subordinates have a readiness to assume responsibility for decision–making.
> If they have a relatively high tolerance for ambiguity.
> If they are interested in the problem and feel that it is important.
> If they have the necessary knowledge and experience to deal with the problem.
> If they have learned to expect to share in decision–

making.[3]

It must be recognized that every style has its own problems or limitations. The democratic approach cannot answer every situation. For example, when an impasse is reached and a stalemate lingers, possibly the only way out is to appoint a committee or give a responsible person the power to act and make a decision. This can often create the illusion that action was taken regardless of what the result may be, due to slow progress or the group's lacking adequate communication or education.

Another weakness of this style is that it can sink to the level of mediocrity because it is so easy to "pass the buck" and shirk responsibility. It is easy to fall prey to the attitude that "he'd rather be popular than be right." This style or emphasis can be effective only when there is a balance between allowing group participation on the one hand and being able to make solo decisions when they are necessary to save time.

Perhaps the greatest weakness of the democratic style is that in times of crisis there is usually much costly delay in action.

Benevolent–Autocratic

This style is characterized by the father–like concern the leader has for his people. We could also call this method the "paternalistic" style. The autocratic leader cannot get too close, but the paternal leader identifies closely with the group.

Here the desire is to keep everyone in the group satisfied and happy. It is assumed that if people feel good because of the paternal leader, the organization will function well.

Identification, however, tends to make the people in the group too dependent and weak. It can degenerate into mere admiration and pseudoworship. Also, when this kind of leader is removed from the scene, the organization flounders.

This "family" approach appeals because it creates the illusion of security and fellowship, but this is at the expense of efficiency and effectiveness. Discipline is hard to maintain, and coordination often suffers with this style.

Autocratic–Bureaucratic

The extreme of the democratic style is the "one rule" type of leadership. This is often found in Christian groups and organizations, because people tend to regard some as being led in this direction by the will of God. Many of our "Christian entrepreneur" types fall into this mode, and in recent years we have witnessed strong and effective ministries irreparably harmed because this kind of leader failed to recognize this as a leadership weakness and thus not delegate responsibilities or have colleagues share in them.

In business, this style is marked by a continual reference to organization rules and regulations, because it leans toward the authority of a person or system. The style assumes that people will not do anything unless told to, and the leader sees himself as being indispensable because he is "the only one who really knows what's going on" and alone can make decisions quickly.

The bureaucratic leader assumes that somehow difficulties can be ironed out if everyone will abide by the rules. As a diplomat he learns how to use the majority rule as a way to get people to perform.

I suppose the concentration of power in one man in historical examples grew out of the critical emergency of military campaigns. When victory was obtained, people were dazzled by the splendor of the achievement, and this easily led to despotism and totalitarianism.

The autocratic style can sometimes be misleading, especially when people are made to believe they have some say in the planning and future of an organization or government. This is illustrated best by the modern Marxist–Leninist movement, which falsely maintains the view that "power belongs to the people." Many of the Communist states are known as "People's Republics." After World War II, Germany was divided; East Germany became known as the German Democratic Republic. One West German official remarked that the new nation was not

German, nor was it democratic nor a republic, but a Soviet colony, ruled by the despots in Moscow. Millions of people in our day know the lie of Communist propaganda and the terror of autocratic rule. Mao Tse–tung more aptly describes such rule in his "Little Red Book": "Power only comes out of the barrel of a gun."

The leader using this style, whether in government, industry, or a Christian organization, answers to no one. He seldom hesitates, and he moves ahead independent of human feeling. He uses people and rides their aspirations to increase his authority. He often gets their consent for decisions, but this is done by manipulation, hiding the true facts, and through the means of control and threat.

There are times, perhaps, where this style provides strength and unity, but on the whole its weaknesses are most glaring.

One of Napoleon's generals allegedly said, "You can do everything with swords except sit on them." The autocratic style is 99 percent inflexible. There is no check and balance system to test weaknesses. The leader may point to the ultimate goal as being positive and beneficial to all. However, if the means to achieve that goal are cruel, harsh, tyrannical, and destructive, then the goal is no greater than the means.

The writer of Proverbs reminds us that people are important and to run roughshod over them is detrimental: "Without people a prince is ruined" (Proverbs 14:28, RSV). We have often heard of the statement made famous during the last century, "Power tends to corrupt; absolute power corrupts absolutely." It does so because people are made to be slaves and paupers as pawns in the hands of weak leaders who can rule only by force. Malice, intolerance, and suspicion are the fruits of this kind of style because resentment issues from feelings of injustice and corrupted power.

One has only to read the Book of Nehemiah to discover the importance of people at work. The leaders in rebuilding the temple and city walls never lost sight of the total goal and overall picture, and they knew they could not do it all. They were able to keep this in focus by using all the people as well as experts who were trained to do specific jobs (cf. 2 Chronicles 2:14ff.).

The bureaucratic leader is narrow, an extremist. He is often fanatical because he thinks provincially, exclusive of other groups. He is often ethnically bigoted. This kind of person has strong convictions, but more often than not he cannot accept those in other groups because he has a "party spirit" and sees them as beneath himself or his group.

His intense dedication tends to make this kind of leader glory in adversity and gives him a martyr complex. But his loyalty to just one group cannot enhance the efficiency of the group for very long.

The style of the autocratic–bureaucratic leader is fraught with weaknesses. Historian Arnold Toynbee stated that the rise and fall of societies has one–to–one correlation with the type of leadership exerted. He reasons that where leaders control by force, that society ceases to grow.

We tend in our society today, because it is an age of specialization, erroneously to equate an expert with authority. But we must be careful. One may become a leader in his own field and achieve; yet, since we are hero worshipers, there is an inherent danger. Frequently, a person who has a Ph.D degree is consulted on matters in fields foreign to his training or expertise; he is often considered an expert in all fields! The truth of the matter is, the higher a person goes in education, often the greater his limitations become. The "expert" does not qualify in unrelated fields any more than another person. In these alien fields he may tend to view all things from his own often limited perspective and can be as mistaken as anyone else regardless of his educational level.

Some writers on leadership have felt that concern for task, work, or ministry tends to be represented by authoritarian leader behavior, while a concern for relationships is represented by democratic leader behavior. This thinking has been popular because it is generally agreed that a leader influences his followers by either of two ways: (1) he can tell his followers what to do and how to do it, or (2) he can share his leadership responsibilities with his followers by involving them in the planning and execution of the task. The former is the traditional authoritarian style that emphasizes task concerns; the latter is the less directive, democratic style that stresses concern for human relationships.

The differences in the two styles are based on the assumptions the leader makes about the source of his authority and about human nature. The authoritarian style often assumes that the leader's power is derived from the position he occupies and that man is innately lazy and unreliable (Theory X); the democratic style assumes that the leader's power is granted by the group he is to lead and that men can be basically self-directed and creative at work if properly motivated (Theory Y). (The concept of theory X and theory Y was first proposed by Douglas MacGregor in his book, *The Human Side of Enterprise* [New York: McGraw-Hill, 1960].) Consequently, in the authoritarian style, practically all policies are determined by the leader, while in the democratic style, policies are open for group discussion and decision.

Leaders whose behavior is observed to be relatively authoritarian tend to be task–oriented and use their power to influence their followers. Leaders whose behavior appears to be relatively democratic tend to be group–oriented and thus give their followers considerable freedom in their work. Often this continuum is extended beyond democratic leader behavior to include the laissez–faire style. This style is, as indicated, very permissive. Few policies or procedures are established; everyone is left on his own; none attempts to influence anyone else. A wretched state indeed!

A good leader will be alert constantly for experts who can consult and render advice on specific matters. He will gain the essentials to get the best results. It is good to remember the economic principle of the division of labor; the leader who tries to do it all is doomed to failure.

Another great drawback of this autocratic–bureaucratic style is that it stifles creative action and discourages innovation and any strong inclination toward change. This kind of leader feels threatened by change initiated by others. Thus he usually supports what is conventional. He cannot even support what is middle ground, because for the most part he can accept only extremes like good–bad or black–white. It is hard for him to accept compromise.

This person often has a personality defect. His ego is so weak that he has to identify with the strong or tough. Because he cannot really accept himself, he has little feeling for others. He is like the playground bully who has to raise a front to defend against his weakness, which he dares not disclose.

The authoritarian often is known to have grown up in a home or in circumstances in which he was constantly put down by a rigid authority figure. He was not given the right to express himself or his feelings—he counted for little. Without proper parental guidance in gentleness, kindness, and words of encouragement and compliments for achievement, he never learned to feel good about himself. In adult life, he expresses this deprivation to others usually without even knowing it.

Finally, there is a vast difference between leading and commanding. The latter seldom gets results from people working in association. Contrast the two attitudes by the following true illustrations.

A supervisor with a surveying firm once said he never listens to personal problems or complaints from his men. If they don't obey they simply are fired—no questions asked—and a new person is hired. Obviously that firm is not highly successful.

A manager in a large canning company has a vastly different approach. "When we hire people, we are looking for people who want a permanent relationship. We want people who are looking for a career who will be happy with us and we with them. And we spend a lot of money and time building a good foundation for that person, hoping to secure a strong common interest. Especially do we want our foremen to express our company's good will to all so everyone will feel a part of the company." This attitude properly characterizes real leadership.

Persons with a command attitude make untenable assumptions — especially the idea that organizations can be "bossed" into survival. The trouble is that commanders direct organizations, but misdirect people because they do not minister to the whole person. They are oblivious to people, because they tend also to believe that their firm exists solely to fulfill the purpose it is specifically organized to carry out. This is a death warrant, since it does not allow for personal responses even though the overall objective of the firm is acceptable. The attitude that "we're only in business to make money" is very likely to produce many bad decisions, because it is not people–oriented.

In the spiritual realm, the parallel would be a church that did nothing but have a Sunday morning worship service. Such a church lacks the insight to see that its chief function beside the worship of God is helping fellow Christians relate to each other. Most people consider this kind of church too austere to join.

The commander, then, always puts the welfare of his organization above that of the people. The true leader strives to make the two one–and–the–same thing. So commanders direct — and leaders guide and develop individuals so that through the group they may better share in shaping their own destiny.

The true leader organizes effort and gives his people a good feeling about what they are doing. There is no intimidation to get people to work; he knows how to keep morale high. Without him there is little zeal or eagerness on the part of people to do something that may even be important. But enthusiasm and effective mobilization of group efforts are called out and sustained by a good leader. Without him it rarely appears.

At World Vision International, my colleague Edward Dayton and I edited a monthly four–page publication, "Christian Leadership Letter." The following material from one of our letters brings the subject of style into sharp focus.

WHICH STYLE IS BEST?

Leaders are different, but so are followers! Which is another way of saying that some situations demand one style of leader, while others demand a different one. Leaders are different. Organizations are different. At any given time the leadership needs of an organization may vary from another time. Since organizations have difficulty continually changing their leaders, it follows that those leaders will need *different styles at different times.* The appropriate style depends a great deal on the *task of the organization,* the *phase of life of the organization,* and the *needs of the moment.*

What are some examples of how the *task of the organization* affects leadership style? A fire department cannot perform without at least some autocratic leadership. When the time comes for the organization to perform, to do what it was designed to do, autocratic leadership is a must. There is no time to sit down and discuss how to attack the fire. One trained person has to decide for the group, and the group must abide by his decision. Later there may be a free discussion on which way will be best next time.

On the other hand, a medical group might best be operated with a permissive style.

An autocratic style may even be needed in a Christian organization. In times of crisis, such as the evacuation of mission personnel or the need to reduce costs radically, the leader often must act unilaterally.

Organizations go through *different phases.* During periods of rapid growth and expansion, autocratic leadership may work very well. For example, the founder of a new Christian organization or the founding pastor of a church is often a figure with charisma who knows intuitively what is to be done and how to do it. Since the vision is his, he is best able to impart it to others without discussion. But during periods of slow growth or consolidation, the organization needs to be much more reflective to become more efficient; participative leadership may be in order. Both considerations need to be tempered by the needs of the moment. Using autocratic leadership may work well for fire fighting (either real or figurative), but it will probably be less than successful in dealing with a personal problem. An emergency in the medical group may demand that someone assume (autocratic) leadership.

FITTING STYLE TO ORGANIZATION

It follows that ideally a leader should have differing styles. He should be a man for all seasons, shifting from the permissiveness of summer to the demands of winter.

On the other side, the organization needs to adopt a *strategy for effectiveness,* taking into account its needs and its "product." Most voluntary groups and nonprofit organizations are founded on a common vision and shared goals. They have a strategy of *seeking success* (reaching their goals). When the organization is young, the founder can depend on his strength of vision to attract others who share his goals. However, as the organization is successful, other means of maintaining a common vision will be needed.

If the leadership style is not modified to include participative sharing of goals, too often the organization will adopt the strategy of *avoiding failure.* When the organization reaches a size at which an autocratic style will no longer work, the leader who is unable to change to a participative style may be forced (perhaps unknowingly) to adopt a laissez–faire approach. Meanwhile, the second level of leadership (now forced to run the organization) is most likely to adopt a bureaucratic style.

WHERE ARE YOU?

What is your leadership style? A cursory examination of some management literature will help you discover this. Hopefully you will discover that you have exercised different styles of leadership at different times. Do you have evidence that you *can* change your style as needed? Or, as you think of the decisions made in the past six months, do you discover that they were always made the same way (by you, by others, or by the bureaucracy)?

268

WHERE IS YOUR ORGANIZATION?

What kind of leadership does your organization need at this time? What is its task? What phase of organizational growth are you in? What are different needs of this moment? Analyze this with help from your board, leadership team, and members. Are different styles of leadership needed for different aspects of organizational life?

Where Do You Go From Here?

Review your calendar of meetings for the past two weeks. What happened in those meetings? Did you go to meetings just to announce your own decision (autocratic style)? Did you go to the meeting with a hidden agenda expecting only to get concurrence of the group (autocratic style)? Did you go to the meeting expecting to work with the group to arrive at a decision (participative style)? Did you go expecting to sit back and let others worry about the problem (permissive style)? Or, did you go intending to use the parliamentary procedures to make sure that the ship stayed on an even keel (bureaucratic style)? Perhaps you didn't go at all (laissez–faire)!

If you discovered that you handled each meeting in the same way, you are probably locked into one style and should consider knowingly attempting to modify your style as a function of the situation you are in. By deciding before the meeting the style you will adopt, you will gain the advantage of being able to observe the response of the other members of the meeting.

If you have been limiting yourself to one style, sudden changes will often result in confusion in others. It may be necessary for you to spell out clearly the ground rules as to how you expect the decision–making process to work.

FLEXIBILITY IS THE KEY

Each style has its advantages and weaknesses and must be evaluated against actual life situations, because there are no hard, fast lines drawn between different styles. Frequently a democratic leader will be paternalistic or autocratic, depending upon the situation.

The well–adjusted mature leader has an advantage because he need not be bound to a single method. He can be flexible without being threatened. Such a wise leader will think carefully about the kind of style best suited for the situation. He will first want to consider his subordinates and how he can best relate to them. Then he can more accurately determine the best style.

In closing, it might be helpful to indicate what we consider the vitally important levels of priority for Christian leadership. The order is crucial.

First—and obvious—is our commitment to the person of God in Christ. This comes through the personal encounter we have had with the Son of God, the Lord Jesus Christ.

The second commitment, far too often confused with the third, is our commitment to the body of Christ. As the apostle Paul said, "Our body has many parts" and we do belong to each other. The measure of our Christian performance is our love for each other. The apostle John exclaimed, "Behold how they love one another!" This is the hallmark of the Christian. Paul had little to say about evangelism in his epistles, but much to say about our love relationship within the body.

Third is a commitment to the work of Christ or the task that God has given to us. The New Testament calls us to be willing to sacrifice houses, families, and lands to follow Christ. But the *work* of Christ will flow forth from the relationships that exist. Too often I have heard Christian leaders say, "What I do as a leader is so important that I must sacrifice my family." If by this he or she means that the work of Christ is more important than the body of Christ, we must protest that this is not the view of the New Testament. The Bible considers our relationship more important than our accomplishment. God will get His work done! He does not demand that we accomplish great things; He demands that we strive for excellence in our relationships.

In our judgment, effective Christian leadership arises from a proper recognition of priorities.

The seven ingredients that lead to superior results.

24

The Pursuit of Excellence

How does Christian leadership differ from that of the secular business world?

Christian leadership is distinctive basically in its motivation, the why of its actions. When everything extraneous is cut away, it seems to come to this: Christian leadership is motivated by love and given over to service. It is leadership that has been subjected to the control of our Lord Jesus Christ and His example. In the best Christian leaders are expressed to the utmost all the attributes of selfless dedication, courage, decisiveness, and persuasiveness that mark great leadership.

DEMANDS THE VERY BEST

No one should be more earnest than the Christian leader in the pursuit of excellence. I have the feeling that often this is a missing note in our evangelical Christian milieu. You will agree with me that God's work demands from us the very best that we have to offer Him but too often we come to an assignment poorly prepared, or we continue to live with sloppy work habits, or we are careless in the handling of our various Christian responsibilities.

Sometime ago when I was in South Africa, I was a guest one day at the home of Gary Player, the professional champion golfer. He is an exemplary Christian, having come to a knowledge of Christ through the ministry of Billy Graham. In his home near Johannesburg, South Africa, there hangs a plaque that says, "God loathes mediocrity. He says, 'If you're going to keep company with me, don't embarrass me.'"

I like that. God does loathe mediocrity. James W. Gardner, former Secretary of Health, Education and Welfare for the United States, wrote a book with the simple title *Excellence* and the subtitle "Can We Be Equal and Excellent Too?" (New York: Harper and Row, 1961). In this work, Gardner attacked the idea that it is almost undemocratic to excel at something over our fellow men. Striving for excellence in one's work, whatever it may be, is not only the Christian's duty but a basic form of his Christian witness. It might be called a foundation of nonverbal communication that supports the verbal.

Far too often in our thinking we don't mind excellence if we can shift responsibility for it onto the Lord. We say, "The Lord has really blessed this ministry, hasn't He?" or "The Lord really gave her great gifts, didn't He?" We become suspicious if someone is praised directly for doing an outstanding job. But we should recognize the human potential and give credit for a job well done.

Melvin Lorentzen has written, "Today we must stress excellence over against mediocrity done in the name of Christ. We must determine to put our best into the arts so that when we sing a hymn about Jesus and His love, when we erect a building for the worship of God, when we stage a play about the soul's pilgrimage, we will not repel men but attract them to God."

Part of our problem in wrestling with Christian excellence may be a defective theology. Many of us find it very difficult to live with the biblical truth that God is doing it all and the parallel truth that man has been given responsibility to act, yet God has commanded him to act to accomplish His will. In believing that God is in control of everything, we have a tendency to play down man's role.

272

STANDARDS ARE NECESSARY

We cannot escape it—in Christian service we are called to excellence. We are called to set standards of excellence for ourselves and all men. In his Philippian letter, the apostle Paul said much about this; indeed, it is a treatise on excellence. In Philippians 1:10, Paul prays that we "may approve things that are excellent." God, as He speaks to us in the Scriptures, never allows the good to be the enemy of the best; "Be perfect [complete] as I am" is the standard.

But where do we begin? Does the call to excellence mean excellence in everything?

In Colossians 3:17 we are admonished, "Whatever you do, in word or deed, do everything in the name of the Lord Jesus, giving thanks to God the Father through him" (RSV). No higher standard can be found. The wise man, Solomon, said in Ecclesiastes 9:10, "Whatever your hand finds to do, do it with your might" (RSV). I contend that nothing less than the pursuit of excellence can possibly please God, yet most of us must admit that there are large segments of our lives in which this is not our experience.

EXCELLENCE PROVIDES A MEASURE

Excellence assumes a standard or measuring stick. Conversely, anything less than excellent Christian leadership is inferior. It assumes there is a way of doing or being something that is less than the best or less than what it could be or less than worthwhile.

This kind of leadership gives us something to aim for—a mark that will render success because God wills it.

EXCELLENCE NEEDS A GOAL

Second, excellence assumes an objective. It demands that we think beyond dreams and concepts; that we think of reality in terms of what can be, what ought to be. We recognize that we will not achieve excellence in everything, but we must pursue it continually.

Christian leadership demands vision. The Christian leader must have both foresight and insight. When he does, he will be able to envision the end result of the policies or methods he advocates. The great missionary pioneers were without exception men of vision: they had the capacity to look beyond the present.

Vision includes optimism and hope. No pessimist ever became a great leader. The pessimist sees a difficulty in every opportunity; the optimist sees an opportunity in every difficulty.

Vision imparts venturesomeness—the willingness to take fresh steps of faith when there is a seeming void beneath.

The Christian leader will be a man of wisdom. He will have heavenly discernment. Knowledge is gained by study, but when the Holy Spirit fills a man, He imparts the wisdom to use and apply that knowledge correctly.

Paul's prayer in Colossians 1:9 was "that you may be filled with the knowledge of His will in all spiritual wisdom and understanding." That is needed for setting goals and achieving them.

EXCELLENCE DEMANDS PRIORITIES

Excellence also assumes priorities. It not only involves doing one thing well, but is concerned with a choice between goals. Some goals are less worthy and less honoring to God than others, goals that fall short of what God expects us to be. It is not that there is only one right way for all people, but rather that the potential for excellence in some areas lies with all people. We are called to live lives whereby we achieve excellence in at least one aspect.

Some time ago a young man came to our World Vision headquarters from a seminary in Indiana. He related in our chapel service that one of his professors recommended that each student become a specialist on one book of the Bible. The seminarian said, "I accepted that challenge, and I determined in my life that I was going to be a specialist in the Book of Ephesians." Of course, that morning he preached from the Epistle to the

274

Ephesians. He had given himself to a thorough study of the book.

Each of us is called to exercise at least one gift to its full capacity. Have you decided what your gift or gifts are? Some have great gifts but perhaps have been too lazy to unwrap them.

A vital priority is discipline. This quality is a part of the fruit of the Spirit (Galatians 5:22). Only the disciplined person will rise to his highest powers. The leader is able to lead others only because he has conquered himself and in turn been conquered by Christ.

Many people think that if they manage themselves, they will be closed in on all sides, as if in a box — bound up and unable to do anything. That image should be dispelled. Managing yourself is being a good steward of your time, talent, and treasure. It is giving proper priority to things so that the most will be accomplished for the Lord.

Self-management is so important because a lack of discipline may prevent completion of the task. The Christian is accountable for his living. A study of the parable of the talents is helpful (Matthew 25:14–30): poor performance yields little reward; God expects us to invest fruitfully what He gives us.

Self-discipline does not box us in. Rather, it frees us to accomplish more with what God has given us. It also provides us with a better feeling about ourselves because of our accomplishments.

A Christian leader is a follower! This is another priority, for the art of leadership is acquired, not only by attending lectures, reading books, or earning degrees, but by first watching another person lead in action, responding to the inspiration of this person, and emulating his example.

The Savior's challenging invitation still rings out: "Follow me and I will make you to become fishers of men" (Mark 1:17, RSV). As men and women heed that invitation and follow Jesus, they begin to qualify for spiritual leadership.

This principle is also seen in the life of Paul, that dynamic leader of the early church. "I beseech you, be ye followers of me" (1 Corinthians 4:16). To another church he wrote, "Brethren, be followers together of me, and mark them which walk so as ye have us for an example . . . Those things, which ye have both learned, and received, and heard, and seen in me, do: and the God of peace shall be with you" (Philippians 3:17; 4:9). But the apostle never asked that he be uncritically followed, as though he were a flawless pattern. "Be followers of me," he urged. But immediately he laid down an all–important limitation: "as I also am of Christ" (1 Corinthians 11:1). It is a matter of following men insofar as they follow Christ.

Thus leaders have to follow, remembering "them which have the rule over you" (cf. Hebrews 13:7).

EXCELLENCE IS A PROCESS

Fourth, excellence is a process. It is more a process than an achievement. Life is a process; management is a process. We can look at an individual or an event at a certain time in history and pronounce it excellent, but it is continually pressing on that marks the person dedicated to excellence.

Paul said, "Brethren, I do not consider that I have made it on my own; but one thing I do, forgetting what lies behind and straining forward to what lies ahead, I press on toward the goal for the prize of the upward call of God in Christ Jesus" (Philippians 3:13,14, RSV).

No leader should live under the delusion that he has finally arrived. Excellence requires constant evaluation, correction, and improvement. The process, therefore, never ends.

EXCELLENCE IS A STYLE OF LIFE

This leads us to a fifth definition of Christian excellence. Excellence has to do with the style of life. Socrates said, "Know thyself." Marcus Aurelius centuries later said, "Control thyself." Ancient sages said, "Give thyself." Jesus said, "Deny thyself."

What is your style? What can it be? We are all different. Some men are ahead of their time, some behind. Some few are musical geniuses, most are not. Some few are great preachers.

276

Some are conceivers of grand ideas. Others are men concerned with detail. But for each of us, excellence demands that we be true to the best that God has placed within us. Our style of life must be marked by excellence. The Christian leader can adopt nothing less as his goal.

Each must develop his own style, but I see several characteristics as absolutely necessary for the Christian leader's style of life. The truly Christian leader must have the indispensable quality that sets him apart from all others—his life is given over to the Holy Spirit. All the other qualifications are desirable; this one is indispensable!

It stands clear in the Book of Acts that the leaders who significantly influenced the Christian movement were men filled with the Holy Spirit. This has been true in all the history of the church.

To be filled with the Spirit is to be controlled by the Spirit—intellect, emotions, will, and body. All become available to Him for achieving the purposes of God. Such an experience is essential for successful leadership. Remember that each of us is as full of the Spirit as we really want to be!

The committed Christian leader's will has been remolded, and he is determined to do God's will at all costs. His will is not passive, but immediately active. He is able to look into the total situation and make a decision—the right one and at the right time. Someone has said that the Christian leader has a will totally willing at all times to will the will of God.

The Spirit–filled life also includes self–effacement, but not self–advertisement. In God's scale of values, humility stands very high. He has always loved to advance the humble. Such a quality should be ever growing.

Paul acknowledged in 1 Corinthians 15:9, "I am the least of the apostles, that am not meet to be called an apostle." Another time he was able to boast, "I have fought a good fight" (2 Timothy 4:7). So there is the right kind of pride, but it is always tempered by humility.

Anger is also needed by Christian leaders. This sounds

like a strange qualification for leadership, but it is a quality present in the life of the Lord Jesus Himself. Mark 3:5 says, "[Jesus] looked around at them with anger" (RSV). Righteous wrath is no less noble than love, since they coexist in God.

Great leaders who have turned the tide in days of national and spiritual decline were men who could get angry at the injustices and abuses that dishonored God and enslaved men. It was righteous anger against the heartless slave traders that caused William Wilberforce to move heaven and earth for the emancipation of slaves.

Further, a Christian leader's style of life should include a willingness or ability to be interested in people. The spiritual leader will have a love for men and a large capacity for friendship. In the Bible, David's fearless command of men sprang from the friendships he had formed; these men of renown were ready to die for him. Paul's letters glow with the warmth of appreciation and personal affection for his fellow workers. Personal friendliness will accomplish much more than prolonged and even successful arguments. The Christian leader must have a genuine respect, a liking for people; if he does, he will look for and major on their good points.

Good human relations is so vital to success. "Plans get you into things," Will Rogers once said, "but you've got to work your way out." But how do you "work your way out"—with people, and through people? One observer of the business scene refers to people as "the portals through which men pass into positions of power and leadership."

Experience repeatedly bears out that you must really care about people to get them to perform at their best level. Industrial psychologists say, "Get to know your people." The more you do, the more they will care about you. Get to know their problems, needs, home life, special interests. If my own experience is any indicator, you will grow to enjoy this.

Misunderstandings remain misunderstandings only as long as they are kept covered. Out in the open they quickly dissolve.

We need some soul–searching on this matter: Are your people genuinely convinced that you are personally interested in their well–being? Do you judge people on their ability and performance rather than on personality traits? How often do you visit with your people on an informal, person–to–person basis? Do your people get a real "charge" out of working with your group? What kind of a friend are you to your people? Do you encourage questions when you communicate—giving the other fellow an opportunity to express his views and reactions? Do your people know how they stand with you?

A lack of interest or an unfriendly attitude are obstacles in the path of achievement and lead to all kinds of personnel problems. You mean one thing; your subordinate thinks you mean another. You fail to explain a newly announced policy; your subordinate applies his own twisted interpretation. You spell out an assignment, but you don't define the measure of authority that goes with it.

A truly friendly approach involves being aware of others, seeing how vitally important it is to get through to your people, and helping them get through to you.

EXCELLENCE REQUIRES MOTIVATION

Sixth, excellence requires genuine, internal motivation. Excellence is not easily achieved: the first 80 percent may be rather easily achieved; the next 15 percent comes much harder; only the highly motivated person on occasion reaches 100 percent.

George Allen, former coach of the Washington Redskins football team, is often quoted as saying, "I demand of my men that they give 110 percent." What is he saying? That on that football field he insists his men give far more than they think they are capable of giving. We have far too many leaders who settle for 70, 80, or 90 percent. When the motivation level is low, achievement is down as well. There is always a one–to–one correlation in this respect.

Motivation will keep a person from going under when the

going gets tough. A good friend, Bob Cook, worked closely with me for many years. Bob said to me one day, when I was wrestling with some problems and was about ready to give up, "Look, Ted, it's always too soon to quit!"

I don't know where you are in life, in leadership, in your role. I don't know your frustrations, your burdens, and the mountains you've got to climb. But I know this: It's too soon to quit! Never give up. Hang in there. This is part of the pursuit of excellence. There is joy in such achievement that is an all–too–rare experience for most of us. One of the mysteries of living is that what is easily achieved brings little inner satisfaction. We need to think big. Motivation guarantees the stamina to conquer and achieve.

EXCELLENCE REQUIRES ACCOUNTABILITY

Finally, all Christian leaders must be accountable to someone else. I believe every leader needs three kinds of people with whom to identify:

(1) *A Timothy.* Paul had his Timothy. You ought to have someone you're giving yourself away to. I have such a colleague; I've had several of them in my career and thank God for them.

(2) *A Barnabas*—son of encouragement. Paul during his career had Barnabas. I have a Barnabas, a retired seminary professor. I go to him continually with problems, situations, difficulties. He prays with me; he counsels with me; he holds my confidence. He's Barnabas to me. Every leader needs someone he can share with intimately.

(3) *A peer group.* For about eight years I have been meeting five other men for breakfast in a restaurant. It is not a prayer meeting, but we pray together. It is not a Bible study, but we refer to the Word of God together. We share with each other. Because of our schedules, seldom are all six of us there, but always three or four, sometimes five. We are accountable to each other, for we uphold each other in many ways. I am accountable to them; they are accountable to me. A leader needs to be a part of a peer group. Generally, we as Christian leaders have missed

this accountability factor. In recent years, the national headlines of well-known ministers caught in the web of sin have underscored the need for each man and woman to be accountable to a carefully selected, honest and Christ–centered peer group.

LET'S SUMMARIZE . . .

We need to commit ourselves to the pursuit of excellence. Bear in mind these seven marks of excellence: Excellence is a *measurement,* and that assumes a standard of *accountability.* Excellence demands a *goal,* and that is the willingness to take risks for others. Excellence demands *priorities,* and that's telling other people or yourself what comes first in your life. Excellence is a *process,* and that means continually checking progress. Excellence has to do with *style,* and that means deciding what gifts God has given you and how to use them. Excellence has to do with *motivation,* and that's what it's all about.

How do we respond to the goal of excellence? Sort out your goals. You can't do everything; you can't be everything; and that's all right. Of those goals you believe are essential, decide which have top priority; do those with excellence. Decide who you are, what you are; decide how God made you and what He wants you to be; do that with excellence. It was said of Jesus, "Behold, He does all things well." Let's strive for that, because the God of the average is not the God of the Bible.

As we aspire to Christian excellence, keep it in perspective. Some things are more clearly excellent than others. Paul in Philippians 1:9 says we will be able to tell how we can judge what is excellent: "It is my prayer that your love may abound more and more, with knowledge and all discernment, so that you may approve what is *excellent* and may be pure and blameless for the day of Christ, filled with the fruits of righteousness which comes through Jesus Christ, to the glory and praise of God" (RSV).

Note the purpose: the glory and praise of God. Note the goal: excellence. Note the steps to the goal: knowledge and discernment, thoroughly mixed together with abounding love. The result will be the fruits of righteousness.

James Russell Lowell expressed this well:

> Life is a leaf of paper white
> Whereon each one of us may write
> His word or two, and then comes night.
>
> Greatly begin! though thou have time
> But for a line, be that sublime—
> Not failure, but low aim, is a crime.

A PARTING WORD

Amidst all leadership problems we need to understand and know that we have a great God. One day many years ago, I was wrestling with a seemingly insurmountable problem: Forty people were depending on me to get them to India for a conference for thousands of young people. We were to leave the day after Christmas, but on Christmas Eve we were informed that the Indian government had canceled our visas.

In the struggle of my heart and mind, I prayed and opened my Bible. Out of the First Epistle of John flashed a message like a neon light—just a three-word statement: "God is greater!" I prayed, "Lord, if You ever had a chance to prove that You're greater than governments and the power of men, You have an awfully good chance right now!" He wrought the miracle, and the problem was resolved. "God is greater!"

Christian leaders must ever press on to the high calling and the tasks that lie ahead. Too many of us are willing to settle for "good enough" instead of "good," and "good" instead of "excellent." Let each of us, in the responsibilities God has given us, fulfill them in such a manner that people will never equate mediocrity with the things of God.

> Press on. Nothing can take the place of persistence. Talent will not. Nothing is more common than unsuccessful men with talent. Genius will not. Unrewarded genius is almost a proverb. Education will not. The world is full of educated derelicts. Persistence and determination alone are overwhelmingly powerful.
>
> Calvin Coolidge

One challenge we face is finding the middle ground between self-confidence and complete dependence on God.

25

The Least of All Saints

(The next three chapters were written by Ted Engstrom's colleague, Ed Dayton, in The Christian Leader's 60–Second Management Guide, which the two co–authored.)

The Bible is replete with people who are put in positions of leadership and management. Their styles cover a wide range. Nehemiah the Planner, Peter the Impetuous, Jethro the Management Consultant, Lydia the House Church Leader. And Paul the Mover. Some of these men and women are more difficult to figure out than others. Some are well organized. Others seem to be anything but organized.

What a mixture Paul appears to be! The "least of all saints" who believed he was imminently qualified. On the one hand, able to bear all things. On the other hand, realizing that he had yet to achieve the goal that lay before him. Great sense of strength. Great sense of weakness.

For many Christian leaders Paul's experience magnifies and models our own. Those of us who have been called to roles of leadership often say to ourselves, "Why did God do all this for me? Why is He giving me these privileges of leadership?" There is a suspicion that not only are we really not deserving of God's grace, but we're really not that good at what we are doing anyway. Which man was the real Paul—the one who led so confidently or the one who was deeply uncertain of his abilities?

Most Christian leaders who have been tested in their role of leadership would probably answer, both! There is the agony and the ecstasy.

It is in the nature of humbleness that those who possess it are not supposed to know it.

True humbleness accepts this mixture of failure and success. It sees that all is a result of God's grace. It balances Paul's "Surely you have heard about the administration of God's grace" that is linked with its subject, "given to me" and to its object "for you" (Ephesians 3:2).

Much of our difficulty in finding a middle ground between self-confidence and complete dependence is the result of the beginning point in our thinking. For most Westerners, this beginning point is the individual—me. When we read Paul, we naturally relate to him as an individual because that's the way we think about the world. This can cause some real difficulties which another perspective may help.

As Christians we get a better perspective on this apparent tension between what we are and what we are called to be if we first understand that leadership is a role and, second, that Christian leadership can only be defined within the context of the body of Christ.

Modern management theorists have attempted to isolate particular attitudes of a leader. There have been many theories of leadership. But in the final analysis, all have failed to produce a coherent system. About the only definition that one can settle on is that "a leader is a person who has followers in a given situation." It is the context that establishes the leader, both the context of the situation and the context of those who are willing and able to follow his or her leadership.

The search for the common attributes of a Christian

leader also fails. When we use the famous leaders of the Old and New Testament, we often overlook the fact that each of these men and women were called to a particular task for a particular group of people. Abraham was called to be the father of a nation. Moses was called to lead God's people, as were Joshua, the judges and the kings that followed. In the New Testament, it is also the people of God, the body of Christ, who are the object of God's concern.

OVER-EMPHASIS ON THE INDIVIDUAL

In our modern Western world, we tend to over-emphasize the individual. We fail to see that we have been called out of our individualism into a community. All of our Western culture and training emphasizes the individual. It is the individual who is educated. It is the individual whose task is described by a job description. It is the individual who has to be motivated. Indeed, the immediate reaction of every Westerner to these sentences is something like, "Well, how else can you think about people if you don't think about individuals?" The fact that other societies, other cultures, may have an entirely different concept of "self" is quite beyond our comprehension.

It is part of our Christian understanding that none of us can be any more than God cares to make of us. We talk about being "clay in the potter's hand." But this seems to run contrary to the need to assert ourselves as leaders. We need a different understanding of leadership, one which doesn't lose the mystery of the sovereignty of God, or His grace, but which places us as Christian leaders in a more biblical perspective.

If leadership is only defined by followers and by the situation, then the reason that leaders are "great" must be because they had great followers and the right situation. In other words, to use biblical language, they were fitted together with others who permitted them to play the role that God had assigned to them.

It is also apparent that none of us are leaders all of the time. Change the followers, change the context, and as far as anyone can tell, we are just another joint or ligament in this marvelous thing called the body of Christ.

In practice this is how most Christian organizations look for new leaders—at least the individuals who will head the local church as pastor or the Christian organization as director or president. We use such language as "called" to a pastorate. We tell one another that "God has provided the person we are seeking." Our job is to "discover" him or her.

But for others further back in the management/leadership stream, we may be less specific and more inclined not to emphasize spiritual gifts. Sometimes we even overlook the question of whether the followers of this new leader are fitted to him or her!

Thus we institutionalize the manager/leader role and divorce it both from the context of the organization and from the part of the body to which this person is to be joined.

THREE IMPORTANT QUESTIONS

As leaders we are the least of all saints. We are also people whom God has set apart for a special situation. Whether that will still be our place and calling next week, next month or next year, is not in our hands (nor should it be).

Consequently, the first question is not whether I am a good Christian leader, but whether I have been called and fitted into this organization for God's purpose at this time.

Second, if there is honor due, it is not to me, but to the role, the function, that I have been assigned to carry. (The same Bible that says honor your leaders also says that we, as the body of Christ, are to give honor to those parts least deserving of it.)

Last, there is the mystery and wonder of why God has chosen to pour out His grace upon us. What a privilege it is to be the men and women whom He intends to use for His purpose in this day.

Use these benchmarks to gauge your progress in getting on top of the load.

26

How to Get Control of Your Job

The Christian leader works with people power, money, experience, information and time. A failure in any one of these five areas will usually keep you from performing adequately. The most important of these is time. People power can be engaged, resources can be raised, experience can be developed, and information can be gained, but time is not a variable.

To be good managers, we must gain control of our position.

FIVE SIGNS YOU'RE GAINING CONTROL

The first sign of control is when we sense that we are *managing our time*. In relation to your job, there are four kinds of time: superior time (demanded by your leaders); peer time (required by those with whom you work); subordinate time (demanded by those who work for you); and discretionary time (that remaining in your direct control). When you sense you have a balance between these, this is the first sign that you are beginning to get control.

The second sign that you are gaining control is when you feel you have *adequate information* to carry out your task. Note that we say adequate. You will never have enough information. But somewhere in the process you should make some projections as to the kind of information you will need and set some goals for obtaining it. Then you will be prepared to accomplish your task.

The third sign of control will be when you sense you have *enough experience* to carry out your task. Again, you'll never have enough experience. But there comes a time when you begin to believe that you now have been through enough of the routines and processes to manage the job.

The fourth sign that you are gaining control is you feel you have *enough resources* to carry out your job. And finally, the fifth sign of control is that you have *enough people power*. In many ways these last two are the easiest to acquire. However, if they do not exist in the organization, you will never be able to carry out your job effectively, so treat them with respect.

THE REAL EVIDENCE

These are just signs. The real evidence is that you are achieving goals. Of course, this assumes that in the very beginning of the job you staked out some goals for yourself and for the organization, and made them known to the degree that they needed to be advertised. You must frequently evaluate your progress and see to it that some of these goals are now past events; they have been accomplished; you are moving on to new things.

At the end of your first month sit down and write some goals for the next three, six and twelve months. These should be goals for yourself, for the part of the organization which you control, and for the total organization. Use these goals to review with your superiors, peers and subordinates what you believe needs to be done. Have them tell you what they believe needs to be done.

One very good question you could use when talking to old–timers in the organization is, "What questions should I have asked you that I haven't asked?" Many times this will elicit all kinds of information that you may not be able to get in other ways.

It is essential that you keep *communicating* upward, sideward, and downward. One of the most overlooked causes of failure is that people don't communicate. They don't tell one another where they are and where they hope to go. This is particularly true in the Christian organization, where volunteerism is often a major component. Many times the expectations of the members are greatly different from the expectations of the leadership. Effective communication can help prevent people from being offended or exploited.

Something *very* basic to good management is a *job description*. If you don't have one, you should! If the organization has never used job descriptions, then do the best you can to write your own and review it with those to whom you report.

MAKE AN ORGANIZATIONAL CHART

If the organization does not have an *organizational chart,* make one. Who reports to you? To whom do you report? Such a chart is useful to show lines of authority and responsibility.

One way to picture the situation at a deeper level is to first ask the question, "To whom do I *relate*?" Then take a blank piece of paper. Draw a circle in the middle. Put your name in that circle. Now draw circles for individuals who are grouped all around you. Draw an arrow from you to them if you need to relate to them and an arrow from them to you if they need to relate to you. Many times both are needed.

Take this same diagram and draw a dotted line to all the people and groups who are dependent on you for their "success." Do the same for yourself: On whom are you dependent for success? Use whatever definition you want of "success." This will help you realize that in order for an organization to operate effectively, the people must be aware that they have an impact on others.

Finally, let me remind you of the most basic contribution to successful management—prayer. Don't let Christian piety become so routine that you fail to base your *life* on it! Let's remember Christ's own words, "Apart from me you can do nothing."

*How 10 minutes of planning can make your
day go better.*

27

*How to Make It
Through the Day*

It's everybody's problem, isn't it? For one person it is a question of "How am I ever going to get all of this done?" For another person it is wondering how to handle the constant interruptions. For a smaller number of people it is a question of just not enjoying the work that is in front of them.

There is a sign over one of the desks in our office that says "A Clean Desk Is the Sign of a Disturbed Mind." You don't have to finish everything every day. It is interesting how people differ in this respect. Some people worry if there is nothing left to do at the end of the day. They wonder if they are going to have a job the next day. Other people feel like they are real failures if they haven't accomplished everything. They go home worrying about the next day's work. Find out what your style is. But remember, if we are part of an organization that is doing an effective and God–honoring task, there will probably always be more work to do.

Make a list of the different things you are supposed to do and the goals you are trying to accomplish. Divide the list up into: (1) things that have to be done every day; (2) things that have to be done every few days; (3) things that have to be done once a week; and (4) things that have to be done less often. Make a rough estimate of how long it will take for each of these to be accomplished. Then you can determine when to begin each and when you should complete it.

It might also be a good idea to prioritize these different kinds of tasks. Which ones are very important, of high value? Assign these an "A." Which are somewhat important, of medium value? Assign these a "B." That means that all the rest are not so important, of low value. Give them a "C." Share your priorities with your boss to make sure you are in agreement.

There probably is no more powerful organizer and tension reliever than the "Things–to–Do" list. If you spend the first ten to fifteen minutes of each day (or it could be fifteen minutes in the evening) writing down all the things that have to be done in the day ahead, this helps to reduce your anxiety and eliminate the question, "What do I have to do next?" Some people like to prioritize such a list using the ABC technique so they can start with the most important things first. Other people take the activities from the list and fit them into their standard day.

If you really want to get organized, a daily planning sheet is essential. Ones that list all of your appointments, as well as record your "things–to–do" under categories such as mail, telephone calls (with numbers), things to plan, things to acquire and so forth, are extremely helpful. You can buy some of these at stationery stores or design your own.

Every so often we get the reverse of an interruption. We suddenly "run out of work." We haven't really, of course. What has actually happened is that we have not planned far enough ahead. We haven't planned for just this kind of a situation. If you know, for instance, that it is worth your while to do filing when you have an extra twenty minutes, then use those gaps for filing. If there is reading that you need to do but it's not immediately important, keep it handy in a reading file near your desk. How about a prayer list? Maybe the Lord gave you that gap so you could address Him specifically about some of the needs you have, or that others have, or just to praise Him.

If you have a diverse work schedule, particularly if you

are getting work from different quarters, you will find it very useful to keep a work log. It does not have to be complicated. Note the item, the name of the item, the person it is for, when you received it, when you promised it, when you began work on it and when you completed it. This will not only help you keep track of things, but it's a great asset if you're sick or unable to come in to the office and other people need to find out what needs to be done.

Experience also contributes to being a good manager. And the way to get experience is to decide how to do your task better, and begin. Now.

Everyday opportunities for modeling Christian excellence and integrity.

28

Being a Good Role Model

By role modeling, we mean a conscious effort on the part of the leader to speak and act in such a way that when the leader is emulated by followers, their actions will be recognized as being appropriate and honoring to Christ.

In what follows, we will not say much about the how–to of role modeling. Rather, we will draw attention to the many ways and situations in which we can model.

• Nothing seems to impress followers more than the way their leaders respond to situations, particularly emergencies. If our followers see a Spirit–filled calmness in the way we meet unforeseen and difficult crises, they will be inclined to follow our example. If our regular response to others' mistakes is, "How stupid can they be!" we should not be surprised if they respond the same way in front of their subordinates.

Remaining calm usually means not responding too quickly. If you are one of those people who tend to overrespond to situations, maybe the old adage about counting to ten will help you have enough time to look at the situation objectively.

• Leaders usually talk too much. If we dominate conversations or find it necessary to take the lead in solving every problem that a group has, if we are quick to define solutions for other people rather than let them find their own, others will follow our lead.

We are all impressed by the leader who seems to have the time and ability to hear others out. But it takes practice, as does learning to respond calmly. Everyone wants to believe that they have been heard. If they perceive that their leader has understood the situation and given their viewpoints careful consideration, then they are more likely to accept it if their leader chooses a solution different from their own.

● The function of leadership is to lead. To lead, one must understand what needs to be done and how to do it. Leaders must believe it is in their own best interest and the interest of the organization to get it done. We can model an attitude which indicates, "Do it my way!" or, we can model an attitude which says, "Here is one way to do it which I have found useful. Do you see a better way?" "Do it my way!" not only prevents others from jointly owning the goal and having a sense of contribution to the solution, it also does not teach people how to solve problems.

The function of leadership is to lead, not bark orders. There are prerogatives and perquisites that go with the role of leadership, but if they are carried as though they were the right of the individual rather than of the position, then leadership will be modeled as a role of personal power rather than a role of servanthood.

Christians claim that we are part of the "body of Christ." We claim that within this body each part has a special function. Indeed, in a way quite opposite to the world's wisdom, we claim that "those parts that we think aren't worth very much are the ones that we treat with greater care" and that "God Himself had put the body together in such a way as to give greater honor to those parts that need it" (1 Corinthians 12:24, TEV).

● If you say something, does your staff believe it will really happen, or is there always a question of whether you really mean it? Integrity is not just a matter of keeping our own personal commitments; it involves an understanding that people can trust us to attempt what we say we will do. Promises should not be lightly given unless we want them to be lightly received. An organization that has a reputation of dealing with its staff in an equitable and honorable manner must be led by an individual who personally keeps his or her word to other individuals and to the group.

● Do people see you as someone who is "transparent" and ready to share your own feelings? Let us not ask others to expose themselves to a degree that we are not willing to expose ourselves. If you want others to take responsibility for their mistakes, then you need to take responsibility for your own.

Sometimes this means that we need to go out of our way to point out when a problem really was our fault. At other times in a Christian organization we may need to actually confess our own breech of Christian conduct.

● The other side of the coin from openness is the need to keep confidences. There is a delicate balance between that which should be shared with everyone and that which should not be disclosed because it was told to you in private. In this dimension we model not only by what we say to our subordinates but what they hear us say to our peers. Also, be careful not to use prayer requests as an opportunity to share confidential information.

● Meetings—how much time we spend in them, and how little time we often take to prepare for them! Meetings are inevitable in any organization and exist for a multitude of reasons. Some need to be prepared for with much more care and concern than others. There don't seem to be any courses on how to be a good meeting *participant*. The way people will learn how to participate in a meeting is by following your lead as they watch you participate.

● What does your office or work area arrangement say about you? Is your office arranged so that visitors must always confront you behind a desk? Are there other chairs or a table to which you can move to make people feel welcome? What does the office layout or the pictures and other decor model for your staff?

• It almost seems as though some of us were born with a "gift of criticism." It may be the result of extremely high ideals or a lack of self–assurance. But the leader who uses the organization as a scapegoat when things go wrong will usually find that his or her staff shows the same disdain. The leader can manifest this in many ways. The most obvious one is at the time of informing people about their salary: "I'm sorry, but *they* said we don't have enough money." Sometimes it happens when your department, committee or part of the organization fails to get a hoped–for responsibility: "I fought for it, but *they* wouldn't hear of it."

• We live in a world of "push and shove," a world that is filled each day with another crisis. The "work" can become all consuming. Individual needs can be put aside unthinkingly. We model: "The work is important, but you (the worker) are not." It is true that in every organization except the local church, the purpose of the organization must come before the needs of the individual. However, this seldom occurs. Most of the time people are more important than the work that we are trying to get done at that particular moment. We need to take the time to affirm others (and let ourselves be affirmed).

We model concern for others in our day–to–day efforts to take time for them and to help with their personal concerns. Modeling can also be demonstrated by the small, thoughtful gestures of remembering birthdays and anniversaries, following up on casual prayer requests, appreciating a special effort, and even complimenting a new hairdo!

It's not easy to ascertain what we are modeling to our staff. Many times they will not be aware themselves. If they have not had experience in several organizations or with several leaders, they may assume the way we act is the way every organization and every leader acts. How do you discover what they really believe about you as their leader?

One way that has been found effective is to ask each member of the staff to give you an anonymous piece of paper that has a sentence on it which begins, "I wish Ed would . . . " Then gather the staff together and read out loud the things that they "wished" about you and attempt to address the issues as best as you can. Criticism can at times be startling and very threatening, but by giving your staff an opportunity to comment on your performance you are already beginning to model a willingness to listen, to change, and to become the kind of leader that God wants you to become.

The Gift of Administration

Some leaders were "born" that way; others were simply *given the nod* and had little choice but to become "leaders." (And then there are always those who couldn't make the meeting and simply got elected!)

In these chapters taken from *Your Gift of Administration* Ted Engstrom addresses both leadership groups.

If you are an "elected" leader, it is my hope that your position will be strengthened as you work through the many skills Ted suggests are required for you to become more proficient in your role.

For the "born" leader, the suggestions and direction Ted offers will hopefully enhance the further development of your already-existing talents.

The Spirit of God is generous with His gifts. May your gift of administration serve you and His kingdom well.

Do you have the gift of administration? These guidelines will help you decide.

29

The Personal Gift of Administration

That there is a valid distinction between *gift* and *office* in the sphere of leadership is nowhere as apparent as in the pages of Holy Scripture.

Perhaps the New Testament passage that most readily comes to mind to illustrate the distinction is in Acts 6, when the apostles in Jerusalem needed special assistants to better care for the church. These assistants were selected to become functionaries to serve Christ's church, and that day their role became an *office* which has lasted in the church for nearly two–thousand years – the diaconate.

But who was selected to fill the role? Just any available saint with a heart for serving God and some free time? Not exactly, though a warm heart and accessible time would certainly figure in. What the apostles wanted and the people agreed to was men who were *gifted*, spiritually equipped to handle the task at hand. Note the biblical text:

> Then the twelve summoned the multitude of the disciples and said, "It is not desirable that we should leave the word of God and serve tables. Therefore, brethren, seek out from among you seven men of good reputation, full of the Holy Spirit and wisdom, whom we may appoint over this business; but we will give oursel-

ves continually to prayer and to the ministry of the word."

And the saying pleased the whole multitude. And they chose Stephen, a man full of faith and the Holy Spirit, and Philip, Prochorus, Nicanor, Timon, Parmenas, and Nicolas, a proselyte from Antioch, whom they set before the apostles; and when they had prayed, they laid hands on them (Acts 6:2–6).

An ideal combination, is it not? Gifted men to take official duty.

Was the work these seven deacons were chosen to do something new? No. In fact, this is what made their work an office. Prior to this account in Acts 6, who had done this work? The men who laid hands on them to inaugurate their new roles—the apostles. And where did the apostles receive the authority to pass the work of care and function on to these who became deacons? From our Lord Jesus Christ, who called and gifted them by the Holy Spirit under the oversight of His Heavenly Father.

PRODUCTIVITY INCREASED

And did this new arrangement prove productive? Without question. When these gifted men took office and began to function and to serve, "the word of God spread, and the number of the disciples multiplied greatly in Jerusalem, and a great many of the priests were obedient to the faith" (Acts 6:7).

We see a similar unfolding of events in Acts 13. Here, Paul and Barnabas were placed in office.

As they ministered to the Lord and fasted, the Holy Spirit said, "Now separate to Me Barnabas and Saul for the work to which I have called them." Then, having fasted and prayed, and laid hands on them, they sent them away (Acts 13:2–3).

At first glance, one would assume they began that day to minister together. But that is not the case, for they had already worked together in Antioch for an entire year (see Acts 11:25–26). Later this discipling duo took care of the relief work in Judea, (see verse 29) finally returning to Antioch from Jerusalem at the close of Acts 12. It was only after this proven ministry had occurred that Paul and Barnabas were officially set apart in Antioch to begin the first of what have come to be called the three missionary journeys of the apostle Paul. Gifted men again took office.

This gift–office distinction is seen even more often in the Old Testament. When God called Moses to lead the nation of Israel out of Egypt, He also chose an able assistant in Aaron. Look at the dramatic use of both gift and office as God establishes an authoritative relationship between these two kinsmen in Exodus 4:15–16. God said:

> Now you [Moses] shall speak to him [Aaron] and put the words in his mouth. And I will be with your mouth and with his mouth, and I will teach you what you shall do [gift]. So he shall be your spokesman to the people. And he himself shall be as a mouth for you, and you shall be to him as God [office].

In Numbers 11, when Moses needed help in overseeing this same nation in the wilderness, God instructed him to select seventy elders to assist him. And look at the Lord's promise in verse 17 for the anointing of these men to serve in the official new capacity. "I will take of the Spirit that is upon you and will put the same upon them [gift]; and they shall bear the burden of the people with you, that you may not bear it yourself alone [office]."

Add to these the appointment of such Old Testament administrators as Joshua, Gideon, David, and Samuel; and the tradition of leadership as both charismatic and official becomes even clearer. Thus it is against this background that the whole matter of spiritual gifts takes on an even richer significance.

In Romans the way gifts relate to office becomes especially clear. Paul writes, "And all members have not the same *office*: So we, being many, are one body in Christ, and every one members one of another. Having then *gifts* differing according to the grace that is given to us, [let us use them]" (12:4–6 KJV, italics added).

GIVEN BY GOD

The word "gifts" here derives from the Greek word *chara*, meaning "joy" or "gladness." Therefore it may be said that a person's *charisma* is a special gift given him by God and that the intrinsic nature of the gift is joy. It follows, then, that when a person discovers his or her gift, the awareness of that gift—and the use of it—brings enthusiastic joy and gladness.

These gifts of grace are special to each recipient. And since they are given, we don't have to strive to possess them. They come from the Holy Spirit who lives within us.

My understanding of Saint Paul in Romans 12:4–6 is that every person possesses at least one of these *charismata,* and that God's gifts work in connection with each Christian's personality— also given to him by God. I call these charismata "personal gifts." There are seven such personal gifts listed in this twelfth chapter of Romans: prophecy, ministry, teaching, exhorting, giving, ruling, and mercy.

For the purposes of this book, I will be addressing primarily the sixth one, described by translators as "he that ruleth" (KJV) or "he who leads." It is this personal gift which designates administrative ability. It derives from the Greek word *proistemi* and is variously translated "rules," "takes the lead," "to be over," "to superintend," "preside over." I call this particular charisma "the gift of administration."

THE GIFT OF ADMINISTRATION

Exactly what is this gift? Is this gift differentiated from other personal gifts? Must one possess the gift of administration in order to be able to function as an administrator?

I would not be completely honest if I did not tell you at the outset that I—and those who know me best—believe my primary spiritual gift is that of administration. I am literally motivated to administer, and I have spent the bulk of my adult life serving in leadership roles.

As a young man I went to work for the Zondervan Publishing House as an editor, because I had a great desire to be a writer and publisher. Although I went to Zondervan believing that my duties would basically consist of writing, I soon found myself serving in an administrative position as production and advertising manager, as well as editor. As I developed schedules, worked with printers, produced books (and got them out on time), I began to be aware of God's call on my life to the *function* of administration.

A dozen years later Dr. Bob Cook and Dr. Torrey Johnson were moved by the Spirit of God to invite me to come to Youth for Christ International as an administrator. I served as that organization's president for a number of years, then the leaders of World Vision (moved—I believe—by the Spirit of God) called me to serve in that organization at first as its executive vice–president. And here I have happily remained since.

As I stated earlier, the word used in the Greek text to designate the gift of administration is *proistemi*. In its usage in Romans 12:8 the word is not referring to an administrative post or office, but to an *administrative gift or motivation*. Or, stated another way, the one who has this gift has an administrative approach to situations.

LIVING IN AN "ADMINISTRATIVE MODE"

As one endowed with the personal gift of administration, I approach practically every situation I face in the "administrative mode." This fact is evident to my wife, to my children, and to my colleagues. Dorothy, my wife, would be the first to testify that I become very restless on the inside if my calendar is not in order. I seek to have my schedule and plans organized well in advance if I am to be at ease. I do not operate well in disorder. I am built to know where things stand, to whom I report, for whom I am responsible, and where we are going down the line.

This is not to say there will be no changes in my plans, for these always occur; but I must have a continuing sense of direction for my days—time allocated and scheduled for worshiping God, for being with Dorothy, for handling work loads, for attempting creative activities. And Dorothy knows from my calendar how our schedules fit and mesh together. This, for me, is operating in an "administrative mode" in a personal sense. And living this way is indescribably satisfying.

This does not mean, by the way, that everyone should aim for the same degree of order, long–range planning, and hierarchical sensitivity that I do. To misquote the apostle Paul, "All are not administrators, are they?"

But it is precisely at this point that we learn from each

other and we complement one another in the Body of Christ. For example, I have a constant need to spend time around what I call the "prophetic types," those who think, preach, and serve radically and creatively. Such people stretch me and help me see my schedule as a guideline instead of a prison. Similarly, prophetic people need people like me. Administrative types help keep prophetic types on track, ordered, scheduled; so their creativity does not become confusion.

A DESIRE FOR ACTIVE LEADERSHIP

There are many people who would give their eye teeth if they never had to lead. Being anonymous and free from endless responsibility is, for them, the next thing to heaven. Others, if they cannot be there in the thick of things—molding, shaping, directing—are of all men most miserable. Is theirs a play for power, a self-aggrandized appetite to rule and lord it over others? Not at all, or at least not for those motivated and energized by the Holy Spirit. For just as an artist wants to paint, a musician wants to play, or an evangelist wants to preach, so one with the gift of administration wants to give active leadership.

I have not always known, by the way, that my personal gift is that of administration. Many of my friends and colleagues have discussed this matter with me. Frequently I have been asked, "But, Ted, how do you *know* that your gift is administration?"

These questioners often seem to listen impatiently to my explanation before interjecting the question they really want to ask: "How can I determine whether I possess the personal gift of administration?"

Such a determination is not a simple, one–two–three question–and–answer routine, especially for an older adult. The reason is that so many of us have developed skills and abilities that—unless examined carefully—can conceal or mask the true nature of one's spiritual gifts.

It is important to realize that we do not determine our gifts all by ourselves. Just as a physician would not do exploratory surgery on himself, so we do not determine by ourselves what our gifts and callings are. In the biblical instances cited earlier in this chapter, we see several factors that help us identify our gifts.

First, the Holy Spirit speaks to God's people. This is the "it seemed good to the Holy Spirit and to us" factor. God will speak to you and others who love Christ. If you are the only one you know who believes you are gifted to administer, beware! Just as it stains one's soul to hear an uncalled preacher preach, so it is equally unsatisfying to be led by an uncalled leader.

Second, if you are called and gifted to administer, you will not have to appoint yourself. Both your peers and those in authority over you will take note and at the proper time call you to serve.

Third, we have vivid examples of godly leaders in the Scriptures who were models of administration. Become familiar with them. Mirror your strengths and weaknesses against their performance.

Finally, there should be an *amen* in your own heart as to your gift of administration. Note I said "should be." There will be exceptions even here. Occasionally some will be drafted to lead who have great difficulty believing they can do it. Moses was such a one. Saint Paul may have been another.

A prominent fourth century bishop, Saint Gregory of Nazianzus, one of the greatest theologians on the Holy Spirit the church has ever known, was most strikingly in this category. He was ordained a pastor against his will. Later, after he steadfastly refused the pleas of his fellow Christians to become their bishop, the people literally brought him before the episcopate for consecration. While he never doubted God, he questioned his own gifts. Nevertheless, he had a brilliant career defending orthodox Christianity against the heretics. But he did insist on taking "early retirement," stepping down in his early fifties to return to seclusion, study, and prayer.

A VARIETY OF SERVICE

Certainly not all who administer do so in the same way. And not all who lead must specifically possess the gift of administration. Other gifts may also be effective in an administrative post.

George, one of my colleagues at World Vision, served in an administrative function as my assistant because he has well–developed leadership skills. While George's primary personal gift may appear at first to be that of administration, such is not the case. I have watched George operate; and while extremely effective, he approaches everything he does in a more nonadministrative manner than do I. The traits which the Scriptures associate with the gift of administration simply are not there. George approaches his daily tasks from the base of his personal gift of exhorting. By contrast, I insist on thorough planning and step–by–step organization of any project before I will proceed. Then, when the project is securely underway, I proceed straight ahead regardless of obstacles that would hinder the attainment of set goals.

George does things differently. He has learned to plan well, and usually does so. But he has a very strong aversion to pushing ahead to achieve the intended deadlines and goals if doing so will impinge upon the pride or feelings of his coworkers. Whereas I will often move ahead and soothe feelings as I go, George will tend to halt the project until the people he is working with are encouraged to continue.

I think you can see what I am illustrating in this thumbnail sketch of the two of us. I love and respect George. He loves and respects me. We have worked together harmoniously for years. We are both effective administrators. But we approach many things differently. And any administrator who approaches the task with a primary personal gift other than administration (say prophecy, ministry, serving, or teaching) will administer the responsibilities differently from one whose personal gift is administration.

TRAITS OF A GIFTED ADMINISTRATOR

Having discussed the sense of teamwork in the church determining the gifts of the Spirit, let us look at some commonly recognized traits of those possessing the gift of administration.

Dr. Hugh Ross, associate minister of evangelism for the Sierra Madre Congregational Church in Sierra Madre, California, leads numerous groups in understanding the gift of administration. He has compiled a representative list of attributes and the various ways of motivating a person who possesses this gift. Often a list of this nature appears as an appendix in a book. But I have found it so useful, I am using it here in the text, with his permission, because I believe that you will find it valuable as well.

Character Qualities and Personality Traits of Those Possessing the Personal Gift of Administration

1. Possesses an ability to integrate several ministries, people tasks, and/or projects toward the fulfillment of a long–range goal.

2. Is sensitive to future needs, particularly to future needs that are not being planned for by others.

3. Has an ability to visualize overall needs and to clarify long–range goals.

4. Has an ability to assist an individual Christian by designing and setting up a ministry that offers that Christian the greatest personal satisfaction because it makes the fullest use of the individual's talents, resources, and gifts.

5. Has an ability to put together individual Christians to form efficient, well–organized teams — teams on which the members work well together, divide their labor efficiently, and enjoy each other's company.

6. Has an ability to discuss the talents, resources, and spiritual gifts of individual Christians.

7. Has an ability to discern and unify available resources toward the fulfillment of a goal.

8. Tends to avoid involvement in anything for which he has no organizational responsibility. Furthermore, his tendency is to remain on the sidelines until the leaders in charge turn responsibility over to him.

9. Tends to assume responsibility if no structured leadership exists.

10. Desires to see that his time and the time of others is used efficiently.

11. Tends to insist on thorough planning and organization

before embarking on a new task or new ministry. Tends to avoid the develop–as–you–go type of ministries or projects. He wants things done right from the beginning.

12. Demonstrates a willingness to wait on a project or ministry until it is properly set up. Once a project is set up, however, he will push for maximum speed in accomplishing its goals.

13. Is strongly motivated to organize anything for which he is responsible.

14. Has an ability to make use of the resources available at the present time, not waiting for future resources to develop.

15. Is motivated to delegate, if at all possible.

16. Has an ability to know what can or cannot be delegated.

17. Is sensitive to recognize and to acknowledge other people's hidden achievements that have helped in reaching a goal.

18. Tends to put high priority on loyalty in selecting people for a team.

19. Tends to be neat and orderly in everything; home, appearance, job, other activities (even recreation), and projects.

20. Is reluctant to pay for organizational services, preferring to perform these himself. He prefers to make proposals rather than ask for bids. He wants to be his own contractor.

21. Tends to assign tasks or solve problems with his eyes on the future impact of his decisions and actions.

22. Is able and willing to endure reaction from others in order to accomplish an ultimate goal in a minimum amount of time. He recognizes that others are not as sensitive as he may be to the overall picture or to the importance of the goal.

23. Is strongly motivated to help others become more efficient in carrying out tasks.

24. Recognizes the importance of maintaining good records and of writing clear instructions. He sees that with these aids a task can be easily repeated in the future or in some different context.

25. Places a high premium on reliability and responsibility. He tends to react to people who do not follow through and help

with the cleanup or with the behind–the–scenes work.

26. Tends to avoid the limelight; however, he definitely enjoys the role of a strategic commander working behind the scenes, pushing pawns on the game board of life.

27. Tends to remain firm and steadfast, regardless of opposition, once he has determined that a particular goal is in God's will.

28. Believes strongly in the importance of keeping commitments even in adverse or difficult circumstances.

29. Appreciates initiative. He values people who can foresee problems and take action to prevent or correct them without having to get detailed instructions.

30. Demonstrates an ability to finalize difficult decisions, though he is very careful and deliberate to first examine all of the pertinent facts.

31. May appear to be a perfectionist because he insists on detailed planning and preparation.

32. May tend to overlook spiritual weaknesses and faults of key persons on the teams that he designs because he focuses almost solely on the personal talents, training, and spiritual gifts that will be useful for achieving a particular goal.

33. If problems exist in his organization, tends to handle them by readjusting the responsibilities and positions of individuals on the team in order to achieve more compatible working relationships (as opposed to first solving individuals' personal problems).

34. May tend to view people impersonally as resources available for helping him achieve goals. People working for him or with him may feel that they are being used.

35. May appear callous to those who misinterpret his willingness to endure reaction.

36. May appear insensitive to the weariness, schedules, and priorities of people on his team because of his strong desire to complete a given task as quickly as possible.

37. May appear lazy or skilled in avoiding work because of his ability and willingness to delegate responsibility.

38. May cause others on his team to feel that they are being misused if he fails to explain thoroughly enough the reasons why their tasks must be done within a certain timespan.

39. Is strongly motivated to look for and move on to a new challenge whenever a project comes to completion. If this motivation is highly exercised, he may get the reputation of being an empire builder.

40. Receives great fulfillment in seeing all the pieces of a project fitting together and in seeing others enjoying the finished product.

As you think back through this listing of forty traits of a gifted administrator, do you find they correlate generally with your own abilities and desires? Did you note the traits that promote negative feelings in others? If you have chafed under the leadership of another, does the list motivate you toward more tolerance and understanding?

If you are currently involved in active administration, you no doubt can see areas in which you need to concentrate on improving as you continue to serve. If you aspire to lead, take heart by being patient with God to establish you in His right time.

From my personal viewpoint, as one who is constantly seeking to learn to understand his personal gift, I can say the only greater joy than knowing and understanding what your gift is, is to find yourself functioning in the Body of Christ in an office or role that fits, because it is the one to which God has called you.

*How to stimulate fresh ideas and insights
in your organization.*

30

Thinking Creatively

Some weeks ago a friend of mine was taking his small daughter on a cruise to California's Catalina Island. It was one of our beautiful, clear southern California days. Suddenly the little girl exclaimed, "Daddy, I can look farther than my eyes can see!"

Think about that. "I can look farther than my eyes can see!" What a wonderfully perceptive child.

CREATIVE IMAGINATION

Too few administrators possess the ability to look any farther than their eyes can see. We might have had it once, as that child still does; but for too many administrators it has been stifled. Stifled in the petty routines of a regimented network of papers and projects and in the prejudices that develop in an organizational world. Yet if we are to be creative administrators – and effective innovators – we must release that dormant ability. We must again learn to look beyond the horizon.

Perhaps even more importantly, we must *want* to look beyond the horizon. For a great majority of administrators this is not easy, and for some it is exceptionally difficult. Most administrators desperately seek an order and pattern to life – one that will leave them with a feeling of constancy, not change. Consequently, they are not receptive to rearrangements. But our imagination should be one of our most cherished faculties, for it will enable every administrator to realize that God "is able to do exceedingly abundantly above all that we ask or think" (Ephesians 3:20).

The imagination of our colleagues should also be cherished, for it follows that in any organization the administrator can never be the sole source of innovation, no matter how great his genius. How, then, can he draw from his colleagues the wealth of their creative thinking except by stimulating their imaginations?

Creative imagination is that part of the mind which generates desires, thoughts, hopes, and dreams. Everything that has ever been achieved started first as an unseen spark in a creative imagination. "In the beginning God created . . . " God spoke into existence His imaginings. He created man in His own image and gave to mankind the gift of imagination so that we can also form, hold, and achieve images.

Then when Jesus came, He liberated man's imagination by telling him, "I assure you that the man who believes in Me will do the same things that I have done, yes, and he will do even greater things than these" (John 14:12, Phillips). As an administrator, you may inhibit the growth of your employee's imagination unless you dare to believe that what Jesus said is true.

The part of your mind that plays the greatest role in achievement is that part of your mind that imagines. We spend years developing the part of our mind that reasons, memorizes, and learns; but almost no time is given to developing the immense potential of our imagination. Yet the untapped power of our imagination is unlimited.

God created the human brain in two distinct parts, each having different functions. The left side of the brain is basically concerned with logic and speech—it thinks. The right side of the brain is related to intuition and creativity—it knows. It is visual in orientation. It is the right side of the brain that some of us tend to neglect.

An interesting experiment was done at Stanford University by Robert McKim, professor of design engineering. He created what he calls an "imaginarium," for the purpose of tapping the vast unknown riches of the mind's eye, because he was concerned about finding ways to expand his students' thinking about design problems. McKim's experiments led him to design his own version of a geodesic dome, which serves as a special environment where people can get away from noise and other distractions. "The person who learns to use his imagination flexibly," McKim explained, "sees creatively."

And this "seeing creatively" is a rich source of ideas and mental pictures that can be developed. A person's imagination reflects an ability to visualize something that has been neither seen nor experienced before. The creative act thrives in an environment of mutual stimulation, feedback, and constructive criticism—in a "community of creativity."

ADMINISTERING CREATIVITY

Every administrator must help provide a creative environment which will make certain that new ideas are brought forward, evaluated, and carried through. We must instill in our people the knowledge that we not only recognize the necessity of new ideas and experimentation, but that we actively encourage the unconventional solution to the conventional problem.

Now I know as well as the next person that the individual who attempts the new and the different, the one who seeks innovation, is likely to make some mistakes. But isn't it infinitely more desirable to assure a man of some reasonable measure of freedom in order to spark some fresh, imaginative thinking than to slap him down when he commits his first error—and perhaps stifle him forever?

Sometimes we forget how eager we were to try out our new ideas. All our people, I'm sure, have new ides, too. They're itching to take a crack at putting them into practice, to swim in a little deeper water and justify their membership on the team. Good. Give them the opportunity. They may come up with some harebrained ideas, some of them simply not workable. But when they do, don't dampen their creative ardor by telling them that they have made a mistake. Instead, advise them tactfully to try again and this time to

317

use a little different approach.

Administrators can help produce ideas by a conscious creative effort, and in this process, it pays to focus our aim. We should first make our target as clear as possible.

CREATIVITY AND RESEARCH

The process of research is to pull the problem apart into its separate components, a great many of which you already know about. When you get it pulled apart, you can work on the things you don't know. The importance of problem definition was stressed by Albert Einstein in these words: "The formulation of a problem is often far more essential than its solution, which may be merely a matter of mathematical or experimental skill."

Let me give you an illustration of how consciously searching for a solution to a problem can spell out opportunity. A few years ago manufacturers were unable to give consumers as good a fit in shirts as in collars. The trouble was that collars had always been washed after being made, but if shirts were washed that way, they would lose some of their fine finish—would look as though they were not new. So, on his own initiative, Sanford Cluett decided to find a way to shrink cloth without putting it in water.

At the cotton mills Mr. Cluett saw that in the finishing process the cloth was always pulled through the various processes of bleaching and mercurization. In fact, the cloth was sewn together into strips as long as fourteen miles and then pulled through the mill. This naturally distorted the fabric. He discovered that if this distortion was taken out, most of the shrinkage would be eliminated. So he built a machine which automatically restored the cloth to equilibrium—in other words, pushed the stretch back. Although the "Sanforized" process was designed for cotton goods only, its success has led to other related creations, thus typifying how we can reach out for targets by grasping problems, and how one target can create another.

When my former World Vision colleague, Bobb Biehl, was seeking to find ways of helping us raise funds for our World Hunger program, he began an experiment with various means of involving entire families in this ministry. He had no thought of anything apart from a direct mail presentation; but as he worked away at his drawing board, he began to think of the primacy the Word of God gives to bread and the emphasis of our Lord on His being the Bread of Life.

The thought struck Bobb that a small loaf of bread symbolized both spiritual and physical life. From this concept came his idea of the "Love Loaves" (little banks shaped like loaves of bread), which have been the means of raising literally millions of dollars for world hunger needs. This serendipitous idea became an integral part of our world famine program.

Creative triumphs have also come from experiments done for the sole purpose of satisfying intellectual curiosity. Michael Faraday went at it blindly when, in 1831, he discovered how electricity could be produced. He had no target. He merely wondered what would happen if he mounted a copper disc between two poles of a horseshoe magnet and made it spin. To his amazement, it produced electric current.

CREATIVE QUESTIONING

Now and then someone asks a question which leads to an especially productive answer. One example of this was reported by the Department of Agriculture a number of years ago. Baby pigs are often crushed by their mothers rolling over upon them. An unknown "thinker–upper" asked whether pig mortality in a farrowing house could not be remedied by simply tilting the floor. This led to a system which is now working well. Since mama pigs like to lie down with their backs uphill and piglets like to travel downhill, the tilted floor tends to keep the baby from under the recumbent mother. Now no more crushed pigs!

I remember the day Bob Pierce called me from Asia during the early days of the Vietnam conflict. He was deeply concerned about the lack of material help for wounded Vietnam War veterans when they were brought into the poorly equipped military hospitals. "What can we do to help them?" he asked. "Think about it," he said, "and let's investigate it when I get home."

From that question came the famous World Vision "Viet Kit" program, with millions of these kits being prepared by church groups, schools, youth societies, and families. Other kits were distributed to Vietnamese children, soldiers, and widows. Bob's question led to redemptive answers.

Questions have long been recognized as a way to stimulate imagination. Professors who have sought to make their teaching more creative have often employed this device. In practical problem-solving we can give conscious guidance to our thinking by asking ourselves questions.

CREATIVE READJUSTMENT OF OBJECTIVES

Administrators also should recognize that innovative aims often change. This is not an unexpected turn of affairs in organized creativity, for problem-solving often calls for reformulating the problem itself and then solving the new problem. It pays to assess our aims and objectives. Countless people have spent endless hours and enormous amounts of creative energy on projects of no useful purpose.

I, too, have at times set forth in search of will-o'-the-wisps. I recall during my Youth for Christ days dreaming largely of a great international Christian youth conference to be held in Jerusalem. We made extensive plans, visited possible sites, spent months in developing plans—only to finally find that the logistics, language barrier, political problems, and finances were all beyond our reach. Much energy and time were expended in the project, which undoubtedly could have been better invested in other programs.

It was a valuable lesson for many of us. I realize that had I analyzed those limitations earlier, I could have invested those creative hours in something of greater promise. Through the years I have found that there are many ways of learning to use creative time in a productive manner.

Alex Morrison, famous golf instructor and author of *Better Golf Without Practice,* instructs his readers to use creative time in a productive manner. He enables golfers to eliminate strokes from their scores simply through mental practice. Morrison demonstrates the correct swing and gives a few pointers in the area of golf. Then he asks the student to spend at least five minutes each day relaxed in an easy chair, eyes closed, picturing himself on the golf course playing the game perfectly.

"You must," says Morrison, "have a clear mental picture of the correct thing before you can do it successfully. That can be acquired through instruction, by watching championship golf, or studying action pictures of golfers you admire." (Incidentally, my problem is that I don't take the necessary five or ten minutes!)

One reason mental practice so often brings prompt improvement is that for the first time, instead of struggling to remember many isolated ideas, you can form a complete pattern. This is why books showing you how to do tasks correctly are so important. The more you study the illustration and picture it in your mind's eye, the more proficient you will become at this and the more quickly difficult tasks are made easier.

INHIBITORS TO CREATIVITY

Most administrators know creative thinking or innovation when they see it. However, it is quite another thing to identify those things which stifle creative thinking, and to root them out. Let me point out a few of the inhibitors I see to genuine creative thought.

First, in our society there seems to be a cultural distaste for innovation. Years ago we admired and rewarded innovation and creativity. Today, however, innovation frequently goes unrewarded. Society is fearful, and so it resents those who might tip the canoe. Security has become the slogan of the secular society.

But in light of the Christian's resources, fear and fearfulness are self–defeating. Besides, they do not come from God, who, instead of fear, has given us the spirit "of power and of love and of a sound mind" (2 Timothy 1:7). Therefore, the person who is rooted in God need never be fearful of exercising his God–given creativity.

Second, within the organization itself there may be a tendency to hold the power of all decision making at the top. This is based on the mistaken notion that the only competent, intelligent individuals are those at the top. Some of the most creative ideas can come from the ranks.

I mentioned earlier the popular Love Loaves which Bobb Biehl developed for World Vision; this program continues to this day. In addition, we have a thirty–hour famine program for young people that teaches them to identify with world hunger needs. This entire successful ministry has been conceived and developed by some of our beautiful middle–management people.

A third barrier to innovation centers in the individual himself. We generally live far below our creative limits. Scientific tests for aptitudes have revealed the relative universality of creative potential. An analysis of almost all the psychological tests ever made points to the conclusion that creative talent is fairly evenly distributed, and that our creative efficiency varies more in ratio to our output of mental energy than to our inborn talent. This would have to be so because the Bible states that we are created to be like God.

As God concluded His creative process in Genesis, He said, " 'Let Us make man in Our image, according to Our likeness' . . . So God created man in His own image" (Genesis 1:26–27). The Hebrew word used here is *demuth,* which denotes likeness in every way. Hence, since God is a creative being, it follows that man is *by nature* also a creative being.

When one fully realizes the creative potential God has given him, he can rejoice. Jesus said, "If you live in Me—abide vitally united to Me—and My words remain in you and continue to live in your hearts, ask whatever you will and it shall be done for you" (John 15:7, Amplified Bible).

So to the degree that His words live in us, we actually have or possess His mind (see 1 Corinthians 2:16) and, consequently, His creativity. Thus the creative Godlikeness, the *demuth* of Genesis 1:27, becomes ours on a practical level; and we can ask for and receive creative assistance from our Father.

The barriers, therefore, to innovation and creativity lie primarily in these three areas: within our society, within organizations, within individuals. If we are to encourage our creative forces, we must be aware of these inhibitors and substitute a climate that facilitates innovation and growth.

PROVIDE AN ATMOSPHERE FOR GROWTH

One thing administrators can do is provide an atmosphere in which the individual's sensitivity can flourish rather than wither away. Innovation comes from awareness of a need or a problem. The problem may exist within the individual himself, or it may be present in the organization or in the public it serves. To solve it requires an openness of mind—a capacity for being receptive to new ideas.

We must also enlarge a man's knowledge about what is going on around him and encourage him to learn more about his own field. We can give him the opportunity to develop and improve the techniques and skills of his area of work.

It is important that every person should master the fundamentals of the job; for while the novice may generate insight and creative ideas on his own, he usually is in no position to use it to the organization's advantage. The novice may not possess the skills and techniques required to follow through on ideas. This is important because, for an idea to be a good one, it must be carried through to its ultimate conclusions. Otherwise it is a passing fancy—a wish, a dream. It must be communicated, it must be implemented, it must be put into effect. Some people can come up with great ideas, but they cannot implement them. They are "idea men" and either cannot or will not carry them through to completion. However, we need these people. In baseball it's pretty hard to bench a .400 hitter who can't field.

We must then develop these idea people's ability to implement, or put others alongside them who have ability in this field. In short, we need to create teams capable of supplementing thoughts with action. We must also provide enough time for the innovator to create. He needs time for preparation, time for the incubation of ideas, time for evaluation and redefinition, and time for complete double–checking and follow–up.

As administrators provide this "community of creativity," the interaction it stimulates will serve as a catalyst to others. And in this community there must be free exchange of ideas, constructive criticism, and disagreement without penalty. In addition, we must give the innovator a sense of belonging to management. For only if he participates in the formulation of goals, and only if he is part of the broad creative effort of the entire organization, can his contributions be real. And don't forget, people support what they help create.

We must recognize the *demuth,* the Godlikeness, of every person at every level in every type of work. We need to remember that each man has within himself the potential for innovation, no matter how little formal education he may have had, no matter how humble his background. We must use every resource of every individual, for the sake of that person, for the sake of the organization, and most importantly for the sake of God's kingdom. We must be careful that we do not put people in straitjackets—that we do not try to make them over in our own image and likeness, causing them to become only a distorted caricature.

Make no mistake about it—a most important job for all administrators is to bring into existence an innovative organization. How well each one of us does this will determine the productive future growth of our organization. A creative organization comes only to those administrators who are intensely committed—first to God and to His call upon their lives, and then to a burning desire to help bring about conditions that will stimulate the natural growth of creativity in other individuals.

*The effective leader is called to serve
those whom he leads.*

31
Called to Serve

Paradoxically, one who leads or administers the work of others is the servant of those whom he leads. When analyzed, though, this apparent contradiction is not a paradox at all. One cannot lead unless he knows where he is going. Only then can a person say, "Follow me," and proceed to lead the way.

KNOW WHERE YOU'RE GOING

And one cannot lead the way until he has clearly defined in his own mind *where* he is going, for *what purpose* he is going, and *how* he is going to get there!

To administrate also means you have decided *who* you will follow. To change Bob Dylan's lyrics just a bit, "You've got to follow somebody." Our Lord Jesus Christ, the King of Kings, served God the Father. "I can of Myself do nothing," Jesus said (John 5:30); and even God the Father does not operate independently of the other two members of the Godhead. Though He is the fountain-head of the Holy Trinity, He always functions together with God the Son and God the Holy Spirit. For us human beings, we either follow Christ in His church or the devil and his servants. It is granted to none of us to function alone.

Of necessity, then, one cannot simply appear on the scene at 8 A.M. some bright Monday morning and say off the top of the head, "Let's go, men . . follow me."

The administrator is not the slave owner.

In a very real sense, the administrator is the servant. In order to lead, one must serve. And not until he has learned how to serve and follow others can he become the optimal leader himself. It was so with the Lord Jesus. With Saint Peter. With the apostle Paul. It is true with all who serve. If they lead, they serve in the fullest sense of the word.

And leadership takes time. It also takes commitment. If the job, the project, the church, the organization is to get moving and stay moving toward its stated goals, the individual at the top must always be moving out in front, setting the pace for service as he leads the followers.

THE BEST LEADERS ARE LED

One could well say, then, that the driver is also the driven. He is driven to lead, and as he leads he is driven to be adequate in knowledge. He is driven to be ahead of the followers. Then he is driven to stay out in front and continue to say, "Follow me."

It is often much easier just to follow.

The apostle Paul was a leader, an administrator, an organizer. Yet in his introduction to the Book of Romans he speaks of himself in the third person: "From Paul, a *bond servant* of Jesus Christ, the Messiah . . ." (1:1, Amplified Bible). And while he said, "Imitate me" (1 Corinthians 11:1), he also confessed in Corinth, "I was with you in weakness, and fear, and in much trembling" (1 Corinthians 2:3).

The Greek word translated "servant" is *doulos,* literally a slave or servant. Peter begins his second epistle with the same introduction: "Simon Peter, a servant [doulos] . . . of Jesus Christ" (2 Peter 1:2).

These great men were leaders, administrators, "out–front" men, yet they served. And Jesus, the greatest leader and follower of all, speaking of leadership to His followers, said, "Let . . . him who is the chief and leader [become] as one who serves" (Luke 22:26, Amplified Bible).

Implicitly, Jesus is saying that leadership in its very essence is serving. It cannot be otherwise. To lead is to serve. And to serve is to become the servant of those one is leading. Leading is not an easy responsibility. Again it is only when I am applying myself to the utmost that I can say before God, as did the apostle Paul, "Follow my example," and then the vital words, "as I follow Christ's!" (1 Corinthians 11:1, TLB). In other words, "pattern your life after mine."

But then one looks at how Paul patterned his life. He summed it up in a phrase, "but *one thing* I do . . . I press toward the goal for the prize" (Philippians 4:13–14).

It is when I have done my homework, it is when I have studied to show myself approved, "a worker who does not need to be ashamed" (2 Timothy 2:15); it is then and only then that I am ready to lead, to administer, and to serve.

Do you see how clearly and pragmatically service helps tie together the charismatic and official elements of leadership? If the stance of serving is taken by the leader, problems are kept minimal. But if the leader seeks to lord it over the followers, trouble will always result.

THE INEVITABILITY OF INCONVENIENCE

Again and again the knowledge has come to me that being an administrative leader involves serving, and serving so very often involves inconvenience. It isn't always convenient to serve people. I have things I want to do. Yet, as the leader, I am responsible to be available at all times to serve those whom I lead.

Sometimes I work my way through the Gospels and meditate upon the way Jesus handled interruptions. You might consider doing the same. He was often involved in meeting the need of one person when another broke in and demanded that He also speak to that need. In every case He paused to heal, comfort, or do whatever was needed, and then proceeded with His original objective.

Never did He rebuke someone with, "Can't you see that I'm busy?"

It is so important to recognize that often what we consider

to be "interruptions" are really occasions for God to break through our routines and get to us, or to enable us to minister to someone's need we may know nothing about.

For Jesus, serving also involved ministering to people who were not always easy to deal with. In His case, there were even lepers to be ministered to. I wouldn't go so far as to suggest having "untouchables" to deal with at times, but I can say that I have often had to administer or arbitrate a situation that was repugnant to me. The personalities involved were abrasive or abusive, and I would much rather have suggested they go elsewhere to settle their disputes. But I needed to appropriate the grace of God and serve, by listening.

John Drakeford's excellent book, *The Awesome Power of the Listening Ear* (Word Books, 1967), identifies the importance of hearing another person—objectively and without prejudging. I have learned that it is not easy. Giving careful attention to what others are saying, and not seeking to give glib answers or suggestions before the other individual is completely heard, is so important. It is a lesson that I, for one, have had to learn—and relearn repeatedly.

THE ROLE OF REASSURANCE

Serving also involves offering reassurances. An excellent example of this in Jesus' ministry has to do with a man by the name of Jairus, who was one of the rulers of the local synagogue. Jairus approached Jesus in a distraught state. He fell at Jesus' feet and said, "My little daughter is dying. Please come and put your hands on her so that she will be healed and live." So Jesus went with him (Mark 5:23–24, NIV).

I am certain that Jairus was immediately relieved, because he knew that Jesus went about healing the sick. But Jesus was suddenly stopped on the way by a woman who needed healing herself. (Now His interruption was interrupted!)

You remember the story. This woman had had an issue of blood for many years. She came up behind Jesus in the crowd "and touched his cloak, because she thought, 'If I just touch his clothes, I will be healed.' Immediately her bleeding stopped" (verses 27–29,

NIV).

Jesus stopped and looked around. He asked who had touched Him. A dialogue ensued with His disciples, then with the woman herself. All of this took time. Meanwhile, Jairus must have despairingly wished they would all go away and let Jesus proceed to his home.

It was while Jesus was still ministering to the woman that some men came to Jairus from his house and told him his daughter had just died. But before Jairus could even respond to them, Jesus turned to him and offered those wonderful words of reassurance, "Don't be afraid; just believe" (verse 35, NIV). Subsequently they reached Jairus's home, and Jesus ministered life to the little girl.

I can only believe that Jesus' words of reassurance strengthened and comforted Jairus along that seemingly endless walk to his home. I also believe that, as administrators, our words of comfort and reassurance when our people become frustrated are often the means of enabling them to continue during difficult times in their lives.

I know how often colleagues of mine have been led by the Spirit to say just the right word to me in times of distress or difficult decision–making. They perhaps did not know they were ministering to me in this way, but God used their word of encouragement at just the right time to bring strength to me in difficult circumstances. As administrators, we can trust Him to do that with each of us as we speak that special, warm word of affirmation when we may not be aware of the burden being carried by an employee or peer.

WE'RE HUMAN, TOO

As I have sought to minister comfort to others, I have sometimes wondered (as have other administrators), "Doesn't anybody ever realize that I am human, too?" There are times when we all would like for someone to pat us on the back and reassure us. But it's during times such as these that God meets my own needs through one of his other servants who possesses both the sensitivity and the ability to do so.

One such man is my dear friend and colleague Dr. Carlton

Booth. He has been around our office for many years as secretary of our board and as a personal counselor. Carlton has been with both me and the organization through the most difficult as well as the blessedly prosperous times. I have never known a man who is so possessed with the ability to minister love, affirmation, and reassurance at just the right time.

I recall when we were going through the deepest of waters in World Vision upon the resignation of our founder/president, Dr. Bob Pierce, and the struggles we faced as an organization simply to survive. Times without number Carlton said to me, "Ted, stay with us; hang in there. God is not through with us. He has His plans for all of us, and for World Vision. Don't give up or give in." His words of perseverance have been so consistently on target and timely, for years I have called him my Barnabas, my "Son of Encouragement"! (Acts 4:36).

REACH OUT AND TOUCH SOMEONE

Serving also means that I must sometimes physically acknowledge others. Personally, I am not much given to touching others—either men or women. It's not so much that I'm averse to physical contact of touching or that intimacy frightens me, it's just that, to put it in the vernacular, "I'm not into touching." Consequently, I don't often go around hugging people or putting my arm around peoples' shoulders. That's just not me.

However, I realize that Jesus ministered to different people in different ways. Some He touched. Others He merely spoke to. His ministry was not stereotyped. His ministering principle was that He was sensitive to the Father's will for people's needs. And He met each person's need *right where that person was*. Recall the woman with the issue of blood, the demon–possessed man—and so many others.

There are times when possibly the physical touch is the only salve that will provide healing. So on those occasions, as the Holy Spirit directs me, I also seek to provide that physical touch. I've seen, as I'm sure you have, how meaningful a warm hand on the arm with an encouraging word can be to the recipient.

Serving isn't something that comes easily to everyone.

Some just don't understand or recognize the important role of service, and to these people it is demeaning to serve or to wait on another. Even the ones who appreciate the ministry of service don't always like to serve continually; and when they do serve, they often want to choose whom they serve.

But for the one who is to administer, I believe it is axiomatic that he is called as much to serve as he is called to administrate. I doubt that the two words can be totally dissected from each other, because implicit in each *is* the other. Neither is complete without the other. In fact, one of Webster's definitions of the word "serve" is "to be used, or be usable."

With this in mind, many of us must rethink our concept of serving. I know of men and women to whom serving carries a negative connotation, the idea of "not being as good as" another person. If you are one of these people, you will tend to resent your service to others. This will necessitate your choosing to accept serving as part of administration by an act of will. Then, through a further act of the will, serving with joy.

LEARNING TO LEAD

Let me share a few suggestions that have helped me to do just that.

1. *Institute plans into your life that are conducive to serving.* It is easy for an administrator to think of himself as the one who gives the orders and calls the shots, and hold himself aloof from the "troops." Such an attitude might work for a time, but it will soon break down. Authority must always move hand in hand with service, because the "troops" need a leader who leads by example—not from a distance and by directive only.

Personally, I have sought to develop a practice in my schedule at the office which has returned meaningful dividends for the time expended. It's my regular "walk around." I frequently set aside a couple of hours on a regular basis when I leave my desk and simply walk around our offices. We have five separate buildings, so I seek to offer myself by going to where the people are. I step into our departments and individual offices, greet the men and women, ask how they are doing and simply chat a bit with different ones.

If there are evident needs, I ask about these and briefly discuss means and methods to meet the needs. If something comes up that cannot or should not be handled on the spot, I make a note of it and try to find a way to handle it upon returning to my office.

Many times, even weeks later, an expression of appreciation will come back to me from someone whom I have taken special notice of with a word of encouragement or a question about family, work, or whatever. Again, a simple affirming "word in season" can mean so much (Proverbs 15:23). And all it takes is a little thoughtfulness!

2. *Begin patterning your serving after Jesus.* After all, He is the ultimate Server. Study His means and methods of serving. Notice His manner of speaking, His compassionate expressions, His availability. I don't, of course, mean for you to begin speaking or praying in King James terminology, but to live as He lived on earth.

3. *Take a periodic self-inventory.* The following exercise will be useful in helping us look at service in a new light. The quiz below may be one that will help you to get a handle on where you are in a "serving frame of reference." If you will complete the six brief items, you will begin to see yourself somewhat more objectively in the matter of serving. Rate yourself on each question with a score from 1 to 10.

- Am I secure enough within myself and in my relationship to Christ to be able to serve others in positive ways without threatening my own self-worth?

- Am I truly committed to serving those whom I lead, to actualize their potential?

- Am I willing to face the new demands and new disciplines that serving will impose on me?

- Am I willing to make daily, decisive acts of self-relinquishment, which is the price often required of those who serve?

- Am I willing to take the place of a learner in general, and a listener in particular, to establish and strengthen relationships between myself and the people I serve?

- Am I willing to accept as God's purpose that the

332

central meaning of my life is serving?

In light of the score you give yourself, ask yourself, "Do I consider myself to be one committed to serving?" If the score is lower than 40–45, ask, "What is blocking or hindering my desire to serve?"

A final question that might enable you to better evaluate yourself and improve your score is, "What definite, precise action should I take in order to serve in a more Christ–like manner?" And then act upon the answer!

If I am to follow Jesus—and, if like the apostle Paul, that is my stated aim—then I will become an administrator who cares enough to serve.

Notes

Chapter 1

1. "A Nation of Liars?" *U.S. News and World Report* (February 23, 1987), p. 54.

2. "Morality Among Supply-Siders," *Time* (May 25, 1987), p. 18.

3. J. David Schmidt, "How to Raise a Billion Dollars," *Christianity Today* (May 15, 1987), p. 36.

4. *The Rebirth of America*, Arthur S. DeMoss Foundation, 1986, p. 143.

5. Jacob M. Braude, *Business and Professional Pointmakers* (Englewood Cliffs, NJ: Prentice-Hall, Inc., 1965), p. 112.

Chapter 2

1. "Marriage Just Got Easier," *Pasadena Star News* (June 29, 1987), p. 1.

2. Elizabeth Loftus, "Trials of an Expert Witness," *Newsweek* (June 29, 1987), p. 9.

3. Paraphrase from "Secular Humanism —Not the Only Enemy," by Donald G. Bloesch, *Eternity* (January 1982), p. 22.

4. James Dobson, Focus on the Family, audio-cassette "Reaching the Unchurched," CS 321, 1986, side two.

5. Ibid., audio cassette.

6. *Christian Herald* (July/August 1987), p. 5.

7. Associated Press, *Pasadena Star News* (August 4, 1987), p. A-8.

8. Cliff C. Jones, *Winning Through Integrity* (New York: Ballantine Books, 1985), p. 84.

9. *Bits and Pieces* (New Jersey: Economics Press, Inc., April 1987), p. 2.

10. Gerhard Gschwandtner, "An Interview with Buck Rodgers: Selling Solutions," *Management Review* (July 1987), p. 48.

11. Ibid., p. 51.

12. Ibid., p. 48.

13. *Bits and Pieces*, p. 12.

14. Nido Quebin, *Get the Best From Yourself* (Englewood Cliffs, NJ: Prentice-Hall, Inc., 1983), p. 60.

Chapter 3

1. Anecdote retold from *What A Day This Can Be*, John Catoir, ed., Director of the Christophers (New York: The Christophers).

Chapter 5

1. Victor E. Frankl, *Man's Search for Meaning* (New York: Pocket Books, 1980), pp. 104-105.

Chapter 6

1. "Advice to a (Bored) Young Man," *Newsweek* (February 13, 1967).

Chapter 7

1. From *Supervisory Control,* newsletter of The Research Institute of America, Inc. (New York, October 1968).

2. *Sales Management* (December 15, 1961), pp. 45-46.

Chapter 8

1. Hal Butler, *Sports Heroes Who Wouldn't Quit* (New York: Simon & Schuster, Inc., 1973), p. 46.

2. Ibid., pp. 52-53.

3. Geoffrey C. Ward, *Success Magazine* (April 1985), pp. 55-56.

4. *Encyclopedia Britannica,* 15th ed., Vol. 28 (Chicago: Encyclopedia Britannica, Inc., 1985), p. 36.

Chapter 9

1. Art Linkletter (Chicago: Nightingale-Conant Corporation, 1983), single cassette recording.

2. Ibid.

3. Lee Iacocca, *Iacocca: An Autobiography* (New York: Bantam Books, Inc.), p. xv.

Chapter 10

1. *U.S. News & World Report* (October 3, 1983), p. 66.

2. Herbert V. Prochnow and Herbert V. Prochnow, Jr., *The Public Speaker's Treasure Chest* (New York: Harper & Row, 1964), p. 286.

Chapter 11

1. John Drakeford, *The Awesome Power of the Listening Ear* (Waco, TX: Word Books, 1967), p. 15.

2. Beth Day, "Standing Room Only for Silence," *Reader's Digest* (June 1958), pp. 187-91.

3. H. Norman Wright, *More Communication Keys to Your Marriage* (Ventura, CA: Regal Books, 1983), pp. 79-80.

4. Kenny Moore, "She Runs and We Are Lifted," *Sports Illustrated* (December 26, 1983), p. 38.

Chapter 12

1. James Dobson, *Hide or Seek* (Old Tappan, NJ: Fleming H. Revell, 1974), pp. 9-10.

2. Taken from *Dreams in Homespun* (New York: Lothrop, Lee, and Shepherd, Co., n.d.).

Chapter 13

1. Martin E. Marty, *Friendship* (Allen, TX: Argus Communications, 1980), pp. 49-50.

2. Neil Clark Warren, *Make Anger Your Ally* (New York: Doubleday, 1983), pp. 145-46.

3. David Ireland with Louis Tharp, Jr., *Letters to an Unborn Child* (New York: Harper & Row, 1974), pp. 33-34.

4. Wayne Dyer, *The Sky's the Limit* (New York: Pocket Books, 1980), p. 52.

5. *Insight.*

6. *Bits and Pieces* (October 1983), p. 24.

Chapter 14

1. James C. Coleman and Constance I. Hammen, *Contemporary Psychology and Effective Behavior* (Glenview, IL: Scott, Foresman & Co., 1974), p. 341.

2. Lloyd Lofquist, *Adjustment to Work* (New York: Appleton-Century-Crofts, 1969), p. 7.

3. Ibid.

4. Ibid.

5. Sigmund Freud, *Civilization and Its Discontents* (*Das Unbehagen in der Kultur*, trans. Joan Riviere, Hogarth Press, 1930), p. 34.

6. Georges Friedmann, *The Anatomy of Work* (New York: Free Press of Glencoe, 1962), p. 127.

7. George Andrew Sargeant, "Motivation and Meaning," *Dissertation Abstracts International*, vol. 34, (September-October 1973), p. 1785-B.

Chapter 15

1. Raymond C. Baumhart, "How Ethical Are Businessmen?" *Harvard Business Review* (July/August 1961), p. 172.

Chapter 16

1. Alan N. Schoonmaker, *Anxiety and the Executive* (New York: American Management Association, Inc., 1969), pp. 130-31.

2. Ibid., p. 136.

3. R. D. Lain, *Politics of the Family* (New York: Random House, 1972), p. 98.

4. Schoonmaker, op. cit., p. 139.

5. Otto Fenichel, *The Psychoanalytic Theory of Neurosis* (New York: W. W. Norton & Co., 1972), p. 445.

6. Martin R. Haskell, *Socioanalysis: Self-Direction via Sociometry and Psychodrama* (Long Beach, CA: Role Training Associates of California, 1975), p. 25.

7. Ibid., p. 38.

8. Fenichel, op. cit., p. 298.

9. Wayne E. Oates, *Confessions of a Workaholic* (Nashville: Abingdon Press, 1971), p. 88.

10. Karl Menninger, *Love Against Hate* (New York: Harcourt, Brace & World, Inc., 1970), pp. 161-162.

11. Oates, op. cit., p. 88.

12. Fenichel, op. cit., pp. 472-473.

Chapter 19

1. Robert M. MacIver, *The Challenge of the Passing Years—My Encounter with Time* (New York: Simon & Schuster, 1962). Lieber Professor of Political Philosophy and Sociology, Columbia University, 1927-1950.

2. Rev. Charles W. Shedd, *Time for All Things* (Nashville, TN: Abingdon Press, 1962).

3. Colleen T. Evans, "My Family Comes First," *Guideposts* (November 1985).

4. Op. cit.

Chapter 20

1. William Oncken, *Managing a Manager's Time,* a film, American Management Association, New York, 1961.

2. Ray Josephs, "Control Your Personal Time Better to Get More Done," *American Business* (February 1960).

Chapter 21

1. Richard Wolfe, *Man at the Top* (Wheaton, IL: Tyndale House Publishers, 1969), p. 43.

Chapter 22

1. Ted W. Engstrom and R. Alec Mackenzie, *Managing Your Time* (Grand Rapids, MI: Zondervan Publishing House, 1974), pp. 87-89.

2. Ibid., pp. 89-91.

Chapter 23

1. "Friends in the Soaring '70s: A Church Growth Era, Oregon Yearly Meeting of Friends Churches" (Newberg, OR, August 1969), p. 121.

2. Ted W. Engstrom and R. Alec Mackenzie, *Managing Your Time* (Grand Rapids, MI: Zondervan Publishing House, 1974), pp. 96-97.

3. Robert Tannenbaum and Warren Schmidt, "Choosing a Leadership Pattern," *Harvard Business Review 36* (March/April 1958), p. 99.

Index